Latino Immigrants and the Transformation of the U.S. South

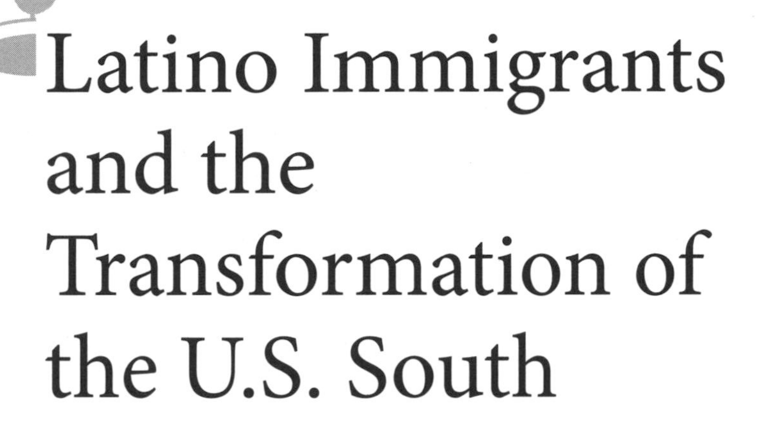

Latino Immigrants and the Transformation of the U.S. South

EDITED BY MARY E. ODEM
AND ELAINE LACY

The University of Georgia Press • Athens and London

Credit for previously published work appears when applicable
on the first page of chapter notes, which constitute an extension
of this copyright page.

Athens, Georgia 30602
www.ugapress.org

Set in 10/13 Minion Pro by BookComp, Inc.
Printed and bound by Thomson-Shore
The paper in this book meets the guidelines for
permanence and durability of the Committee on
Production Guidelines for Book Longevity of the
Council on Library Resources.

Printed in the United States of America
13 12 11 10 09 C 5 4 3 2 1
13 12 11 10 09 P 5 4 3 2 1

Library of Congress Cataloging-in-Publication Data

Latino immigrants and the transformation of the U.S. South
/ edited by Mary E. Odem and Elaine Lacy.
p. cm.
Includes bibliographical references and index.
ISBN-13: 978-0-8203-2968-0 (hbk. : alk. paper)
ISBN-10: 0-8203-2968-1 (hbk. : alk. paper)
ISBN-13: 978-0-8203-3212-3 (pbk. : alk. paper)
ISBN-10: 0-8203-3212-7 (pbk. : alk. paper)
1. Latin Americans—Southern States.
2. Hispanic Americans—Southern States.
3. Latin America—Emigration and immigration.
4. Southern States—Emigration and immigration.
5. Immigrants—Southern States—Social conditions.
6. Alien labor, Latin American—Southern States.
I. Odem, Mary E. II. Lacy, Elaine Cantrell.
F220.S75L363 2009
304.8089'68075—dc22 2009001007

British Library Cataloging-in-Publication Data available

CONTENTS

vii Acknowledgments

ix Introduction / *Mary E. Odem and Elaine Lacy*

1 ONE. Cultural Enclaves and Transnational Ties: Mexican Immigration and Settlement in South Carolina / *Elaine Lacy*

18 TWO. New Scenarios of Migration: Social Vulnerability of Undocumented Veracruzanos in the Southern United States / *Rosío Córdova Plaza*

34 THREE. The Dalton Story: Mexican Immigration and Social Transformation in the Carpet Capital of the World / *Víctor Zúñiga and Rubén Hernández-León*

51 FOUR. Globalization and Latin American Immigration in Alabama / *Raymond A. Mohl*

70 FIVE. Hispanic Newcomers to North Carolina: Demographic Characteristics and Economic Impact / *James H. Johnson Jr. and John D. Kasarda*

91 SIX. Race, Migration, and Labor Control: Neoliberal Challenges to Organizing Mississippi's Poultry Workers / *Angela C. Stuesse*

112 SEVEN. Latino Immigrants and the Politics of Space in Atlanta / *Mary E. Odem*

126 EIGHT. New Americans in a New South City? Immigrant and Refugee Politics in Nashville, Tennessee / *Jamie Winders*

143 NINE. Popular Attitudes and Public Policies: Southern Responses to Latino Immigration / *Elaine Lacy and Mary E. Odem*

165 List of Contributors

169 Index

ACKNOWLEDGMENTS

This collection grew out of a conference on Mexican immigration to the U.S. South that took place in Atlanta, Georgia, in May 2004. The conference was a collaborative effort of the Mexican Consulate in Atlanta and four universities in the Atlanta area: Emory University, Georgia State University, Kennesaw State University, and the University of Georgia. The scholarly gathering brought together Mexican and U.S. immigration scholars to discuss and share research about the recent and massive shift of Mexican immigration to new destinations in the Southeast. We were participants in the conference and edited the conference proceedings, which were published by the Institute of Mexico in Atlanta under the title *Mexican Immigration to the U.S. Southeast: Impact and Challenges*. We wish to acknowledge the contributions of the organizers and participants in this conference, especially Dr. Remedios Gómez-Arnau, the Mexican Consul General in Atlanta; Dr. Arthur Murphy of Georgia State University; and Lucila Ruvalcaba of the Institute of Mexico.

With the encouragement of editors at the University of Georgia Press, we've produced a revised and expanded collection of articles that focuses more broadly on Latin American immigration to the U.S. South. The volume includes a number of articles from the conference proceedings that have been extensively revised, plus three new chapters and an expanded introduction. We thank Nicole Mitchell and Derek Krissoff for their support and for sharing our enthusiasm about this project. We are grateful to Jennifer Reichlin and Deborah Oliver, whose careful editing has improved the clarity and flow of the individual chapters and the volume as a whole.

Mary Odem would like to acknowledge the support of the Pew Charitable Trusts and the Emory Center for the Study of Law and Religion, and the research assistance of Joy Henderson and Svetoslava Milhusheva of the Emory SIRE program. Elaine Lacy would like to express gratitude to the University of South Carolina's Office of Sponsored Awards Management and the University of South Carolina Aiken's Partnership Board. She also thanks Dr. Michael Scardaville for his editorial assistance and generous encouragement.

And finally, we owe a big thanks to the contributors to this volume. They endured several rounds of revision and cooperated with our numerous suggestions and demands. We learned a great deal from their research on Latin American immigration in various southern contexts.

Elaine Lacy
Mary E. Odem

Introduction

MARY E. ODEM AND ELAINE LACY

In the last decade of the twentieth century the South became a major new immigrant destination in the United States. Largely bypassed in the last great wave of immigration to this country (1890–1920), the region is now home to millions of immigrants from Latin America, Asia, and Africa. This collection of essays examines the migration and settlement of the largest group of foreign-born newcomers to the U.S. South—those from Latin America. Globalization and economic restructuring in both the United States and Latin American countries have led to the mass migration to the southern United States of peoples from Mexico, Guatemala, El Salvador, Colombia, Venezuela, Brazil, and elsewhere in Central and South America.

In towns, cities, and suburbs throughout the Southeast, one now finds Mexican *panaderías*, *tiendas*, and restaurants, Colombian bakeries, Spanish-language newspapers and radio programs, Latino nightclubs featuring a variety of Latin music, and December processions in honor of Our Lady of Guadalupe. Apartment complexes and mobile-home parks in the region are home to immigrants from Maya villages in the Guatemala highlands, urban neighborhoods in Mexico City, Lima, and San Salvador, and rural towns throughout Mexico and Central America. The mass migration of Latin Americans to the U.S. South has triggered an unprecedented series of changes in the social, economic, and cultural life of the region and inaugurated a new era in southern history. This multidisciplinary collection of essays explores these transformations in rural, urban, and suburban areas of the South from the late 1980s to 2008. Based on a variety of methodologies and approaches, the chapters present in-depth analyses of how immigration from Latin America is changing the U.S. South and how immigrants are adapting to the southern context.

The South has long been thought of as a distinct region in the United States, one with its own customs, political style, social relations, and cultural and religious traditions. The region's distinctiveness, many believe, was rooted in its history of slavery, secession, and defeat in the Civil War. After the war the South continued to follow a separate historical path marked by uneven economic development, rural poverty, and an entrenched system of white supremacy and racial segregation. Since the 1960s the region has undergone sweeping transformations in its racial laws and practices, politics, and economic conditions brought about by the civil rights revolution and significant economic development and investment.

The pervasive changes have led many scholars and observers to ponder whether the South is, in fact, still a distinct region. Some argue that the region has been so thoroughly incorporated into the American mainstream that it is no longer useful to talk about "southern distinctiveness," while others point out that the South continues to differ from the rest of the nation in noticeable ways, such as higher levels of political conservatism, evangelical Protestantism, and poverty.[1] The chapters in this book do not settle the question of "southern distinctiveness," but they do illuminate one of the significant ways the region has been changing in recent decades. Learning how immigrants are adapting to life in the South and how southerners are reacting to the new immigration will contribute to the discussion of the changing nature of southern identity.

The South has been defined in different ways, depending on whether one is talking about the Old South, the Confederacy, the Jim Crow South, the Deep South, or the South as delineated by the U.S. Bureau of the Census. For purposes of this volume we define the South as those states that share a history of slavery and the legal institution of racial segregation and its undoing by the civil rights movement. Because of our interest in new immigration states we omit Texas and Florida, for they have a longer and different history of Latin American immigration. The remaining ten states—Georgia, North Carolina, South Carolina, Virginia, Tennessee, Alabama, Mississippi, Arkansas, Louisiana, and Kentucky—included only small populations of Latinos prior to the 1980s, made up mostly of Cubans who had fled their country's revolution and Puerto Ricans. Beginning in the 1980s in Georgia and North Carolina, and in the 1990s for most other states, Latino numbers skyrocketed in the South, driven largely by mass immigration from Mexico, Central America, and South America (figure 0.1 and table 0.1).

Several studies have examined the rise of Latino populations and their impact on the South. The first edited collection on this theme, Arthur Murphy, Colleen Blanchard, and Jennifer Hill's *Latino Workers in the Contemporary South* (2001), explores the incorporation of Latinos in key sectors of the southern economy and addresses developments in Texas and Florida as well as new immigrant destinations in Georgia and North Carolina. *Latinos in the New South: Transformations of Place* (2006), edited by geographers Heather Smith and Owen Furuseth, analyzes the ways in which Latino immigration is reshaping urban and rural places in the region, with a particular emphasis on North Carolina and Tennessee. The first book-length study of Latino immigrants in

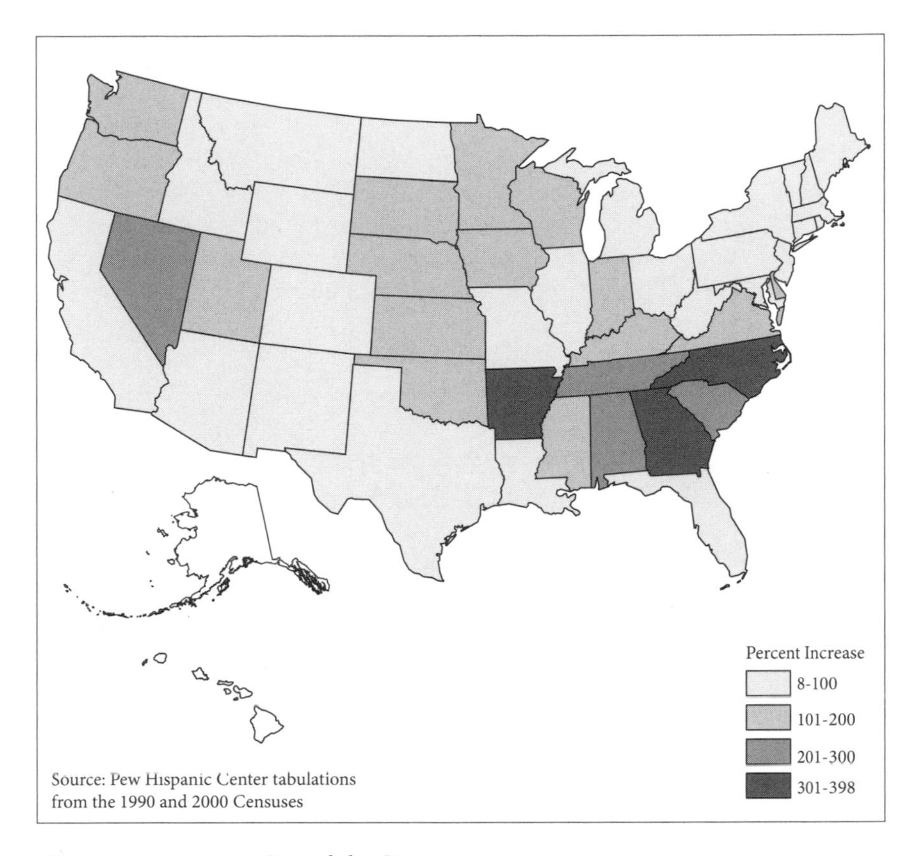

Figure 0.1. Hispanic Growth by State, 1990–2000.

the South, Leon Fink's *The Maya of Morganton* (2003), explores the changing face of labor and labor struggle in the North Carolina poultry industry.[2]

Recently published studies of the impact of globalization on the U.S. South also have addressed the theme of immigration. James Cobb and William Stueck's *Globalization and the American South* (2005) includes broad overviews of Latin American and Asian immigration to the region, while *The American South in a Global World* (2005), edited by James Peacock, Harry Watson, and Carrie Matthews, presents case studies of immigrant newcomers, from Mexican farmworkers in the rural South to Japanese professionals in North Carolina's Research Triangle.[3] Articles about Latino immigration to the region have also appeared in several collections that explore the new geography of immigration in the United States at the national level. For example, *New Destinations* (2005), edited by Víctor Zúñiga and Rubén Hernández-León, examines the dispersion

Table 0.1 Hispanic Population in Southern States, 1990–2006

	Hispanic Population			*% Change (+)*		
State	*1990 census*	*2000 census*	*2006 survey*	*1990–2000*	*2000–6*	*1990–2006**
North Carolina	76,745	378,963	597,382	393.8%	57.6%	678.4%
Arkansas	19,876	86,866	138,283	337.0%	59.2%	595.7%
Georgia	108,933	435,227	696,146	299.5%	60.0%	539.1%
Tennessee	32,742	123,838	187,747	278.2%	51.6%	473.4%
South Carolina	30,500	95,076	148,632	211.7%	56.3%	387.3%
Alabama	24,629	75,830	111,432	207.9%	46.9%	352.4%
Kentucky	22,005	59,939	83,015	172.4%	38.5%	277.3%
Virginia	160,403	329,540	470,871	105.4%	42.9%	193.6%
Mississippi	15,998	39,569	46,348	147.3%	17.1%	189.7%
Louisiana	93,067	107,738	123,281	15.8%	14.4%	32.5%
Total South	584,898	1,732,586	2,603,137	196.2%	50.2%	345.1%

* States are ranked by total growth in the Hispanic population from 1990 to 2006.

Source: U.S. Census, 1990, 2000, 2006 American Community Survey

of Mexican immigrants from traditional settlement areas in Texas and the Southwest to new regions of the country, including the Southeast.[4]

This book builds on and adds to the knowledge and insights these earlier studies offer. We focus exclusively on southern states where mass immigration from Latin America began in the late twentieth century; therefore, unlike the other volumes on Latinos in the South we do not address developments in Texas and Florida. Further, we broaden the coverage of new immigrant destinations in the South by including chapters on areas that have not been addressed in existing publications, such as South Carolina and Mississippi. This book also expands on a number of themes addressed in existing studies, including factors driving migration, economic and cultural incorporation, settlement patterns, and the social and cultural transformation that results from mass immigration. In addition we explore other themes that have received less attention, such as immigrant transnationalism, shifting racial dynamics, southern responses to immigration, and recent debates and conflicts over immigration reform.

The collection is multidisciplinary in scope, bringing together essays by historians, economists, sociologists, anthropologists, and geographers. Further, it includes essays by both U.S. and Mexican scholars, providing a binational perspective on the processes and implications of migration. The authors present analyses of the dynamics and impact of Latino immigration using a rich variety of research methodologies—ethnographies, interviews, surveys, focus groups, statistical analyses, and newspaper and archival research. Together the chapters address the diverse regions in the South that have been affected by this demographic change, including rural areas, small towns, medium-size cities, and large metropolitan areas.

Contributors explore a range of topics related to immigration in the various places where immigrants have settled: ethnic and racial tensions among poultry workers in rural Mississippi and forestry workers in Alabama; the "Mexicanization" of the urban landscape in Dalton, Georgia; the costs and benefits of Latino labor in North Carolina; the challenges of living in transnational families; Catholic religious practice and community building in metropolitan Atlanta; and the creation of Latino spaces in rural and urban South Carolina and Georgia. Before we delve further into the central themes and arguments of the book, it is useful to examine how the South became a major new immigrant destination.

Emergence of the South as a New Immigrant Destination

Historically the South did not attract immigrants in large numbers until the late twentieth century, largely because of its slower pace of industrial development and the presence of a large number of poor blacks and whites who provided a steady pool of low-wage labor. During the last great wave of immigration to the United States at the turn of the twentieth century, small groups of immigrant workers from Europe and China settled in the region, but the vast majority headed to urban areas in the Northeast, Midwest, and West to become part of the industrial workforce, and to areas of expanding commercial agriculture such as the Southwest to work as farm laborers.

Since the 1980s, however, economic restructuring and growth and new immigration policies have drawn Latin American immigrants to the South in ever increasing numbers, turning the region into the most rapidly growing immigrant destination in the country. Economic globalization has contributed to the transformation of the southern economy, leading to the decline of some industrial sectors and expanding economic investment in others. Global competition has caused plant closings and layoffs in the steel, textile, and apparel industries as production has shifted to lower-cost areas in Southeast Asia, China, and the Philippines. At the same time, domestic and foreign corporations have been drawn to the South because of the relatively low taxes, cheap nonunion labor and significant government subsidies provided to attract investment. Foreign automobile makers (Mercedes, Honda, Hyundai) have built factories in Alabama, North Carolina, South Carolina, and Tennessee. In addition, poultry, pork, and seafood processing plants have opened throughout the rural South. The poultry-processing industry in particular has flourished in the region; nearly half of all poultry processing in the country is now concentrated in Georgia, Alabama, Arkansas, and North Carolina. Southern cities such as Atlanta, Birmingham, Greensboro, and Charlotte have become important locations for commercial banking and financial industries, high-tech research and manufacturing, and biomedical research. Many of the country's largest corporations now have their headquarters in the Southeast, including Wal-Mart, Home Depot, Bank of America, and Federal Express. Rapid population growth accompanied business expansion in southern cities, creating high demand in the construction and service industries and consequently a demand for low-wage labor.[5]

Economic globalization and neoliberal policies have also led to the restructuring of Mexican and Latin American economies, and created conditions that increased international labor migration. Driven by a complex set of social and economic forces, migration between Mexico and the United States has gone on continuously since the early twentieth century except for a brief hiatus during the 1930s. Mexican migration in recent decades has been shaped by neoliberal restructuring of the Mexican economy that began in the early 1980s. Pressured by the World Bank, International Monetary Fund, and the U.S. government, Mexico embarked on a program of neoliberal economic reform that opened the country to full participation in the global market economy. Led by President Carlos Salinas de Gortari, the Mexican government dismantled trade barriers, lowered tariffs, phased out subsidies, eliminated restrictions on foreign business ownership, and privatized state enterprises. President Salinas sought to institutionalize these reforms in the North American Free Trade Agreement (NAFTA), which was signed by the governments of United States, Mexico, and Canada in 1994.[6]

NAFTA furthered the economic integration of Mexico and the United States and fostered transportation and communication networks between the two countries. The treaty's free-market policies, however, displaced workers and farmers in record numbers through the downsizing of government bureaucracies and state enterprises and land consolidation and capital-intensive production in rural areas. Mexican manufacturing suffered from the termination of tariff protections, and Mexican agriculture was damaged by the flood of cheap American food products into the country. Economic pressures mounted with the devaluation of the Mexican peso in 1994, resulting in lowered wages and increased unemployment. The subsequent economic crisis sharpened the need for income and credit throughout Mexico, in middle-class as well as poor and working-class households, and encouraged out-migration not only from traditional sending states but also from new sending states.[7]

In Central America globalization and economic restructuring along with political violence and unrest led to mass international migration during the 1980s and 1990s. U.S. and to a lesser extent European investment supported the expansion of agricultural exports and industrial development in Central America, particularly in Guatemala and El Salvador, which created new job opportunities but also led to the widespread displacement of small farmers and indigenous communities, prompting both internal and foreign migration. During the 1980s El Salvador and Guatemala were torn by civil wars as right-wing governments engaged in violent repression of labor unions, peasants, activist organizations, and indigenous communities. With the support of U.S. military aid and training, both El Salvadoran and Guatemalan military forces assassinated suspected militants and carried out large-scale massacres in regions thought to support guerilla forces. At the height of the violence, thousands of Salvadorans and Guatemalans fled their home countries, many heading for the United States. Deteriorating economic conditions in the aftermath of war combined with neoliberal economic restructuring in the 1990s created high levels of unemployment and underemployment and prompted large-scale migration from Central America.[8]

As economic destabilization pushed increasing numbers of Mexicans and other Latin Americans into the migration stream, changes in U.S. immigration policy, principally passage of the Immigration Reform and Control Act (IRCA) of 1986, contributed to a major shift in the destinations of Mexican and Central American migrants from traditional destinations in Texas and California to new U.S. locations.[9] IRCA's key features included stronger border controls, new sanctions on employers who hired undocumented immigrants, and the legalization of immigrants who could demonstrate that they had resided and worked in the United States for at least five years. Under IRCA approximately 3 million immigrants gained permanent legal residence. Of these, 2.3 million were Mexicans; the remaining 700,000 included immigrants from El Salvador, Guatemala, the Philippines, Colombia, Haiti, and several other countries. Free to move about the country, increasing numbers of newly legalized immigrants left the crowded job and housing markets in California and the Southwest to pursue better opportunities elsewhere.[10]

The new border controls under IRCA also had an impact on the geography and nature of Latin American immigration. The beefing-up of border enforcement diverted migrants from traditional crossing points in California (San Diego) and Texas (El Paso) to more remote desert regions in Arizona and New Mexico. Instead of stemming the flow of illegal immigrants, the new policies actually encouraged undocumented workers to stay for longer periods in the United States or to make the move permanent in order to avoid the now more costly and dangerous border crossings.[11]

The southeastern United States became a magnet for immigrant workers in the 1990s because of plentiful jobs for unskilled and semiskilled workers, a lower cost of living, and the relative absence (at the time) of anti-immigrant sentiment. Faced with a shortage of laborers, employers in the carpet, food-processing, and construction industries recruited Latino immigrant workers, initially from Texas and California and later directly from Mexico and Central America. The agricultural industry used both recruiters and temporary work visa programs to draw immigrant workers to the Southeast.[12] In Atlanta the construction trades relied heavily on the recruitment of skilled and unskilled workers from Mexico and Latin America to complete the numerous building projects for the 1996 Olympic Games.

By the late 1990s chain migration facilitated employer recruitment efforts. Once migrants from a certain sending area in Latin America concentrate in a new receiving area in the United States, a migration stream develops that channels further migration to the same location. As an immigrant community grows, it develops resources and social networks that ease the process of settlement and adaptation for new migrants.[13] Many migration channels have been established between sending communities in Mexico and Central and South America and receiving communities in the Southeast.

Together, economic globalization, new immigration policies, labor recruitment, and chain migration have produced a rapid and dramatic rise in Latin American immigration to the Southeast. Largely as a result of this migration, the Latino population in the region grew exponentially during the 1990s. The census reported Latino growth rates of between 300 and 400 percent for North Carolina, Arkansas, and Georgia, between 200 and 300 percent for Tennessee, South Carolina, and Alabama, and smaller but still significant growth rates for other southern states between 1990 and 2000 (see table 0.1). In comparison, at the national level, the Hispanic population grew from 22.4 million in 1990 to 35.3 million in 2000, a growth rate of 58 percent.[14] The dramatic growth of the Latino population in the Southeast has had profound social and economic consequences for the region.

Reflecting ongoing Latino migration, census estimates in 2006 reported continuing high Latino growth rates throughout the Southeast, with North Carolina, Arkansas, Georgia, and Tennessee leading the way into the twenty-first century. By 2006 the population of Latinos in the ten southern states had increased to a total of over 2.5 million, their numbers ranging from 46,348 in Mississippi to 696,146 in Georgia. Latino migrants continue to settle in a variety of localities throughout the Southeast. Many have moved to small towns and rural areas to work in agriculture and food-processing, while others have settled in metropolitan areas, with the greatest number in the sprawling Atlanta metro area (467,418 in 2006). Latinos have also concentrated in North Carolina's urban areas along the I-85 corridor, with 133,959 in Raleigh–Durham–Chapel Hill, 126,608 in Charlotte, and 114,120 in Greensboro–Winston-Salem as of 2006. Smaller but still substantial numbers of Latinos have settled in other southern cities, including Greenville, Birmingham, and Nashville (table 0.2).

Latino newcomers comprise a diverse group in terms of nationality, family status, socioeconomic background, race/ethnicity, and legal status, among other characteristics. Unlike traditional Latino immigrant destination areas, where one group initially dominated the immigrant community (such as Puerto Ricans in New York City, Mexicans in Los Angeles, and Cubans in Miami), Latino immigrants in the South come from a variety of countries in Central and South America and the Caribbean. The largest national group by far is Mexican, but the population also includes many Puerto Ricans, Guatemalans, Salvadorans, Colombians, and Dominicans (table 0.3). Except in Virginia and Louisiana, Mexicans comprise over 60 percent of the total Hispanic population in the ten states, and Central Americans, mainly from Guatemala, El Salvador, and Honduras, make up the second-largest group of Latinos everywhere but Virginia (where Central Americans outnumber Mexicans) and Kentucky (where Puerto Ricans outnumber those of Central American origin). South Americans from

Table 0.2 Hispanic Population, Selected Southern Metropolitan Areas, 1990–2006

	Hispanic Population			*% Change (+)*		
Metro Area	*1990*	*2000*	*2006**	*1990–2000*	*2000–6*	*1990–2006*
Atlanta, GA	57,169	268,851	467,418	370.3%	73.9%	717.6%
Birmingham, AL	3,989	16,598	30,981	316.1%	86.7%	676.7%
Charlotte, NC	10,671	77,092	126,608	622.4%	64.2%	1086.5%
Greensboro-Winston-Salem, NC	7,096	62,210	114,120	776.7%	83.4%	1508.2%
Greenville-Spartanburg, SC	5,120	26,167	50,280	411.1%	92.2%	882.0%
Nashville, TN	7,665	40,139	72,664	423.7%	81.0%	848.0%
Raleigh–Durham–Chapel Hill, NC	9,019	72,580	133,959	704.7%	84.6%	1385.3%

* The 2006 data correspond to the revised metro-area definitions adopted by the OMB in 2003.

Source: U.S. Census Bureau, 2006 American Community Survey

Table 0.3 Origin of Hispanic/Latino Population, Ten Southern States, 2006

State	*Mexican*	*Puerto Rican*	*Cuban*	*Dominican Republic*	*Central American*	*South American*	*Other*
Alabama (Hispanic pop. 111, 432)	63.8%	7.7%	4.8%	0.1%	13.6%	4.0%	5.9%
Arkansas (Hispanic pop. 138,283)	75.9%	1.9%	0.5%	0.5%	11.9%	2.1%	7.2%
Georgia (Hispanic pop. 696,146)	65.4%	7.4%	2.7%	1.3%	12.6%	6.1%	4.7%
Kentucky (Hispanic pop. 83,015)	67.2%	8.2%	7.7%	0.3%	6.3%	4.3%	6.1%
Louisiana (Hispanic pop. 123,281)	40.8%	6.6%	7.1%	1.7%	21.8%	5.9%	16.1%
Mississippi (Hispanic pop. 46,348)	65.6%	4.8%	2.6%	0.8%	13.8%	3.2%	9.3%
North Carolina (Hispanic pop. 597,382)	66.6%	7.5%	1.8%	1.2%	13.2%	5.0%	4.8%
South Carolina (Hispanic pop. 148,632)	63.0%	10.1%	1.7%	0.4%	11.6%	7.8%	5.4%
Tennessee (Hispanic pop. 187,747)	67.5%	6.9%	1.7%	1.0%	12.0%	4.3%	6.7%
Virginia (Hispanic pop. 470,871)	25.1%	10.9%	2.7%	1.2%	31.4%	18.3%	10.5%
Total (Hispanic pop. 2,603,137)*	57.8%	7.8%	2.7%	1.1%	16.3%	7.6%	6.8%

* Total Hispanic population in 2000 in these ten states was 1,732,586.

Source: U.S. Census Bureau, 2006 American Community Survey

Colombia, Brazil, Peru, and Venezuela also contribute to the expanding Latino population in the South.

The region's Latino population includes legal residents, U.S. citizens, temporary workers, and undocumented immigrants. Some have migrated to the South from other regions in the United States, while others have arrived directly from Mexico, Central, and South America. They come from rural areas and small towns in Latin America, as well as major metropolitan areas like Mexico City, Caracas, Bogotá, and Guatemala City. A large number migrated without family members, leaving children, spouses, and parents in their home countries. Single male migration is especially common in the early stages of labor migration, but over time greater numbers of women and children have joined the migration stream to the South. Immigrants come from regions that have been sending migrants to the United States for generations and from new sending areas in Mexico and Central and South America.

Chapters and Main Themes

IMMIGRANT TRANSNATIONALISM

Latino immigrants in the South exhibit a range of migration patterns. Depending on a variety of factors—legal status, income, purpose for migrating, location of the nuclear family, and conditions in the homeland—migrants may live and work in the United States for several years before returning home, circulate regularly between their home towns and the United States, or settle for an extended period if not permanently in this country. Whether they are circular migrants, temporary workers, or long-term residents, most engage in various kinds of transnational activities that connect them to their countries of origin. Contrary to popular perceptions, theirs is not a simple story of leaving one country for good and settling in another, abandoning their former lives. As several authors demonstrate in this book, many immigrants develop strong social, economic, and/or familial ties in both places of settlement in the U.S. South and places of origin in Latin America. Transnational linkages are not new to today's immigrants, but technological developments in travel and communication have greatly facilitated their ability to sustain strong relationships with families and community members who live thousands of miles away.

In chapter 1 Elaine Lacy analyzes patterns of migration and settlement among Mexican immigrants in South Carolina, based on extensive field research and semistructured interviews with two hundred migrants. She finds that many Mexican immigrants in South Carolina lead transnational lives: even as they become incorporated into the local economy and, sometimes, local society, they stay closely connected to families and friends in Mexico through telephone communication, regular remittances to family members, and involvement in hometown projects and events. Such transnational connections help them to deal with the material and emotional challenges of living and working in a foreign country. Lacy argues that many Mexicans in South Carolina are developing a "sense of belonging on both sides of the border."

In chapter 2 Mexican sociologist Rosío Córdova Plaza explores what living in a transnational social space means for family and gender relations among rural migrants from the state of Veracruz, Mexico. Córdova Plaza's fieldwork in Veracruz, which includes sixty-four in-depth interviews with both return migrants and family members of migrants who are still in the United States, offers valuable insight into the lives of rural migrant families. The author analyzes the tensions in gender and marital relations as migrants attempt to maintain families and marriages across national borders. Working in fields, factories, and construction sites in the Southeast while their families remain in Mexico, Veracruzano male migrants experience loneliness, fear of arrest by U.S. authorities, and anxiety about losing the affection and respect of wives and children. Successful migration, however, can offer them considerable material and psychological benefits by providing a source of subsistence and bolstering their authority in the home and social prestige in the community.

ECONOMIC INCORPORATION AND IMPACT

Another theme contributors address is the widespread reliance on Latino immigrant labor in southern industries, and the social and economic consequences of this development. The restructuring of the southern economy and the resulting growth and prosperity of the last two decades have depended to a large extent on the recruitment of laborers from Mexico and other countries of Latin America. Employers in some industries throughout the urban, suburban, and rural Southeast turned to Latino immigrants as a flexible, low-cost labor pool that has not only boosted corporate profits but also reduced costs for consumers. Immigrant labor has fueled the economic growth and competitiveness of key southern industries such as poultry processing, forestry, textiles, carpets and rugs, construction, landscaping, hospitality, and agriculture. Reliance on Latino immigrant labor, both documented and undocumented, is now a structural feature of the southern economy that has had and will continue to have significant social, economic, and political consequences for the region.

The contributions in this book analyze the consequences of this development from different perspectives. In chapter 5 economists James Johnson and

John Kasarda assess the economic impact of Latino immigration in the South, focusing on North Carolina. Their work addresses a heated political debate among southern politicians and citizens about the costs and benefits of Latino immigration. Those opposed to immigration charge that immigrants, especially the undocumented, drain state resources especially in education and health care, while proponents contend that immigrants, even the undocumented, pay taxes, create new jobs, and provide a needed source of labor. Johnson and Kasarda provide a systematic assessment of Latinos' economic impact using an economic model that measures their costs and contributions to the state budget, as well as their impact on the state's economic productivity and competitiveness.

While Johnson and Kasarda address the state-level economic impact, Raymond Mohl (chapter 4) examines how the incorporation of Latino labor has affected southern communities and workers in Alabama. He finds that the effects of new immigration have proven contradictory and complex. Latino immigrants recruited to work in food-processing and forestry industries have helped revive rural areas and small towns that suffered from population and economic decline. At the same time, employers' reliance on Latin American workers has created tensions between immigrant and U.S.-born workers, both black and white. Even though policy experts and economists disagree sharply about whether the use of immigrant labor has resulted in job losses and wage depression for American workers, many U.S.-born workers in Alabama, especially African Americans and white workers at the lower end of the wage scale, feel threatened by the new immigrants.

PLACE-MAKING AND COMMUNITY BUILDING

Several chapters explore how Latino immigrants are transforming the physical and cultural landscapes of the South through their cultural traditions and adaptive strategies. In chapter 3 Mexican sociologists Víctor Zúñiga and Rubén Hernández-León explore community-level changes that Mexican immigration has brought to Dalton, a small city in northwestern Georgia that has become an international center for the production of wall-to-wall carpeting. Among other changes, immigration has shifted existing social and spatial boundaries in this predominantly white city. While some Dalton residents object to the newcomers, their presence is evident: Mexican restaurants, taco stands, tortilla factories, churches, religious symbols, and soccer teams can be found throughout Dalton and its environs. Local businesses are reaching out to Latino residents as well. Wal-Mart, the largest discount chain in Dalton (and in the region), now caters to Mexican customers by providing aisles of Mexican products and Spanish-language announcements.

Elaine Lacy's chapter examines the ways in which immigrants affect the social landscape in South Carolina, specifically through the formation of Mexican enclaves in urban and rural parts of the state. Typically centered around apartment complexes, mobile-home parks, churches, *tiendas*, and/or restaurants, these enclaves are especially important for immigrants in new sending areas where there are no large established Latino communities to cushion the settlement process. Ethnic enclaves in the South allow immigrants to feel more at home and to participate in social networks where they share resources and information about jobs, housing, health care, and schooling.

Latino immigrants have sometimes encountered resistance from local authorities in their efforts to create ethnic cultural spaces, as Mary Odem demonstrates in chapter 7 about religion and community formation in metropolitan Atlanta. Odem explores the early community-building efforts of Latino Catholic immigrants in Chamblee-Doraville, one of the first and most densely populated immigrant neighborhoods in metro Atlanta. In the early 1990s immigrants from Mexico, El Salvador, Guatemala, Peru, and other countries sought to establish a religious space where they could practice their faith in a familiar environment but encountered opposition from police, local citizens, and Catholic officials. Through a process of struggle and negotiation they eventually convinced the archdiocese to establish a Latino Catholic mission in Chamblee-Doraville that became an important source of spiritual and social support for immigrants, especially for undocumented immigrants and those facing family separation and economic hardship.

CHANGING RACIAL DYNAMICS

The ways in which Latino newcomers are transforming existing racial relations, practices, and categories and are becoming incorporated into the South's racial system are of great interest to scholars and policy makers alike. Given the relatively short duration of Latino settlement in the South, it's too soon to make generalizations about the direction of racial transformation in the region. Several chapters, however, provide important insights into the changing racial and ethnic dynamics in various southern localities. Zúñiga and Hernández-León demonstrate that carpet industrialists' recruitment and accommodation of Latino immigrant workers has undermined the system of white privilege that long protected factory jobs for southern white workers in northwest Georgia. Mohl's chapter explores ways in which the mass immigration of Mexicans and other

Latin Americans has given rise to new patterns of racial and ethnic conflict in Alabama, where both African Americans and whites express resentment over economic competition, neighborhood change, and the "otherness" of the Latino newcomers.

Angela Stuesse in chapter 6 analyzes the impact of neoliberal economic policies on race relations and collective organizing in the poultry industry in rural Mississippi. The economic restructuring of the poultry industry in recent years has created a racially diverse workforce in which immigrants from Mexico, Guatemala, and South America now work alongside African Americans as low-wage laborers. Using participant observation, interviews, and focus groups, Stuesse analyzes attitudes and interactions among diverse groups of workers. She argues that neoliberal labor practices have heightened existing racial tensions not only between African American and immigrant workers, but also among different racial and national groups of Latino workers. While employers exploit racial and national divisions among workers, local labor leaders and social justice activists are pursuing new forms of organizing to unify black and Latino poultry workers to defend their rights.

In chapter 8 geographer Jamie Winders points to the importance of analyzing interactions between diverse groups of immigrants, as well as between the native born and foreign born, in order to understand the changing racial dynamics in the South. She examines the negotiations and conflicts between new populations of immigrants from Latin America and refugees from the Sudan, Somalia, and Bosnia in Nashville, Tennessee. Through an analysis of their encounters in various spatial and institutional contexts, including neighborhoods and nonprofit organizations, Winders explores how these groups are transforming the ways residents of southern cities think about and address issues of diversity, race, ethnicity, and cultural belonging.

SOUTHERN RESPONSES TO LATINO IMMIGRATION

A final theme explored in the collection is the diverse and shifting ways that southern citizens, politicians, and the media have responded to Latino immigrants. During the 1990s public officials and the media paid little attention to immigrants, tending to emphasize their economic contributions and strong "work ethic." Even though conflicts with local authorities arose in some of the more densely populated immigrant neighborhoods across the region, as Odem demonstrates in her chapter on Atlanta, for the most part these remained localized events. The political environment for immigrants in the South, however, changed significantly in the early twenty-first century, as Lacy and Odem discuss in chapter 9. Southern attitudes and policies toward immigrants have become increasingly hostile in recent years, a shift that the authors attribute to deteriorating economic conditions in the region and heightened national preoccupation with terrorism and "illegal immigration." Public outcry about "illegals" stealing jobs and burdening taxpayers and about increasing crime rates led state and local officials across the Southeast to pass laws and ordinances limiting unauthorized immigrants' access to jobs, social services and housing. At the same time, a number of nonprofit organizations, immigrant advocacy groups, and churches have worked to defend immigrants' rights. According to authors Zúñiga and Hernández-León certain regions in the South were less prone to nativist reaction. The Dalton area in northwest Georgia did not experience the overt anti-immigrant sentiment found in other cities and towns with large immigrant populations, largely due to the influence of local carpet manufacturers and their political allies.

The issue of immigration will no doubt remain at the forefront of southern politics for the foreseeable future. Despite the desires of many southern politicians and citizens, it is not possible to reverse or stop the process of immigration; the South has become a multiethnic region with a diverse and still-expanding immigrant population. The question is not *whether* Latino immigrants will become a part of southern society, but rather *how* they will be incorporated into the region. We hope that the articles in this volume will contribute to the knowledge and understanding of this newest group of southerners and of the process of their incorporation.

A Note on Terminology

The terms *Hispanic* and *Latino* are often used interchangeably in U.S. discourse, but they are not identical terms. According to the *American Heritage Dictionary* the term *Hispanic* comes from the Latin word for "Spain" and refers to all Spanish-speaking peoples in both hemispheres. *Latino* refers more exclusively to peoples of Latin American origin. In this book we use the term *Latino* when discussing people of Latin American background because of its greater accuracy. However, the U.S. Census more often uses the broader term *Hispanic* and includes in its calculations of Hispanics all Spanish-speaking peoples (that is, those from Spain as well as those from Latin America). When referring specifically to census data contributors generally use the term *Hispanic*.[15]

Notes

1. John Egerton, *The Americanization of Dixie: The Southernization of America* (New York: Harper's Magazine Press, 1974); Larry J. Griffin, "Southern Distinctiveness, Yet

Again, or Why America Still Needs the South," *Southern Cultures* 6 (fall 2000): 47–72; James C. Cobb, *Redefining Southern Culture: Mind and Identity in the Modern South* (Athens: University of Georgia Press, 1999); Edward Ayers, "What We Talk About When We Talk About the South," in *All Over the Map: Rethinking American Regions*, by Edward L. Ayers, Patricia Nelson Limerick, Stephen Nissenbaum, and Peter S. Onuf (Baltimore: Johns Hopkins University Press, 1996), 62–82; Matthew Lassiter, *Suburban Politics in the Sunbelt South* (Princeton, N.J.: Princeton University Press, 2006); "The End of Southern History: Integrating the Modern South and the Nation," conference organized by Matthew Lassiter and Joseph Crespino, Emory University, March 23–24, 2006.

2. Arthur D. Murphy, Colleen Blanchard, and Jennifer A. Hill, eds., *Latino Workers in the Contemporary South* (Athens: University of Georgia Press, 2001); Heather Smith and Owen Furuseth, eds., *Latinos in the New South: Transformations of Place* (Hampshire, England: Ashgate, 2006); Leon Fink, *The Maya of Morganton* (Chapel Hill: University of North Carolina Press, 2003).

3. James C. Cobb and William Stueck, eds., *Globalization and the American South* (Athens and London: University of Georgia Press, 2005). See also James L. Peacock, Harry L. Watson, and Carrie R. Matthews, eds., *The American South in a Global World* (Chapel Hill and London: University of North Carolina Press, 2005).

4. Víctor Zúñiga and Rubén Hernández-León, eds., *New Destinations: Mexican Immigration in the United States* (New York: Russell Sage Foundation, 2005). See also Audrey Singer, Susan W. Hardwick, and Caroline B. Brettell, eds., *Twenty-first Century Gateways: Immigrant Incorporation in Suburban America* (Washington, D.C.: Brookings Institution Press, 2008); Greg Anrig and Tova Andrea Wang, eds., *Immigration's New Frontiers* (New York: Century Foundation Press, 2006). For other works on Latinos in the South see Stanton Wortham, Enrique G. Murillo Jr., and Edmund T. Hamann, eds., *Education in the New Latino Diaspora* (Westport, Conn.: Ablex, 2002).

5. James C. Cobb, *The Selling of the South: The Southern Crusade for Industrial Development* (Baton Rouge: LSU Press, 1982); James C. Cobb, "The Sunbelt South: Industrialization in Regional, National, and International Perspective," in *Searching for the Sunbelt: Historical Perspectives on a Region*, ed. Raymond A. Mohl (Knoxville: University of Tennessee Press, 1990), 25–46; Alfred E. Eckes, "The South and Economic Globalization, 1950 to the Future," and Raymond A. Mohl, "Globalization, Latinization, and the *Nuevo* New South," in *Globalization and the American South*, ed. Cobb and Stueck, 36–65 and 66–99.

6. Douglas S. Massey and Kristin Espinoza, "What's Driving Mexico-U.S. Migration? A Theoretical, Empirical, and Political Analysis," *American Journal of Sociology* 102 (1997): 939–99; Douglas S. Massey, Jorge Durand, and Nolan J. Malone, *Beyond Smoke and Mirrors: Mexican Immigration in an Era of Economic Integration* (New York: Russell Sage Foundation, 2002), 47–49, 73–83; David G. Gutierrez, "Globalization, Labor Migration, and the Demographic Revolution: Ethnic Mexicans in the Late Twentieth Century," in *The Columbia History of Latinos in the United States Since 1960*, ed. David G.

Gutierrez (New York: Columbia University Press, 2004), 43–86; Peter Andreas, "The Escalation of U.S. Immigration Control in the Post-NAFTA Era," *Political Science Quarterly* 113 (winter 1998–99): 591–615.

7. See all references in the previous note.

8. Nora Hamilton and Norma Stoltz Chinchilla, *Seeking Community in a Global City: Guatemalans and Salvadorans in Los Angeles* (Philadelphia: Temple University Press, 2001), 17–35; Saskia Sassen, "Why Migration?" *Report on the Americas* 26:1 (July 1992): 14–19.

9. For a discussion of the history and implications of IRCA, see Massey, Durand, and Malone, *Beyond Smoke and Mirrors*. For a discussion of IRCA's implications for the Southeast see Mohl, "Globalization, Latinization, and the *Nuevo* New South."

10. David M. Reimers, *Unwelcome Strangers: American Identity and the Turn Against Immigration* (New York: Columbia University Press, 1998); Roger Daniels, *Guarding the Golden Gate: American Immigration Policy and Immigrants Since 1882* (New York: Hill and Wang, 2004), 219–59; Massey, Durand, and Malone, *Beyond Smoke and Mirrors*, 24–51, 105–41; Jorge Durand, Douglas S. Massey, and Emilio A. Parrado, "The New Era of Mexican Migration to the United States," *Journal of American History* 86 (Sept. 1999): 518–36; Betsy Cooper and Kevin O'Neal, "Lessons from the Immigration Reform and Control Act of 1986," Migration Policy Institute, *Policy Brief*, no. 3 (Aug. 2005); Julie A. Philips and Douglas S. Massey, "The New Labor Market: Immigrants and Wages after IRCA," *Demography* 36:2 (May 1999): 233–46; Barry R. Chiswick, "Illegal Immigration and Immigration Control," *Journal of Economic Perspectives* 2:3 (summer 1988): 101–15.

11. Douglas S. Massey, "March of Folly: U.S. Immigration Policy after NAFTA," *American Studies* 41 (summer/fall 2000): 183–209; Massey, Durand, and Malone, *Beyond Smoke and Mirrors*.

12. Mohl, "Globalization, Latinization, and the *Nuevo* New South"; Sandy Smith-Nonini, "Federally Sponsored Migrants in the Transnational South," in *American South in a Global World*, ed. Peacock, Watson, and Matthews, 59–79.

13. Massey, "The Social and Economic Origins of Migration," *Annals of the American Academy of Political Science* 510 (1990): 10–71; Massey and Espinoza, "What's Driving Mexico-U.S. Migration?"; Massey, "International Migration at the Dawn of the Twenty-first Century: The Role of the State," *Population and Development Review* 25 (June 1999): 303–22.

14. U.S. Bureau of the Census, American Community Survey, 2007.

15. *American Heritage Dictionary of English*, 4th ed. (New York: Houghton Mifflin, 2006), http://dictionary.reference.com/browse/Hispanic; accessed March 18, 2007.

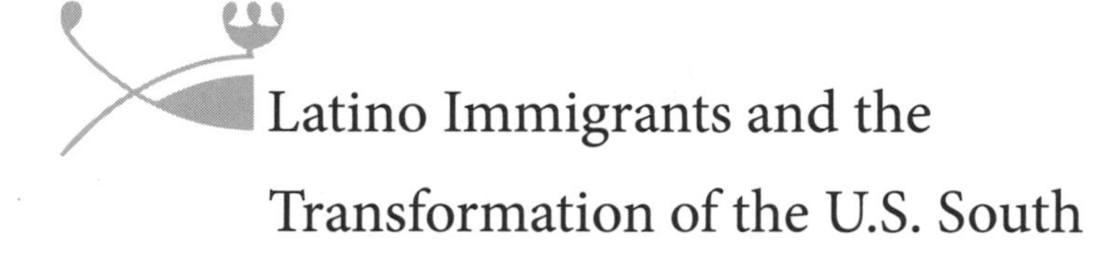

Latino Immigrants and the Transformation of the U.S. South

CHAPTER ONE

Cultural Enclaves and Transnational Ties

Mexican Immigration and Settlement in South Carolina

ELAINE LACY

In early 2004 Griselda López Negrete, a fifteen-year-old high school honors student of Mexican origin living in Aiken, South Carolina, faced deportation because her deceased mother, who had brought Griselda to South Carolina at age two, was undocumented. Griselda, whose English carries a soft southern accent, could be forced out of the only home she remembers. Her plight brought sympathy and support from many quarters for the DREAM Act (Development, Relief and Education for Alien Minors Act), proposed federal legislation that would prohibit such deportations of young immigrants whose parents brought them into this country as young children and who have been in the United States more than five years.[1]

Griselda's story made international news, but aside from reporting that her mother died when Griselda was eight years old, journalists made no mention of others in the large Negrete family, most of whom are legal U.S. residents. Many of Griselda's cousins, aunts, and uncles are part of a close-knit Mexican community in Aiken where streets are named after places in their state of origin, Michoacán. Griselda's grandfather came to Aiken in the early 1980s to work grooming horses, and, following an age-old migratory pattern, he sent for family members and friends. Eventually over half of his home village of San Juan Palmira emigrated to the United States, most of them to the Aiken area. Some of the Negretes and other former residents of San Juan Palmira return to Michoacán regularly, and remittances from the migrants provide support for the small community to this day.[2] They and thousands of other Mexicans living in South Carolina, most of whom have arrived from southeastern Mexico in the last decade, have become integrated into South Carolina life in a variety of ways while continuing to maintain formal and informal ties to their places of origin.

Migration scholars describe a three-step process of migration: the actual movement of people across borders, which can involve large segments of the sending community; the settlement phase, which requires adjustments on both sides of the border; and the consolidation stage, in which migrants become assimilated or incorporated into the host society in some form.[3] Since Mexican migration to South Carolina is a relatively new phenomenon, we are witnessing predominantly stages one and two of this process. Migration to the state differs in some ways from the pattern in other new settlement areas: first, new immigrants tend to migrate directly from Mexico rather than moving from other parts of the country; second, no large multigenerational Mexican communities exist here that could provide them with social capital; and finally, they must negotiate what W. E. B. Du Bois referred to as the "color line," in a state with a large African American population and a history of racism.[4]

This chapter provides a social and demographic profile of the Mexican community in South Carolina, based largely on a fourteen-county study of Mexican immigrants funded through the University of South Carolina (USC) and conducted by the author between 2003 and 2005. A key objective of the study was to establish a baseline profile from which to measure changes in the Mexican community in South Carolina over time. Approximately two hundred subjects were asked over sixty questions related to their demographic profile, community of origin, social networks, economic status, "transnational" activities, cultural practices, and future plans, among other topics.[5] The research methodology and complete findings are available in a published report.[6]

Findings from these interviews form the basis of the following description of Mexican migration to and settlement patterns within South Carolina, and the discussion of transnational cultural spaces in which many Mexican immigrants continue to live. Despite the short history of Mexican migration to South Carolina, I argue that Mexican immigrants' settlement patterns and transnational practices call for reconsideration of traditional notions of assimilation and citizenship.

Mexican Migration to South Carolina

According to the U.S. Census, South Carolina's Latino population grew by 400 percent between 1990 and 2006 (from roughly 30,000 to about 150,000), while in the same period their numbers increased nationally by 50 percent (from just over 22 million to roughly 44 million).[7] Census estimates in 2005 placed South Carolina among the states (all but one in the Southeast) with the highest growth rate of Hispanic residents since 2000, and between 2004 and 2005 the state's foreign-born population, most of whom are Latinos, increased at the highest rate in the nation. The actual number of Latinos in South Carolina is likely at least twice that reported by the U.S. Census Bureau. Their complex household makeup and cultural differences in "household" definitions, the legal status of many Latino immigrants, individual and family mobility, language barriers, and fear or distrust of government are the most commonly cited reasons for this undercount.[8] Latinos comprise an official minority in South Carolina, and state policy makers and service providers find themselves generally unprepared to accommodate this new population group.

The majority (63 percent, according to census data) of South Carolina's Hispanic population is of Mexican origin.[9] Immigration to South Carolina from Mexico, which began in earnest in the 1980s, grew out of conditions outlined in the introduction to this volume: economic shifts related to globalization and neoliberal policies, along with Mexico's periodic economic crises, led to massive emigration from Mexico, facilitated over time by social networks; and U.S. immigration policy and regional economic conditions within the United States set the stage for migration from traditional Latino settlement areas in Texas, California, Florida, New York, and Chicago to new immigrant "gateways."

Profile of Mexican Immigrants to South Carolina

The findings of the USC study and other research conducted by the author both formally and informally since the early 1990s reveal that the majority of Mexican immigrants to South Carolina are typical of recently arrived Mexican migrants elsewhere in the United States. Most leave Mexico largely out of economic necessity, they work long hours in relatively low-skilled, low-wage jobs, many live with or near family or friends from Mexico, and they maintain a variety of ties to their communities of origin, living within what many scholars refer to as transnational communities.

On the other hand, Mexican immigrants in South Carolina differ in important ways from those in traditional areas of settlement in the United States. While the Negrete family patriarch from Michoacán and other Mexican migrants relocated to South Carolina from other U.S. states or settled out of the East Coast migrant agricultural stream in the 1980s, the majority (over 70 percent) of those in the USC study have arrived since the late 1990s, and 65 percent came to the United States directly from Mexico.[10] Further, well over half arrived from new "sending" areas in the southeastern portion of Mexico, particularly from the states of Veracruz, Chiapas, Hidalgo, and Puebla.[11]

In the 1980s and early 1990s the overwhelming majority of Mexican migrants in South Carolina were young single males. Today more women and children are joining husbands and fathers in the United States or are coming on their own. According to census data, in 2006 44 percent of Hispanics in South Carolina were female, up from 40 percent in 2000.[12] In the USC study 31 percent of subjects were female. The median age among males in the study (all of whom are age eighteen and over) was twenty-nine (SD 10.5) and among females, thirty (SD 10.1). These immigrants are therefore older than the national average for newly arriving Hispanic immigrants: the census reported the average age of Mexican immigrants at entry level into the United States as twenty-one.[13]

Over half (56 percent) of the males in the USC study were married, and 53 percent of those brought their wives to the state. Some female respondents indicated that tighter border security after September 11, 2001, and the resulting difficulty of their husbands' visits home influenced their decision to reunite the family by moving to the United States. Of married Mexican immigrants, 86 percent had children, and 58 percent have children with them in South Carolina. Only 19 percent of women in the study were unmarried.

The median educational level of those interviewed was nine years for both males and females. Over one-third (36 percent) received six years or less of schooling, and illiteracy even in Spanish is widespread. The overwhelming majority of Mexican immigrants are members of the working class who work in the state's secondary labor market, most of them filling jobs in construction, poultry processing, manufacturing, restaurants, landscaping, the hospitality industry, and agriculture. Ninety-nine percent of respondents in the USC study are employed, and the average income is $1,200 per month. As has been the case in other parts of the United States, Mexican workers in South Carolina are preferred by some employers, reportedly because they are highly productive and willing to work for low wages, they will readily take jobs that employers find difficulty filling with native-born labor, they tend to shun unions (in South Carolina), and they eagerly work overtime.

In the 1990s most Mexican immigrants settled in South Carolina's metropolitan areas, but today they are also prevalent in communities throughout the state. Counties with the largest Mexican populations include Greenville and Spartanburg in the upstate (along the I-85 industrial and commercial corridor), where immigrants work predominantly in construction, factories, landscaping, and agriculture; Beaufort, Charleston, and Horry Counties along the coast, where they fill mostly construction, restaurant, hospitality, landscaping, and agricultural jobs; and Richland and Lexington Counties in the central part of the state, where construction, poultry packing, restaurant, and landscaping jobs abound. Roughly 70 percent of respondents in the USC study lived in crowded conditions in mobile-home parks and apartment complexes in small communities, towns, and cities in fourteen counties in South Carolina.

Many Mexican immigrants prefer to live in the state's smaller communities not only because of established social networks, but because of the relative *tranquilidad* of such locales.[14] Some who have relocated from other states report that they fled cities including Los Angeles and Atlanta to escape crime, violence, and gangs. Others, especially those from rural Mexico (who make up the majority of immigrants in the state), enjoy the similarities in climate, setting, and relative security between South Carolina and the southern Mexican states. Mexican immigrants have revitalized a number of small communities in the state, providing labor to local industries, students for local schools, and a boost to the towns' economies.

Settlement Processes

Since at least the 1920s migration scholars have described the role of social networks in migrants' decisions to migrate, in the process of migration itself, and in the course of settlement and incorporation.[15] Among the most valuable aspects of social networks is that they can provide social capital, that body of knowledge and skills that can facilitate the migration and settlement processes. Most Mexican immigrants in South Carolina, however, lack access to social capital for a variety of reasons.

First, the longer immigrants are in the United States, the more social capital they accumulate.[16] Our respondents' average length of time in the United States was 4.5 years (SD 4.7), and the average number of years in South Carolina was 3.5 (SD 3.7), a relatively short period. Further, most Mexican immigrants in South Carolina come directly from Mexico, which limits their access to social capital.[17] The fact that over half of immigrants arrive from new sending areas in Mexico also limits their access to information about the social, cultural, and economic terrain of their new destinations. Finally, unlike traditional receiving areas, South Carolina includes no large, multigenerational Mexican community that could provide new immigrants with social and emotional resources as well as political and economic clout. Long-established ethnic communities help preserve cultural norms and values, shape the process of acculturation into a new society, and provide access to local ethnic networks. These well-established networks in traditional receiving areas provide social capital in the form of information about and access to jobs, credit, services, and ways of navigating the host country's cultural, legal, and economic terrain.[18]

Also contributing to the challenges of the settlement process is the fact that South Carolina, like many other states experiencing the recent influx of new immigrants, is unprepared in many ways to accommodate them. In 2007 many of the state's law enforcement units, hospitals, and courtrooms still lacked qualified translators and interpreters. Public schools in many parts of the state are without sufficient certified English for Speakers of Other Languages (ESOL) instructors or the means to assist students with poor English skills. Few low-cost health care options are available. Word has spread within the Mexican community in South Carolina about the availability of such services in Georgia and North Carolina, and some respondents in the USC study consider their absence in South Carolina another form of discrimination.

Typical of the lack of support services is the state's inadequate public transportation, which limits immigrants' employment opportunities as well as access to health care, English classes, and opportunities to interact with the larger society.[19] Like most other states, South Carolina requires proof of legal residency to secure a driver's license. Many drive without licenses or, as one woman in the USC study said, "manejamos con licencia de Dios"—we drive with a license from God (respondents' translations by the author). Limited transportation options also contribute to feelings of isolation and depression, especially among immigrant women. Over half of respondents in the study listed lack of transportation and/or the inability to drive legally among the most serious problems they face.

Another critical challenge in the settlement process is the language barrier. Despite a virtually unanimous desire to learn English, subjects cite lack of access and transportation to classes, long work hours, or illiteracy even in their own languages as impediments to language training. As one young man said, "the reason I don't speak more English is that I work 12 to 16 hours every day, every week so I can have something in the future, for my kids and my wife" (translated). Still, roughly one-quarter of respondents in the USC study said they are taking or had taken formal English classes, and another 23 percent were attempting to learn on their own with help from tapes or books in English, or by watching English-language television. Their inability to speak English or speak it well contributes to another challenge in South Carolina: discrimination.

Roughly 40 percent of Mexican immigrants in the USC study stated that they had experienced discrimination in South Carolina. Such discrimination manifested itself in the form of denial or reluctant provision of services in shops, restaurants, and other public facilities; in employment, including being passed over for the most select tasks, being denied pay or other benefits they had been promised, or harassment from others in the workplace; in housing; various forms of ill-treatment by law-enforcement personnel; or, most commonly, being subjected to verbal abuse from strangers. As other studies reveal, perceived discrimination brings on other problems during the settlement process, such as depression, feelings of isolation, and delayed assimilation.[20]

As numerous observers have noted during the last decade, such treatment reflects resurgent nativism in U.S. society. Some reactions to Mexican immigrants in South Carolina may be categorized as economic nativism, which targets particularly undocumented immigrants because of the perception that they take jobs, housing, educational, health care, and other resources that should go instead to legal residents. Some males in the USC study report being accused of taking jobs away from U.S. citizens. In addition, cultural nativism targets "the detrimental cultural consequences of immigration."[21] This type of nativism is evident in the national English-only movement, and in South Carolina it is most often expressed by the demand that Mexican immigrants learn English (and speak it clearly), the charge that they carry diseases, drink too much, and live in filth.

Anti-immigrant sentiment is also driven by ethnic differences in South Carolina. The "in-between" ethnic or racial status of most Latinos means that their "relationship to the U.S. color line is not clear and is still being determined."[22] In a state where most think of ethnicity strictly in terms of Blacks, Mexicans have become targets of both Blacks and whites. Some respondents consider such attacks racially motivated, but others believe that provincial attitudes are to blame. Comments such as "because I am Mexican the police watch me," "white kids in Saluda hate Mexicans," and because we are Mexican "they treat us as inferiors" are common.

How do Mexican immigrants in South Carolina navigate the settlement stage of migration, given the enormous challenges? In examining processes of settlement and consolidation among Latino immigrants elsewhere in the United States, scholars have identified a process they refer to as cultural citizenship.[23] As William Flores makes clear, "culture interprets and constructs citizenship." Cultural citizenship denotes daily activities that enable Latinos in the United States to "claim space in society and eventually claim rights. . . . The motivation is simply to create space where the people feel 'safe' and 'at home,' where they feel a sense of belonging and membership."[24] Community building comprises an important part of cultural citizenship, since "for Latinos, community is essential to survival, not only in terms of neighborhood or geographic locale, but also in terms of collective identity."[25] The concept of cultural citizenship is useful in understanding the processes of community building, and in comprehending the behavior of Latinos and other immigrant or marginalized groups as they carve out cultural spaces that help them not only to adapt but eventually to make political or social claims on the dominant society.

The sense of belonging to a larger Mexican community is evident among subjects in the USC study. Regardless of whether they consider their relocation to the United States permanent or temporary, the overwhelming majority (over

90 percent) self-identify as Mexican or with their state of origin in Mexico. Less than 1 percent refer to themselves as *Hispano* or Latino. Suzanne Oboler, among others, has raised the issue of Self and Other in identity formation among immigrants.[26] As she points out, identity formation is often situational and may arise as a reaction to the dominant ideology. Discrimination directed toward an ethnic or immigrant group often results in what has been called a reactive ethnicity, feelings of solidarity with the broader group.[27] As one Veracruzano said, "I don't want to be called Mexican, because they get blamed for everything around here, so it's better to be known by the state you come from."

Despite the relative short history of Mexican migration and settlement in South Carolina, immigrants are beginning to carve out spaces in which they feel "at home" and "safe," and where they can express their culture and develop their own group identity. For example, as has been the case with other immigrant groups to the United States, Mexican enclaves have formed in virtually every community with a Mexican population in South Carolina, usually around apartment complexes and mobile-home parks. Often a Mexican *tienda* and authentic Mexican restaurant are not far away. Ninety percent of respondents in our study live with or near family, friends, or other Mexicans in such enclaves. They engage in enclave behaviors typical of first-generation immigrants over time: over 60 percent of subjects in the USC study speak little to no English, and over 95 percent speak exclusively Spanish at home and during leisure time with friends. Job-related enclaves have also appeared: the majority of our respondents speak Spanish at work, because most work with other Mexicans or Latinos, usually Central Americans. Respondents access almost exclusively Spanish-language media, including television and newspapers. Lack of transportation, poor English-language skills, and feelings of discrimination from the larger society reinforce enclave behaviors. Such enclaves help maintain and strengthen cultural ties, and they provide a sense of community and mutual support.

The role of immigrant women in fostering cultural citizenship is critical. As Pierrette Hondagneu-Sotelo points out, women immigrants are central in "developing culturally distinct immigrant communities."[28] Immigrant women construct social networks within their cultural enclaves, they purchase and prepare familiar food items, and, as mothers, they pass on Mexican culture to their children (such as the practice of celebrating their daughters' *quinceañeras*). Half of the women in the USC study do not work outside the home and therefore devote more time to such activities.

Other loci of Mexican community in South Carolina include churches, commercial establishments, and restaurants. Since the mid-1990s scores of churches (in a state with more churches per capita than most) have begun to offer services in Spanish. Roughly half of those in the USC study participate in church activities, many of them attending Protestant churches. At least forty churches across the state offer services exclusively in Spanish.[29] Mexican and other Latino entrepreneurs are also engaged in community building by drawing people together in shops and restaurants where social relationships are nurtured. The scores of Mexican *tiendas* that have appeared since the mid-1990s in South Carolina serve as both community and cultural centers. In addition to socializing with other Mexicans, customers can gain information about jobs, housing, transportation, utilities, health care, and other topics that facilitate settlement. *Tiendas* also promote cultural citizenship by selling Mexican food products, clothing and music, paraphernalia related to Mexican *fútbol* teams, art, and other cultural icons such as candles emblazoned with the Virgin of Guadalupe, Mexico's patron saint.[30] One can also rent Mexican movies and pick up free copies of some of the nine Spanish-language newspapers published in the state that serve as technical means of representing a larger, "imagined community," as Benedict Anderson called it.[31] These newspapers carry job notices, advertise services for the Latino population, and report local and international news of interest to the entire Latino community in a culturally familiar manner. Further, *tiendas* facilitate the creation and maintenance of transnational communities: in these stores Mexicans can wire money to Mexico, purchase telephone cards to call friends and family there, and buy bus and plane tickets to travel to their country of origin.

Transnational Communities

Frequent contact with or travel to and from Mexico, or both, are common practices among Mexican immigrants to South Carolina, despite tighter border security since the September 11, 2001, terrorist attacks in the United States. Most immigrants maintain a variety of social, cultural, and economic connections to their communities (and country) of origin, thus behaving as members of transnational communities. The topic of transnational activities among migrants has generated widespread discussion and debate among scholars. Although definitions vary somewhat according to scholarly discipline, and some scholars dispute claims made by others that the early-twenty-first-century immigrants' transnational ties are stronger than those at the turn of the last century, there is widespread recognition that migrants around the world today occupy "transnational social fields" through border crossings, regular communication, remittances, and institutional or other connections, or some combination of these.[32] Some who study transnational processes also consider the nonmigrants in sending communities as part of the transnational social field.

The overwhelming majority of Mexican immigrants in our study maintain a variety of linkages to their communities of origin. Over 90 percent report that they communicate by telephone with family and friends in the sending community once or twice per month, and 57 percent report that they talk with family and friends in Mexico at least weekly, sometimes more often. About 90 percent remit earnings to family in Mexico, and for those who do so on a regular basis, their average remittance is about $450. Most reported that the remittances were used to assist family members with basic living expenses and with health and educational costs. A few said they were purchasing land or building or remodeling homes, while others said a portion of their remittance monies went toward community improvement projects in their home towns or to the local church.[33] A number of respondents in the USC study report that their remittances are being invested or saved for their use when they return to Mexico, which most hope to do. Such investments represent an ongoing emotional tie to "home."

Only 22 percent of respondents state with some certainty that they plan to live permanently in the United States. The remainder either express uncertainty or say they will stay a few years, just long enough to save a certain amount of money or until their children are educated. As studies elsewhere have demonstrated, however, the majority of Mexican immigrants who plan to return to Mexico, especially those who have children in the United States, eventually settle permanently on this side of the border.

Most Mexican immigrants in the USC study are undocumented, yet despite the danger and expense there is a great deal of *ida y vuelta*—coming and going across the border.[34] Some go to Mexico for the December–January holidays and return after a few months, whereas others remain in Mexico a year or more before returning to South Carolina. Almost 40 percent of subjects report that they own property in Mexico, and several mentioned continued ties to churches in their sending communities. Well over 90 percent stay informed of events in their communities and Mexico as a whole through regular telephone communication and by watching news of Mexico on Spanish language television. Many expressed the desire to live in both Mexico and the United States in the coming years.

The "sojourner mentality" expressed by so many of the state's Mexican immigrants is evident among other Latin American immigrant groups today, and, according to some theorists, contributes to a strategy that many adopt: becoming cultural citizens of transnational spaces. As Louis Mirón argues, rather than "simply acculturating to the dominant traditions of the United States, as the nativism of the 1990s would have it," many Mexicans "strive to acquire the cultural capital necessary to maneuver across national spaces that connect the

United States and their homelands."[35] This involves acculturating to host country traditions just enough to "maneuver within the space bounded by such conventions," but at the same time maintaining a cultural repertoire necessary to negotiate transnational space.[36] Strong evidence exists that Mexicans in South Carolina are adopting just such a strategy. While most express the desire to return to Mexico, many see themselves going back and forth permanently, and as cultural citizens of that transnational space they have a sense of belonging on both sides of the border.

This cultural repertoire includes bilingualism: over ninety-five percent of subjects in the USC study reported a desire to learn English themselves, and roughly the same number said they would want their children to be bilingual. It also entails retaining previous cultural forms while at the same time creating completely new ones. As other studies have demonstrated, this includes crafting new words that are neither Spanish nor English, such as "yardas" for lawns, "parqueaderos" for mobile-home parks, and "trailas" for mobile homes. Musical preferences within South Carolina's Mexican community include not only Mexican favorites, (which, like other elements of Mexican culture are regional), but U.S. music as well. Immigrants from southeastern Mexico tend to prefer ballads, *cumbia* and other *música tropical*, along with U.S. pop music, country music, rap, and hip hop. A number of respondents, especially younger males, add to their musical repertoire *ranchera* and *norteña* music, which has become the musical anthem of the experience of illegal border crossing.[37]

Mexican immigrants also retain certain cultural values and practices while adopting U.S. practices they consider necessary for success here. Some respondents, for example, report that they have learned to become more "organized" and more punctual since moving to the United States. One respondent said that he is learning to live the "American dream," to work hard and make a lot of money, and to "enjoy his rest, like Americans do." At the same time, others express the desire to maintain aspects of Mexican culture such as maintaining close family relationships and not succumbing to materialism.

High on the list of South Carolinian's concerns over recent immigration is that the new immigrants are not being incorporated or assimilated at the same pace and in the same manner as did previous waves of immigrants to the United States. Many believe, as Harvard University Professor Samuel Huntington has argued, that Mexican immigrants' proximity to their homeland, their lack of language skills, lack of education and income, and tendency toward enclave behavior result in a failure to assimilate, at times by design.[38] Other scholars argue, however, that globalization has altered the processes and implications of migration, and that transnational behaviors do not limit incorporation into new settlement areas.[39] The work of Peggy Levitt and others demonstrates that migrants can and do become incorporated into their host societies while maintaining social, political, and economic ties to their places of origin.[40] Mexican immigrants' settlement and consolidation processes suggest that we must reconsider traditional notions of assimilation. Rather than reverting to earlier nativist-inspired ideas that immigrants should make a clean break with their homelands and adopt "American" culture, we must recognize that, as Levitt argues, "some [immigrants] are keeping their feet in both worlds," and are, in a variety of ways, becoming incorporated into U.S. society.[41] Roberto Suro argues, "[Latinos'] proximity [to their places of origin] means that assimilation is not continuous or direct, but rather a rhythmic, periodic process in which immigrants retain aspects of their foreign identity even as they learn English and otherwise adopt American ways."[42]

The relatively large, longstanding Mexican community in Aiken, South Carolina, that includes the Negrete family is no longer an anomaly in a state where new immigrants arrive, mostly from southeastern Mexico, every day. Pushed by desperate and deteriorating economic conditions and pulled to South Carolina by jobs, a mild climate, and more importantly, migration networks, most of these migrants are coming directly to South Carolina rather than moving from other U.S. states. The resulting measure of their social capital and the fact that they are settling in a state without a long-standing, multigenerational Mexican population that could help facilitate settlement and consolidation poses tremendous challenges for the new immigrants. Further challenges arise because of South Carolina's relative lack of preparedness to meet the new immigrants' basic needs and because of the region's complex ethnocentric, ethnic, and racial landscape.

Mexican immigrants to South Carolina are meeting the challenges of settlement in part through the practice of cultural citizenship, that is, by participating in enclave networks, building communities, and otherwise carving out spaces within the state where they can develop and maintain a collective identity and feel "at home." *Tiendas* and restaurants contribute to these practices by providing familiar cultural products and serving as social gathering places for Mexican immigrants, and Mexican immigrant women contribute as well through social networking and helping in various ways to develop culturally distinct communities.

The overwhelming majority of Mexicans in South Carolina engage in transnational activities, whether through frequent communication, remittances, or travel back and forth across the border. Very few express the desire to live in South Carolina permanently. Most either have not decided where they will settle permanently, or they plan to return to Mexico or hope to live in both places.

This "sojourner mentality" contributes to a tendency seen among Mexican immigrants in South Carolina and elsewhere to develop a repertoire of cultural practices that enable them to be cultural citizens of transnational spaces. This may mean picking and choosing from among cultural practices and artifacts from both sides of the border, or combining elements, thus creating totally new cultural products and practices.

The adoption of U.S. cultural forms and practices, even if they are blended with Mexican cultural forms and practices, indicate that Mexican immigrants are being incorporated into U.S. society, albeit through a process of negotiation and accommodation. At the same time, Mexican immigrants, like other Latinos in the United States, will certainly bring changes to South Carolina culture and society. As William Flores writes, Latinos are "renegotiat[ing] . . . what it means to be a citizen with a distinct Latino infusion into the defining fabric of the United States."[43] The increasing prevalence in South Carolina of the Spanish language of Mexican restaurants, *tiendas*, and food products on grocers' shelves, of Mexican workers in industries beyond agriculture, and the thousands of Mexican children in public schools will slowly alter the cultural landscape. The richness of Mexican culture is already evident in numerous ways, including local celebrations of the Virgin of Guadalupe Day and Día de los Muertos, and in Mexican recipes in newspapers around the state. As Mexicans continue the migration and settlement phases and begin the consolidation stage, more changes are sure to come.

Notes

A version of this paper appears as "Comunidades mexicanas en Carolina del Sur: Vidas transnacionales y ciudadanía cultural," in *In God We Trust: Del campo mexicano al sueño americano*, Rosío Córdova Plaza, María Cristina Núñez Madrazo, and David Skerritt Gardner, eds. (Mexico City: Plaza y Valdés Éditores/Universidad Veracruzana, 2007).

1. These young immigrants would also be able to apply for permanent residence if they graduate from high school and attend college in the United States or serve in the U.S. military. Griselda López Negrete was approved for legal permanent residence status in the United States in January 2008 because her U.S. citizen father (by adoption) petitioned for her.

2. Pat Butler, "Path to Prosperity Leads Mexicans to Jobs in S.C.," *Columbia (S.C.) State*, 19 April 1998; Butler, "One Man Clears Paths to Aiken's Stables," *State*, 22 April 1998; Butler, "Dream Thrives for Some, Dies for Others: Hispanic Immigrants Re-create Mexican Hometown in Aiken County," *State*, 23 April 1998; author's interview with Pedro Negrete, 25 Jan. 1996, Aiken, S.C.

3. Robert C. Smith, "How Durable and New Is Transnational Life? Historical Retrieval through Local Comparison," *Diaspora* 9 (fall 2000): 203–33.

4. W. E. B. Du Bois, *The Souls of Black Folk* (Chicago: A. C. McClurg, 1903; New York: Dover, 1994).

5. The literature on transnationalism is vast. Among the most noteworthy works on the meaning and characteristics of the transnational experience are those of Arjun Appadurai, Wayne Cornelius, Nancy Foner, Nina Glick Schiller, Nathan Glazer, Luin Goldring, Michael Jones-Correa, Michael Kearney, Peggy Levitt, Douglas Massey, Alejandro Portes, and Robert C. Smith.

6. Elaine C. Lacy, *Mexican Immigrants in South Carolina: A Profile* (Columbia: USC Consortium for Latino Immigration Studies, 2007), at http://www.sph.sc.edu/cli/pdfs/final_final[1].pdf. The study was funded by a grant through the University of South Carolina Research and Productive Scholarship Program and by the Aiken Partnership Fund at USC Aiken. Other primary data in this essay are derived from a series of informal interviews with Latino immigrants conducted by the author between 1994 and 1996.

7. U.S. Bureau of the Census, 1990 Census and 2007 American Community Survey.

8. Mary C. Davis et al., *Estimations of Matching Error in Census Undercount Estimates* (Washington, D.C.: U.S. Bureau of the Census, 1992); Barry Edmonston, *The Undercount in the 2000 Census* (Baltimore: Annie E. Casey Foundation, 2002); Mary Romero, *Ethnographic Evaluation of Behavioral Causes of Census Undercount of Undocumented Immigrants and Salvadorans in the Mission District of San Francisco* (Washington, D.C.: U.S. Bureau of the Census, 1992); E. L. McLean and S. S. Newton, "United States and South Carolina, General Characteristics, 2000," working paper WP072301. Department of Agricultural and Applied Economics, Clemson University, Clemson, South Carolina, 2001.

9. U.S. Bureau of the Census, American Community Survey 2007.

10. In the 1990s well over 90 percent of South Carolina's migrant and seasonal farmworkers were Latinos who were engaged in planting and harvesting tobacco, peaches, tomatoes, soybeans, and other fruits and vegetables in all forty-six counties of the state for nine months of the year. Institute for Families in Society, *South Carolina Statewide Hispanic Health Needs Assessment* (Columbia: Institute for Families in Society, USC, 1998), 4.

11. Lacy, *Mexican Immigrants in South Carolina*; data from the Mexican Consulate in Raleigh, N.C.

12. U.S. Bureau of the Census, Census 2000 and American Community Survey 2007.

13. U.S. Bureau of the Census, Census 2000.

14. In using the term *tranquilidad* to describe a location, some respondents in the USC study apparently were referring to the lack of crime and anti-immigrant sentiment. In some cases the respondent was alluding to the relative absence of immigration enforcement personnel.

15. See, for example, Douglas Massey et al., *Return to Aztlan: The Social Process of International Migration from Western Mexico* (Berkeley: University of California Press, 1990); Monica Boyd, "Family and Personal Networks in International Migration: Recent Developments and New Agendas," *International Migration Review* 23 (1989): 638–70; Jacqueline Hagan, *Deciding to Be Legal: A Maya Community in Houston* (Philadelphia:

Temple University Press, 1994); Pierrette Hondagneu-Sotelo, "Regulating the Unregulated: Domestic Workers' Social Networks," *Social Problems* 41 (1994): 50–64; Alejandro Portes and Ruben Rumbaut, *Immigrant America: A Portrait* (Los Angeles and Berkeley: University of California Press, 1990); Jacqueline Hagan, "Social Networks, Gender, and Immigrant Incorporation: Resources and Constraints," *American Sociological Review* 63 (1998): 55–67.

16. Maude Toussaint-Comeau, "The Occupational Assimilation of Hispanic Immigrants in the U.S.: Evidence from Panel Data," *International Migration Review* 40 (2006): 508–34; Mark A. Leach, "The Incorporation of Mexican Immigrants in New Destinations: A Research Agenda," unpublished paper, Summer Institute on International Migration, University of California, Irvine, 2005; Michael E. Fix and Jeffrey Passel, *Immigration and Immigrants: Setting the Record Straight* (Washington, D.C.: Urban Institute, 1994), at http://www.urban.org/publications/305184.html.

17. Leach, 2005; Rubén Hernández-León and Víctor Zúñiga, "Mexican Immigrant Communities in the South and Social Capital: The Case of Dalton, Georgia," University of California, San Diego, Center for Comparative Immigration Studies, working paper 64, 2002.

18. Alejandro Portes and Rubén G. Rumbaut, *Immigrant America: A Portrait* (Berkeley: University of California Press, 1990), 53–55, 87–88.

19. Most areas of South Carolina are virtually without public transportation, and many of the few public bus companies have cut back on services because of budget constraints. Language and other cultural barriers and lack of information about bus schedules and destinations may also account for the fact that public transportation is underutilized by Latino immigrants to the state. For a discussion of difficulties associated with public transportation in the Columbia area see Kristen Hudgins, "Prisoners in Our Own Homes: Latinas and Access to the Public Transportation system in Columbia, South Carolina," M.A. thesis, University of South Carolina, 2005.

20. Brian Karl Finch, Bohdon Kolody, and William Vega, "Perceived Discrimination and Depression among Mexican-Origin Adults in California," *Journal of Health and Social Behavior* 41 (2000): 295–313; James P. Smith, "Assimilation across the Latino Generations," *American Economic Review* 93 (2003): 315–19.

21. Louis F. Mirón, Jonathan Xavier Inda, and JoAnn K. Aguirre, "Transnational Migrants, Cultural Citizenship, and the Politics of Language in California," *Educational Policy* 12 (1998): 660–61.

22. Héctor R. Cordero-Guzmán, Robert C. Smith, and Ramón Grosfoguel, *Migration, Transnationalization and Race in a Changing New York* (Philadelphia: Temple University Press, 2002).

23. William V. Flores and Rina Benmayor, eds., *Latino Cultural Citizenship: Claiming Identity, Space, and Rights* (Boston: Beacon Press, 1997). The broader definition of citizenship is described by Flores and Benmayor: "The traditional legal definition of citizenship, a status conferred upon individuals by place of birth or by decree of the state and implying membership, with all of its accrued rights, benefits, and responsibilities, was too narrow for our purposes. Instead, we found the sociological and political notion

of citizenship as political subject a broader and more useful concept to describe the current realities of Latino communities. In this way, immigrants who might not be citizens in the legal sense or who might not even be in this country legally, but who labor and contribute to the economic and cultural wealth of the country, would be recognized as legitimate political subjects claiming rights for themselves and their children and in that sense as citizens" (6).

24. Ibid., 15.

25. Ibid., 16.

26. See Suzanne Oboler, "The Politics of Labeling: Latino/a Cultural Identities of Self and Others," in Carlos G. Vélez-Ibáñez and Anna Sampaio, eds., with Manolo González-Estay, *Transnational Latina/o Communities: Politics, Processes, and Cultures* (Lanham, Md.: Rowman & Littlefield), 73–90.

27. See, for example, Rubén G. Rumbaut, "Severed or Sustained Attachments? Language, Identity, and Imagined Communities in the Post-Immigrant Generation," in Peggy Levitt and Mary C. Waters, eds., *The Changing Face of Home: The Transnational Lives of the Second Generation* (New York: Russell Sage Foundation, 2002), 74; Suzanne Oboler, "The Politics of Labeling"; Charles R. Chandler, Yung-Mei Tsai, and Renee Wharton, "Twenty Years After: Replicating a Study of Anglo-and Mexican-American Cultural Values," *Social Science Journal* 36 (1999): 353–67.

28. See Pierrette Hondagneu-Sotelo, *Gendered Transitions: Mexican Experiences of Immigration* (Berkeley: University of California Press, 1994), chapter 6.

29. *Directorio de negocios hispanos de Carolina del Sur* (Columbia, S.C.: Hispanic Connections Inc.), 2004.

30. Caroline Brettell, "Meet Me at the Chat Corner: The Embeddedness of Immigrant Entrepreneurs," unpublished paper, New York University Symposium on Immigration, Oct. 2003.

31. See Benedict Anderson, *Imagined Communities: Reflections on the Origins and Spread of Nationalism* (London: Verso, 1983).

32. For a discussion of transnational social fields see Linda Basch, Nina Glick-Schiller, and Cristina Szanton-Blanc, *Nations Unbound: Transnational Projects, Postcolonial Predicaments, and Deterritorialized Nation-states* (Langhorne, Pa.: Gordon & Breach, 1994).

33. The story of how remittances from the Negrete family of Aiken, S.C., helped their community of origin has been documented by journalist Pat Butler. See "Path to Prosperity Leads Mexicans to Jobs in S.C.," *Columbia (S.C.) State*, 19 April 1998. The author also learned of these activities from one member of that family in an interview 25 Jan. 1996, Aiken, S.C.

34. Although few respondents admitted to regular border crossings, over half said they knew many people who come and go, especially during the holiday season or for medical care.

35. Mirón, Inda, and Aguirre, "Transnational Migrants," 660.

36. Ibid., 666.

37. Rubén Martínez, *Crossing Over: A Mexican Family on the Migrant Trail* (New York: Picador, 2001).

38. Huntington's ideas appear in "The Hispanic Challenge," *Foreign Policy* 141 (March–April 2004): 30–45, and Samuel Huntington, *Who Are We? The Challenges to America's National Identity* (New York: Simon & Schuster, 2005).

39. Richard Alba and Victor Nee, "Rethinking Assimilation Theory for a New Era of Immigration," *International Migration Review* 31 (winter 1997): 826–74; José Itzigsohn and Silvia Giorguli Saucedo, "Immigrant Integration and Socio-Cultural Transnationalism," *International Migration Review* 36 (autumn 2002): 766–98.

40. See, for example, conclusions for various studies in the following: Levitt and Waters, eds., *Changing Face of Home*; Vélez-Ibáñez and Sampaio, eds., *Transnational Latina/o Communities*; and Paul Kennedy and Victor Roudometof, eds., *Communities Across Borders* (London: Routledge, 2002), among many others.

41. Levitt, "Keeping Feet in Both Worlds," in Christian Joppke and Ewa Morawska, eds., *Toward Assimilation and Citizenship* (New York: Palgrave, 2003), 178.

42. Roberto Suro, "Recasting the Melting Pot: Later-Generation Latinos Are Writing a New Immigration Story," *American Demographics* (March 1999): 30–32.

43. See Flores in Flores and Benmayor, *Latino Cultural Citizenship*, 277.

CHAPTER TWO

New Scenarios of Migration

Social Vulnerability of Undocumented Veracruzanos in the Southern United States

ROSÍO CÓRDOVA PLAZA

> Lots of Veracruzanos began arriving in about '98 or '99. That's why last time I went to Mexico I went to Veracruz, because many of the people who work with us are from there. I went to the ranches of many people who live here. We went to Cuitláhuac, Yanga, Córdoba . . . we went to all of those areas.
>
> *Mary, from Guanajuato, owner of a Mexican store in Newberry, South Carolina*

In the last thirty years increasing globalization has led to changes in population movements. The magnitude of movements from poor to rich countries means that we are experiencing the largest migratory wave in history. The outstanding characteristics of these migratory flows include their global nature, with at least one-half of the world's nations involved, the diversity of migrants' geographic and social origins, their acceleration and increasing volume, and their increasing feminization.[1]

A good illustration of population movements is that of Mexican migration to the United States, not just because of its century-plus duration but also because it is the world's largest in terms of the number of immigrants.[2] Mexico suffered a net loss of more than 2.4 million individuals in the 1980s alone.[3] As observers have pointed out, shifts have occurred not only in the origin of Mexican emigrants (they now leave almost every region of Mexico), but also in migrant destinations: they increasingly migrate to predominantly urban regions of the United States that had not received immigrants before—including the U.S. Southeast.

As noted elsewhere in this volume, factors that have shaped Mexican emigration since the 1980s include Mexico's economic crises since the early 1980s, the U.S. economy's year-round demand for nonagricultural workers, changes in U.S. laws associated with the 1986 Immigration Reform and Control Act (IRCA) that resulted in family reunification, and the maturity of migratory networks.[4] These factors have sparked a change in the way Mexican undocumented workers integrate themselves in the United States spatially and economically.

This study provides an analysis of the vulnerability of undocumented Mexican workers in the United States in the early twenty-first century and of their perceptions of the impact of migration on their personal and familial lives. Primary data for this study were collected through sixty-four in-depth interviews with returning migrants (both male and female) in Tuzamapan, Veracruz, between April 2002 and March 2003, and with migrants in ten towns and cities in South Carolina in June 2004. In this chapter I provide a brief overview of the background of Mexico–United States migration and an assessment of conditions that led to the shift in the types of workers who migrate to the United States. I also discuss factors that increase the vulnerability of migrants in the United States, the manner in which their situations change at various stages of the adaptation process, and how the migrant experience affects notions of gender norms and behaviors.

Binational Tensions

As various studies have demonstrated, despite stricter U.S. immigration policies that would seem to indicate ironclad border security, the number of unauthorized migrants who have succeeded in settling in that country has increased every year since 1988.[5] This phenomenon is driven by two factors: Mexico's development has been tied to the U.S. economy for decades, and since 1988 Mexico's worsening economic crisis has severely impacted the national economy both in urban areas as well as rural, causing high unemployment rates. As a result, rural-to-urban migration within Mexico is no longer an option to find employment.[6] On the U.S. side employers have benefited from the porous border and have hired large numbers of undocumented works as a cheap labor force. Many of these workers have practically no power to negotiate with employers and have to endure poor working conditions including long shifts, low salaries, lack of access to social security, job instability, lack of safety equipment, and risk of exposure, among other dangers.[7]

As a result, undocumented labor has become a structural feature of the economy in some U.S. states.[8] In addition, growing persecution, detentions, and deportations of unauthorized migrants in the United States create a climate of insecurity and fear among these migrants while allowing politicians "to back up their [tough] statements on border security, even though most people who try to enter the United States illegally succeed in doing so."[9] The apparent contradiction between discouragement and attraction also serves as a mechanism for politicians to earn votes during elections and as an instrument to pressure Mexico, whose subordination to the interests of its northern neighbor have been pledged even at the cost of its own, with direct and negative implications for migrants.

Migration from Veracruz to El Norte

In recent years Veracruz residents' participation in migrant streams has increased to such dimensions and at such an accelerated rate that it has captured the attention of both researchers and municipal and state officials. In 1997 Veracruz ranked twenty-seventh among Mexican states sending migrants to the United States; in 2002 the state ranked fourth.[10] It is estimated that between 400,000 and 800,000 Veracruzanos emigrated to the United States in the late twentieth and early twenty-first centuries.[11] Migration to the neighboring country has become an attractive option for many Veracruzanos and in many cases the only option. Many cannot find employment in the state's depressed job markets. Research into the causes and extent of this large and diverse state's unemployment and underemployment is ongoing, but more needs to be done in order to gain a better understanding of the depth of the problems of poverty and economic displacement.[12]

The factors that propel Veracruzanos into the international migratory circuits are intimately related to the state's agricultural and mining crises. As a producer of raw materials, Veracruz falls into the pattern that Agustín Escobar and his team described.[13] That pattern characterized Mexican regions that feed new migratory flows at the end of the millennium as places with significant indigenous and peasant populations and with marked income inequality, and as municipalities that are highly marginal (on a national marginalization index) and whose economies have revolved around plantation and commercial agriculture and are tied to the world's raw-materials markets. Further, the restructuring of Veracruz's industrial sector in recent years resulted in a loss of almost twenty thousand jobs.[14] As result, emigration to the United States serves as a viable alternative, especially for the population that is in their productive years. This out-migration is resulting in a rapid transformation of the structure and dynamics of the state's rural societies, resulting in severe depopulation of some areas.[15] One rural farmer interviewed in 2003 said,

> Before, they said that we began a crisis in the month of July, but now that crisis is ongoing. Nowadays, the crisis starts in January and ends approximately around the months of October, November and December when it's time to harvest again. That's why the young people are choosing to go abroad to work, because here there are no sources of work that grab young people's attention. If you go to the countryside, you will only see us—the elderly—working. (Braulio, age 59)

At the same time, the principal destinations of emigrants from Veracruz reflect changes in the destinations of Mexican migrants to the United States. California, Texas, and Chicago are waning in their attraction, giving way to Georgia, Florida, Alabama, North Carolina, and South Carolina.[16]

Even though their social networks are in the process of solidification, these networks provide Veracruz migrants with orientation to new receiving areas, temporary housing, and help in finding work. This assistance is of vital importance to the neophyte migrant as he inserts himself into the destination community. Although a few travel with a passport and tourist visa, the majority of migrants cross the Mexico-U.S. border without proper documentation, traveling through the desert and facing grave dangers, as evidenced by the significant number of Mexican migrant deaths every year. Between 2001 and 2006, 959 Mexicans died crossing the border, most of them in the Arizona desert. Many of the victims were from Veracruz, which has been recognized as a state sending many undocumented migrants to the United States.[17] The inherent dangers of traveling without papers and the increasing cost of the trip mean that return migration is not a regular occurrence, and the danger and cost therefore affect the ways in which one lives in "transnational space."[18]

Migration and Victimization

Even though an inexpensive Mexican labor force has been of vital importance in U.S. economic development since the mid-nineteenth century, when southwestern cattle ranches and California fruit cultivation were expanding, the fluctuations in the level of border security and in the treatment migrants have received in the United States is linked to that country's shifting political necessities. Since the U.S. Border Patrol was created in 1924, undocumented workers have been considered "illegal aliens," and except for the just over two decades in which the Bracero Program operated (the program that legalized the temporary transfer of Mexican agricultural workers to the United States), labor migration has become a point of conflict in bilateral relations.[19] It has become an especially sticky point in recent years.

The U.S. government's efforts to enhance border security in recent years are in response to a series of highly complex circumstances that have had unfortunate consequences for migrants. The attacks of September 11, 2001, and the subsequent "War on Terror" have placed all immigrants under suspicion of being a potential terrorist. The U.S. government's April 2003 order called for the indefinite detention without bail of undocumented individuals for reasons of "national security" while they are awaiting a hearing is a case in point.

A tendency to associate immigrants with crime is common in receiving societies, a tendency manifested in varied and ambiguous ways. On the one hand, it is understood that poverty, lack of opportunities, and economic and social deprivation in their home countries have forced certain individuals to migrate, but on the other hand, they are accused of driving down labor costs and taking U.S.-born workers' jobs—even though they are dirty, denigrating, poorly paid jobs that U.S. workers often avoid. Additionally, Mexican immigrant workers are often suspected of harboring bad intentions: because of their poverty, they are believed to be more likely to commit crimes. They are categorized as "illegals" and therefore are associated with violation of the law and accused of every imaginable crime.[20]

Madriz's 1997 study of U.S. women's perceptions of violence notes that the most clear-cut representations of the criminal are highly racialized, and centered on "illegal" Latinos and poor blacks who are considered disturbed, savage and inhumane. At the same time, that negative perception can extend to the entire home country. For example, the Mexican channel Televisa's news program *En Contraste* on June 24, 2003, aired a portion of an interview with a U.S. Border Patrol officer who, in discussing control of the flow of undocumented Mexicans into the United States said, "Mexico is a corrupt country and we don't want that corruption invading us." The symbolism of the Other plays a fundamental role in perpetuating and justifying conditions of exploitation and the violation of the rights of migrants.

Further, their regular movement back and forth between the two economically asymmetrical nations puts Mexican migrants in constant danger of assault, exploitation, racism, hostility, xenophobia, and an increasing danger of losing their lives. One reason for the increasing deaths of migrants is Operation Guardian, a U.S. governmental program started in the mid-1990s to discourage the entry of undocumented persons. Instead of curtailing unauthorized immigration, the program has merely redirected migrants from the traditional crossing points in urban areas to high-risk zones in the desert and mountains. The results are clear: the number of migrant deaths increased 400 percent between 1994 and 1999, and the figures increased to a staggering 500-plus deaths in 2006.[21]

Fear and the Undocumented Migrant Status

The climate of fear that the situation described above generates in migrants is made worse for many migrants from Veracruz, who come predominately from rural areas. The migrants in this study lack knowledge of English, have limited education and vastly different cultural backgrounds from those of North Americans, and perhaps most importantly, most enter the United States without proper documentation. The process of adaptation to a new society requires of migrants the acquisition of skills and the understanding of codes far removed from their lives in their home communities.

The principal anxieties of migrants in this study were related to two potential dangers that are interconnected, resulting in a clandestine existence in the United States. On the one hand, they fear falling into the hands of the police, a fear supported by their own or others' experiences. Many migrants perceive the police as racist, and they know the police could jail and/or deport them. In addition, they fear being victims of a crime, mainly at the hands of African Americans, without being able to ask for any police protection because of their questionable legal status.

The risk and fear of being a victim of a criminal act are understood to be just as important as the crime itself in generating a sense of vulnerability.[22] Further, migrants' sense of vulnerability has been found to be directly related to a series of individual, social, and environmental factors that may come not so much from personal experience as from the context in which they find themselves and the way they are inserted into it. Individual factors include gender, age, socioeconomic status, length of residence in the destination community and prior personal experiences with crime in their places of origin. Social factors include the degree of consolidation into the social network to which the migrant belongs, familiarity with the laws of the receiving society, and previous knowledge of crime levels and accumulated experiences with crime. Environmental factors include the media's portrayal of criminal behavior, the neighborhood's safety, its ethnic composition and the degree of protection or harassment on the part of the police. These considerations are important because perceptions of crime and police protection comprise the way in which immigrants understand and practice their rights and responsibilities, even when they are limited.[23]

This study reveals three phases in the process of migrant workers' adaptation to the receiving society. Although the phases are determined based on the length of stay, each can have a variable duration depending on a combination of the above-mentioned factors. The first phase is isolation, followed by camouflage, and finally acclimation.

The initial period of the Mexican migrants' experience, or isolation phase, is permeated by a sense of extreme fragility and insecurity. The migrants feel unable to leave their residences alone, to ask questions of strangers, place phone calls, or even answer the telephone. Their activities depend in great part on the willingness of others in the social network to go somewhere with them or to help meet their needs. During this phase, they are easy prey to fraud and abuse, given their lack of knowledge of U.S. laws and norms, and because of their lack of proficiency in English. As one return migrant stated,

> Many nights I couldn't sleep because I was thinking about how I was going to get a job, how I was going to get to such-and-such a place, how I was going to buy a car, how I was going to get my papers, how I was going to get a license. Because if you don't have a car there in the United States, you can't function; you're forced to have a car. (Pedro, age 45)

Migrants in the early stages of settlement feel a lack of freedom to get around or to participate in recreational activities in public places where—it is feared—their status as aliens could become evident and they could run the risk of falling into the hands of the immigration authorities, popularly known as *la migra*. Getting fake documents allows them to get work, but they are in perpetual fear of discovery. Another return migrant said, "The truth is, as Los Tigres del Norte sing: 'Although the cage is made of gold . . .' There you are locked in and nothing more. It's not the same as here . . . Mexico is a free country and over there we are not free" (Ignacio, age 30).

Still another expressed the fear and frustration that goes along with an undocumented status:

> There are no words—you just have to swallow hard so as to not cry and look ahead. People think and say it's easy, but it's not. Once you are at the border, the situation gets hard, because while you're in Mexico with money, you do what you want. From there, dealing with Americans is difficult; you can't communicate. You go as an illegal, and you will always be marked by the law as soon as you cross the dividing line between Mexico and the United Sates. And with the fear that *la migra* will catch you, you are scared at every moment. There I am not brave. (Arnulfo, age 38)

Underscoring the relative feelings of safety in numbers in the early stages of settlement, another return migrant described a typical work week:

> I arrived home from work. We cooked dinner, each would make something and the other would clean up the house. The next day early, at 6 in the morning, up and at 'em again. [We ventured out] only on Sundays to deposit the money or go grocery shopping, but all of us went together. (Fernando, age 23)

In a second stage, that of camouflage, migrants are more familiar with their surroundings and have acquired indispensable communication skills and an ability to do things on their own. Likewise, they know what can or cannot be accomplished with fake documents, and try to avoid situations where their presence is obvious. They have also learned to identify potential dangers in terms of individuals, groups or places. In this stage many migrants decide to risk purchasing and driving an automobile, given the importance of cars in the Southeast where public transportation is limited. Lack of transportation can increase a migrant's vulnerability, but many feel they have few options. A migrant who had returned to Veracruz observed,

> I also got a car there, because they're indispensable for workers. You wind up with a job an hour from where you live, you have to get there by interstate and it's far away, and you don't have a car. Sometimes someone with a car will give you a ride, but they charge $20 or $30, depending on how far. And if they're not going to work, you lose that day. You have to just buy a car. (Luis, age 48)

Another risk factor in the camouflage stage is that of purchased documents. Migrants often find this process somewhat schizophrenic because the fake Social Security cards they are forced to purchase in order to work and rent housing are, in many cases, in other people's names and match up with real Social Security numbers. A worker who had returned to Veracruz said, "There one uses all fake papers. To go cash checks at the bank, . . . they want papers . . . and how are you going to do that, if you are a 'wetback'?" (Alberto, age 22).

Another migrant explained what the undocumented must know about these documents:

> Yes, we had problems renting the apartment because they ask for your social [Social Security card] to rent, and a roommate showed a fake social. That's how she got the apartment. But it's only good for some things. You can't show it to Immigration, nor to the consulate. You can't go around carrying it in your purse because the police will take it away; they have a special machine where they check it. It does work at jobs though, because the manager says if you don't have papers you can show those . . . Sometimes [the managers] are Mexican and good hearted—but sometimes not. I was lucky that it was laid back there [where I worked]. (Lorena, age 23)

During the acclimation phase, immigrants have gained the knowledge necessary to understand the system and can more confidently secure services such as education and health care. Additionally, they are more able to overcome obstacles related to their disadvantaged status, and even ask for law enforcement's involvement in cases of abuse and mistreatment. Once acclimated, individuals can become involved in organizations that work for immigrant rights or help someone get access to services. The sense of vulnerability gives way to an appreciation of the benefits that the United States can offer. Another migrant who returned to Veracruz said,

> The United States is respectful of the law. There the law really is enforced but here in Mexico, no. No, there when somebody breaks the law they may even kill him for not respecting [the law]. That's what is nice about the United States. . . . If you make a mistake, well, they lock you up because the law is stricter than it is here. (Gerardo, age 42)

In this stage, migrants learn more about what they are able to do in the United States. Another man who had returned to Veracruz said,

> Look, there are a lot of Mexicans [there] who scare their own people or even tell you that *la migra* is running around loose, that *la migra* this and that . . . it's not true. You can walk around in Los Angeles, Chicago, New York, wherever you want. You can go into any place—to the market, here and there, wherever you want—as long as you have money and a way to communicate; you can go into any place. You can even go to Las Vegas even though you are illegal. . . . What happens is that a lot of people—I don't know why—scare the rest of the people. . . . I'm telling you, in the trip that I made from Los Angeles to Chicago, I went through Las Vegas, I went through several cities with no problem. (Adrian, age 30)

Living in the Transnational Social Space

Aside from the adaptation necessary to enter the labor market successfully and live in relative peace, migrants experience the constant stress of having left their families behind, often for a long period of time. The telephone calls and the wiring of money and shipping of goods, photographs, and videos are indispensable to keeping the memory of those absent alive. In some cases, exerting authority over great distances is also necessary for the head of the household and provider: decisions must be made regarding the expenditure of money and the rewarding or punishing of children, and wives must be given instructions. The fear of losing the family's affection and the sense that one has to maintain control over family members becomes another source of anxiety. As one migrant husband and father who had been in the United States said,

> It feels bad, leaving for such a long time. . . . I was only there seven months and you come back and your children don't recognize you. I spoke to mine and they didn't recognize me; with time they started to grow fond of me again. But those

> [fathers] who have been away three or four years, I think their children lose affection for them. They even lose the respect of their wife sometimes. One is over there and sometimes the family doesn't even know if you are alive. (Luis, age 28)

For some, the stress of separation is compounded by worries over money and fidelity. Another young man said,

> If you leave, well . . . God forbid you have to deal with a bad woman. You say, "I'm over here busting my ass to earn more or to do something." And you send money and your wife says, "you know that in such-and-such a week, I will be out of money." And one starts to think, "Why does she spend so much? Who is she hanging out with?" And then you start to imagine that she's going out with someone else, and everyone has to pay for her sins. Thank God I ended up with a good woman. She has tried hard to save for the house. But I know of similar cases and you do become scared, and even more over there. That's why I left her with my in-laws so they can take care of her for me and so they could keep tabs on what she's doing. (Antonio, age 31)

Many male migrants look back on their experience in the United States as successful, despite the difficulties they encountered. An economically successful migratory experience strengthens masculine values insofar as it allows the man to show off his positive attributes and his ability to survive in a hostile environment.[24] Not surprisingly, the stories male migrants tell typically involve the difficulties they suffered and the actions they took to overcome them, thus sublimating an experience that had put them in a position of extreme vulnerability but which they demonstrated an ability to gracefully transcend. As one return migrant recounted,

> I feel most proud about having had a command of a little English, which is the most difficult thing. That's the only sense of pride that I have. Also, [I am proud] that I could experience the luxury of traveling in an airplane. Imagine that I, a mere farmer, would travel in a plane. I never would have dreamed of arriving at an American airport and asking for a plane ticket to go to Mexico. I thank the Lord for giving me the vision to go and come back. I think the desire and the dream is what leads one to do everything. (Alfonso, age 38)

Another return migrant expressed pride over what his efforts in the United States accomplished:

> When I left [Mexico] my house was flooded with water, and these damned bugs were under the mattress . . . you can't imagine it. My wife, my three children, and I all slept in the same bed. I don't have a piece of land, I don't have a business, I

don't have anything except my wife, my children, and the grace of God. So for me [going to the United States to work] was a vision that I had for myself. I wanted my life to change and I asked God to give me a chance to give to my children what I never had. [After I made some money] I told them, "Don't be arrogant, you brats. We are the same people. Just because we have a nice house doesn't mean that you have a lot." I also provided for their education while I was over there. (Javier, age 48)

On the other hand, many migrants remember their experiences in the United States with bitterness, especially those who did not meet their expectations and even lost the collateral that they put up for the trip. One such migrant said,

Life over there is very hard. The Americans humiliate you a lot; I mean they don't like Mexicans. They speak badly about you. They treat you really ugly. You work and the Americans act the fool; they almost don't do anything. And we Mexicans are always working hard. And you don't earn much over there either, so you shouldn't be saying, "I'm going to get rich." You suffer a lot; they humiliate us in a bad way. They say those things in English, insults, but since we didn't understand . . . (Jorge, age 23)

In general, however, those interviewed saw themselves as victims of adverse circumstances beyond their control, yet which they overcame through their integrity, valor, and preparedness to face danger and humiliation, all attributes that to them connote a "real man." Along those lines, one of the masculine imperatives is to provide for the protection of their family and make sure that the weak (women and children) don't have to suffer the trials and tribulations of living in another country. For that reason, many male migrants choose not to cross the border with their families:

I don't take my family because of the dangers in the crossing, like for example, the desert. The cities are very different from those here. At work, sometimes they mistreat you. If a grownup feels bad, imagine how it would feel to see your wife and children suffering the same as you. No way. Better that they stay here. (Gerardo, age 42)

Another reason males discourage migration by women is the perceived difference in gender relations on the other side of the border. The U.S. forms of interaction, which are less hierarchical and offer more protection to women against violence from men, are perceived as abnormal. In that sense, even some women fear the possibility of disobeying their husband and thus disrupting the "natural" order of reality:

Yes, my son tells me that there everything is different from here. Over there if a man ends up hitting his wife or lays a hand on her, the cops come and take him

> away. They charge three hundred dollars to get him out. There, a man can't yell at a woman "you're a whore's daughter." And over there if the woman behaves badly toward her husband and the husband goes and hits her, they lock him up. (Esther, age 44)

Another woman explains why her husband doesn't want her to go to the United States with him:

> He complains that over there the women are totally different from those here because over there the woman is the boss, and over there the woman cashes the check. And the woman who was good here changes and becomes very different there. Over there you can't hit a woman because the police will take him in and here they hit us and we have to take it. So, what are we going to do? (Laura, age 29)

Although scholars disagree over whether and how migration changes gender relations, at least in communities where it occurs family migration is perceived as a threat to the social order and triggers divisions in the family environment, mainly because of their perceptions that women in the United States have few constraints placed on them, including sexual constraints.[25] As one woman explained,

> Most of the women who go [to the United States] are single, and the married ones go looking for their husbands. But unfortunately, over there I think there is more freedom because they tell us that there are spouses who don't live together anymore, each one goes their own way. Most of them are girls who don't have kids and they arrive there and . . . see that their husband is going out with other women. [She says] "if he's doing it, why can't I?" And she goes out with one then the other. (Lucía, age 56)

These concepts about what gender roles should be and of family authority within the social order permeate the way in which being here or there is experienced, as well as the rights and responsibilities of both men and women in maintaining what María Eugenia D'Aubeterre refers to as a "long-distance spousal relationship."[26]

The south-to-north migration phenomenon is a complex process, composed of many political, economic, demographic, social, cultural, and ethical dimensions. If we add to that the undocumented and irregular nature of Mexican economic migration to the United States, the polarization of interests, considerations, discourses, and practices sharpen even more, from the most intimate areas of family life to the national and multilateral policies of the states involved.

It is clear that an asymmetrical relationship such as that existing between Mexico and the United States places the former in a state of subordination to the interests of its neighbor to the north, while the latter can strengthen or loosen border security, depending on political or economic conditions. Further, the situation seems to be getting even worse: it is not clear what the middle-term solution would be to bring about economic stability in Mexico. As always, the most vulnerable population will continue to suffer as a result of the failures of a state that is incapable of creating the minimum conditions to guarantee full employment and dignity for its citizens. As an example, the last step in the deregulation of corn and bean tariffs as result of the North American Free Trade Agreement went into effect in 2003, and the tariff was completely removed in 2007. Those reductions in tariffs have and will continue to result in a deterioration in the standard of living for Mexican peasants, and will also have a pronounced impact on a region like Veracruz, which relies heavily on agriculture and ranching, spurring an even greater impetus to emigrate as a subsistence strategy.

In general terms, with the increase of undocumented migration there is every indication that the abuses and violations of migrants' human rights documented elsewhere will persist, and the criminal activities against migrants will continue to rise. However, when observed on a microsocial scale, workers find that economic migration provides considerable benefits even when they are victims of abandonment, humiliation, and suffering. Masculine values as they are understood in the local sphere—the role of the provider, strength, integrity, and diversified sexuality—are supported by successful migration that allows them to sublimate the experience of victimization, to recover their prestige in their communities of origin, and to reinforce their capacity to overcome adversity.

On the other hand, the effects of the migrant as victim differ depending on gender. Given that changes in gender relationships after arriving in the United States are perceived in certain sectors as threats to the social order, feelings of fear and vulnerability are used as instruments to keep individual behavior in check by a demanding society that dictates that women be responsible for their role in the family and that tries to sequester them in domesticity. If their roles in the household change after migration, her home culture suspects that female migrants have dubious morals and blames them for family breakups, at least initially. In the transnational social space controls are developed to maintain patriarchal control over women.

The suffering and adversity that Mexican economic migrants to the United States undergo is not minimal, but these work on various fronts and at different levels. Migrants are the weakest link in the production chain, are an indispensable component in the destination communities' economies, and are victims of abuse and exploitation. But at the same time, their search for better living conditions can lead to a reassessment of their self-esteem, a reinforcement of the cultural pillars of masculinity, and as a source of subsistence for their family and the community.

Notes

A version of this essay appeared as "¿Delincuentes o víctimas? Migrantes rurales indocumentados mexicanos en las ciudades de Estados Unidos," in *La ciudad y el miedo*, ed. Obdulia Gutiérrez (Girona, Spain: University of Girona, 2005), 39–47.

1. John Gledhill, "El reto de la globalización reconstrucción de identidades: Formas de vida transnacionales y las ciencias sociales," in *Fronteras fragmentadas*, ed. G. Mummert (Zamora, Mexico: Colegio de Michoacán, 1999): 34–42; Enrico Marceli and Wayne Cornelius, "The Changing Profile of Mexican Migrants to the United States: New Evidence from California and Mexico," *Latin American Research Review* 36: 105–31; Alejandro Canales, "Migración y trabajo en la era de la globalización: El caso de la migración México–Estados Unidos de la década de 1990," *Papeles de Población* 33 (July–Sept. 2002): 48; Fernando Lozano, "Interrelación entre la migración internacional y la migración interna en México," *Papeles de Población* 33 (July–Sept. 2002): 86–89; Alma Rosa Muñoz, "Efectos de la globalización sobre las migraciones internacionales," *Papeles de Población* 33 (July–Sept. 2002): 25–36; Carola Suárez-Orozco and Marcelo Suárez-Orozco, "Immigrant Children and the American Project," *Education Week* 20 (2001): 56–58.

2. Jorge Durand, "Tres premises para entender y explicar la migración México–Estados Unidos," *Relaciones* 83 (2000): 19.

3. Agustín Escobar, Frank Bean, and Sydney Weintraub, *La dinámica de la emigración mexicana* (Mexico City: CIESAS/M.A. Porrúa, 1999), 8.

4. Marceli and Cornelius; Douglas Massey, Jorge Durand, and Nolan Malone, *Beyond Smoke and Mirrors: Mexican Immigration in an Era of Economic Integration* (New York: Russell Sage Foundation, 2002).

5. Escobar, Bean, and Weintraub; Massey, Durand, and Malone.

6. It is estimated that the accumulated employment deficit under President Ernesto Zedillo's administration (1994–2000) reached 4 million and wages lost 47.2 percent of their purchasing power. Likewise, of a workforce population of 36.5 million Mexicans, only around 10.9 million have steady jobs and the rest are employed in the informal sector. See Javier Brena et al., "Segunda década perdida para los salarios y el nivel de vida," *Memoria* 137 (July 2000): 20–23.

7. Heikki Mattila, "Protection of Migrants' Human Rights: Principles and Practice," *International Migration* 38 (2000): 54.

8. Wayne Cornelius, "Escenarios de inmigración mexicana hacia el siglo XXI," *La Jornada*, 18 May 1999. Cornelius highlights the employers' advantages in these hiring

practices: migrants' social networks provide a readily available workforce; migrants' perceived work ethics and abilities as compared to Anglos and other racial minorities; and few sanctions for employers.

9. Escobar, Bean, and Weintraub, 12.

10. Mario Pérez Monterosas, "El capital social en la migración emergente de Veracruz a los Estados Unidos. El caso de Puente Nacional 1990–2002," unpublished report, Xalapa, Mexico: IIH-S/UV, 2003. María Eugenia Anguiano lists Veracruz among the "emerging" Mexican states in terms of emigration. Others include Puebla, Guerrero, Chiapas, and Hidalgo. See Anguiano, "El flujo de la emigración veracruzana a la frontera norte mexicana y a los Estados Unidos," in *In God We Trust: del campo mexicano al sueño americano*, eds. Rosío Córdova, Cristina Nuñez, and David Skerrit (Mexico City: Plaza y Valdés Éditores/Universidad Veracruzana, 2007).

11. Pérez Monterosas, 3.

12. Veracruz, with an area of 72,410 square kilometers, is the eleventh largest state, with 745 kilometers of coastline. It is likewise a multicultural state, with a 10.35 percent indigenous population, mainly Nahua, Tepehua, Aguacteca, Popoluca, Zoque, Chinanteca, Huasteca, Mazateca, Totontaca, and Otomi, which makes it the state with the third largest concentration of indigenous groups in absolute numbers (INEGI, 2001.)

13. Escobar, Bean, and Weintraub. Although the primary sector's proportion of the economically active population dropped from 47 percent in 1980 to 39.4 percent in 1990, then to 31.7 percent in 2000, Veracruz continues to be one of the Mexican states with a large number of the population working with agriculture and livestock. Hipólito Rodríguez, "El espacio productivo de Veracruz en la más reciente época del libre cambio," *Ulúa* 1 (2003), 143.

14. Escobar, Bean, and Weintraub, 158–59.

15. Mario Pérez Monterosas, "Miradas y esperanzas puestas en el norte: Migración del centro de Veracruz a los Estados Unidos," *Cuadernos Agrarios* 19–20 (2000): 73.

16. According to a survey by investigators working on the University of Veracruz project, "The Impact of International Migration in Rural Areas: The Case of the Sugar and Coffee Sectors in Central Veracruz," which included 456 households in ten communities in central Veracruz between 2003 and 2004, about 30 percent of Veracruz's emigrants came from the southeastern region of the state. Unpublished report, Instituto Investigaciones Histórico-Sociales, Universidad Veracruzana, 2005.

17. John Pomfret, "An Increasingly Deadly Trail," *Washington Post*, 6 June 2006.

18. Ludger Pries, "Migración laboral internacional y espacios sociales transnacionales: bosquejo teórico empírico," in *Migración laboral internacional*, eds. Saúl Macías and Fernando Herrera (Mexico City: BUAP, 1997), 17–53. For Pries this concept underscores the fact that "these human collectives in space increasingly behave less and less unidirectionally, but rather they are made up of ever-increasing, long-lasting, and distinct pendulum swings which create new social realities above or beyond the spatial geographic separation of the departure or arrival regions" (18).

19. The Bracero Program was in place between August 1942 and December 1964. Due to the scarcity of U.S. workers resulting from enlistments for World War II or U.S.

workers' movements from agricultural to better-paying industrial jobs, the U.S.-Mexican border was opened for the immigration of Mexican agricultural workers. At the end of the war it was also an imperative to maintain an abundant workforce to move toward the new model known as the welfare state. See Ana María Aragonés, "¿Nuevo Programa Bracero en la era de la globalización?" *Memoria* 141 (2000): 18. According to http://www.farmworkers.org/pbracero.html, roughly 5 million workers registered in the Bracero Program.

20. Cecilia Menjívar and Cynthia Bejarano, "Latino Immigrants' Perceptions of Crime and Police Authorities in the United States: A Case Study from the Phoenix Metropolitan Area," *Ethnic and Racial Studies* 27 (Jan. 2004): 120–48.

21. Figures from 1994 in Cornelius, 11; 1999 figures in Claudia Smith, "Operación Guardián: migrantes en peligro mortal," *Memoria* 141 (2000): 10; 2006 figures in "Building Up the Border," PBS Online, at http://www.pbs.org/newshour/bb/latin_america/jan-june06/fences_2-15.html.

22. Yaw Ackah, "Fear of Crime Among an Immigrant Population in the Washington D.C. Metropolitan area," *Journal of Black Studies* 30 (2000): 555.

23. Menjívar and Bejarano, 121–22.

24. Elsewhere I have stated that for the local gender system, the sustaining masculine role includes qualities that allow a man to be independent beyond the economic and sexually efficient. Therefore, "a man will be considered a real man . . . when he keeps his word, does not betray his friends and is generous toward them, won't succumb to pressure, nor shows fear of threats . . . showing respect to superiors and the appropriate show of force against equals or subordinates who show a lack of respect, disobedience or abuse represent the sign of masculine honor." See Rosío Córdova Plaza, *Los peligros del cuerpo: Género y sexualidad en el centro de Veracruz* (Mexico City: Plaza y Valdés Éditores/BUAP, 2003), 187.

25. See, among others, Pierrette Hondagneu-Sotelo, "Overcoming Patriarchal Constraints: The Reconstruction of Gender Relations among Mexican Immigrant Women and Men," *Gender and Society* 6 (Sept. 1992): 393–415; María Eugenia D'Aubeterre, "Mujeres y espacio social transnacional: Maniobras para renegociar el vínculo conyugal," in *Mujeres y relaciones de género en México*, eds. Dalia Barrera y Cristina Oehmichen (Mexico City: Gimtrap/UNAM, 2000), 63–85; Gloria Marroni, "El siempre me ha dejado con los chiquitos y se ha llevado a los grandes . . . Ajustes y desbarajustes familiares de la migración," in ibid., 87–117.

26. D'Aubeterre, 71.

CHAPTER THREE

The Dalton Story

Mexican Immigration and Social Transformation in the Carpet Capital of the World

VÍCTOR ZÚÑIGA AND
RUBÉN HERNÁNDEZ-LEÓN

During the late twentieth century Mexican immigrants began to arrive in the rural and urban South as part of what scholars have called the "new era of Mexican migration to the United States."[1] The dramatic rise in Mexican immigration to the South has transformed many southern communities by introducing a new ethnic group, changing the face of the working class, and creating new international linkages for the region. In this chapter we examine the community-level changes that Mexican immigration has produced in Dalton, a small city in northwestern Georgia. Well known in the industrial and commercial arenas as a global center for the production of wall-to-wall carpets, the city has been in the headlines in recent years because of its swift demographic and social transformation. Driven by the influx of Mexican immigrants and other Latinos during the late 1980s and 1990s, the Latino population of Dalton expanded from 6.5 percent of the total population in 1990 to more than 40 percent in 2000. The same year, more than half of the students in the city's public schools were of Latino origin. Needless to say, such momentous transformation has left few local institutions and social spaces untouched.[2]

In our examination of the impact of Mexican immigration on the Dalton community, we focus on three main areas of sociocultural change: the positioning of key local actors; social and spatial group boundaries in the urban landscape; and the cultural representations and narratives about Dalton. We begin with a discussion of the approach and methods of our study and then address why Mexican immigrants began to immigrate to Dalton in large numbers, and how this immigration has transformed social relations, spatial boundaries, and cultural symbols in the city. Finally, we address the current backlash against immigrants in Georgia, expressed by the passage of Georgia Senate Bill 529 (Ga. SB 529) in 2006, and reflect on its implications for Mexican immigrants in Dalton.

Background and Methods

This chapter is part of a larger study of Mexican immigration, settlement, and incorporation in the city of Dalton and Whitfield County that we began in 1997.[3] From the outset we approached the rise of a Mexican community in the "Carpet Capital of the World" from both macro and micro perspectives. We view Dalton as an instance of the larger transformation of Mexican migration to the United States in the post–Immigration Reform and Control Act (IRCA) and post–North American Free Trade Agreement (NAFTA) era. We are also interested in the specific local and regional transformations that international migration has generated in this corner of the South. Even though international immigration is by definition an extralocal phenomenon, immigration-driven social change is ultimately locally mediated. Massive Mexican and Latino immigration has prompted an intense debate among social actors in Dalton about the meaning of community. At the same time, by settling and becoming a visible and permanent presence, Mexicans have become the newest social actors in Dalton and are beginning to participate, at times hesitantly, in the city's social and political life.

We have not only studied but also participated in the process of change that has unfolded in Dalton as a result of Mexican immigration. In 1996 a group of Dalton civic leaders and public-school authorities contacted the University of Monterrey in Monterrey, Mexico, where we were faculty members, to seek assistance with how to deal with the sudden rise of Latino immigrant children in the public-school system. Several subsequent meetings between Dalton leaders and University of Monterrey faculty and officials resulted in an agreement between the university and the school districts of Dalton and Whitfield County. Known as the Georgia Project, this binational effort aimed to improve the capacity of local schools to address the needs of their growing Latino student body in several ways: through the recruitment of bilingual teachers from Mexico to work in local public schools; the design of a bilingual curriculum; and the establishment of a summer institute at the University of Monterrey for local Georgia teachers to learn Spanish and to study Mexican history and culture.[4] Our involvement in the design and implementation of these programs, as well as in the local, often contentious debates about them, made us both observers and participants in the process of social transformation in Dalton.

In studying Mexican immigration and settlement in Dalton and Whitfield County, we have followed an inductive and exploratory approach characteristic of community studies. In accordance with this approach we have considered diverse hypotheses and taken note of different, often contradictory, accounts of a wide array of social actors. We conducted nearly five years of field research and employed multiple forms of data collection, including interviewing, life history, participant observation, focus group, and survey research. We conducted research in factories, schools, churches, households, weddings and dances, shopping centers, community meetings, and on soccer fields, interviewing and conversing with a wide range of people, including carpet and poultry workers, teachers and school officials, religious and political leaders, entrepreneurs, corporate executives, managers and supervisors, service providers, and journalists.

In addition to ethnographic research we also collected survey data to develop a quantitative profile of the Mexican and Latino immigrant population in Dalton. In 1997 we implemented a self-administered household survey of Latino parents with children enrolled in the Dalton public schools, resulting in a nonrandom sample of approximately 850 men and women. While not representative of the entire Latino immigrant population, the survey supported the findings of the qualitative research.

From Historical to New Destinations

As noted in the introduction to this book, IRCA changed the dynamics of Mexico-U.S. migration by granting legal permanent residence to 2.3 million formerly undocumented Mexican sojourners. IRCA's amnesty provision changed the temporary and seasonal migratory patterns as well as the calculations and long-term prospects of migrants and their families, giving them the possibility of settlement in this country. The rippling effects were immediately felt in the historical concentrations of Mexican immigrants in the Southwest and Chicago and in their labor and housing markets. As millions of Mexicans shifted their orientation from a pattern of temporary to permanent migration, their sheer numbers provoked a saturation of agricultural and urban labor markets. Scholars have shown how in California's agricultural labor markets dominated by Mexican immigrants, wages declined as a result of an excess of farm labor supply in the aftermath of IRCA.[5]

The in-depth interviews we conducted in Dalton provide a similar picture for urban labor markets. Mexican immigrants settled in Los Angeles began to experience intense job competition from coethnics, resulting in fewer employment opportunities and declining wages in the late 1980s and early 1990s. Don Dámaso Pérez, a migrant from the Mexican state of Guerrero who arrived in

Dalton in the mid-1990s, recounted that "Everybody was coming to California and it got full. And then work was scarce. It got saturated. So people started to do what I did; there [are] a lot of people [in Dalton] that have come from California."[6] In the case of the housing markets, the shift toward settlement appeared to increase the demand for home ownership and to drive housing prices up in urban concentrations of Mexican immigrants in longstanding places like Chicago and Los Angeles.[7] Coethnic competition and labor and housing market saturation created difficult conditions that "pushed" immigrants from historical to new destinations. One Mexican migrant explained that he left Los Angeles for northern Georgia because "there's no future in L.A."

In California, since 1960 the state with the largest concentration of Mexicans, IRCA and its aftermath also produced a backlash against immigrants. Coinciding with the end of the Cold War and the loss of thousands of defense-related jobs, the backlash and its climax—the passage of Proposition 187—created an unwelcome environment for newcomers, prompting many to leave California.[8] IRCA not only made the usual destinations less attractive but also made the search and exploration of new destinations possible. Undocumented no more, many Mexicans could emerge from the protective cover of the ethnic neighborhood to explore distant, less-competitive labor markets and less-expensive housing markets located in places as distant from California as Atlanta, Nashville, and Omaha. Others used their new permanent resident status to settle out of the agricultural migratory streams of the East Coast and explore opportunities in urban-industrial and service labor markets with year-round employment, higher wages, and less taxing conditions than they had found in California and other traditional urban destinations. Many of them settled in towns and small cities in the Southeast, such as Dalton, which they had learned about through their sojourning and networks.[9]

Nontraditional destinations produced their own appeal. Here it is worth stressing that new destinations are diverse; they include "company towns" like Dalton, Georgia, and Marshalltown, Iowa, as well as large metropolitan areas like Atlanta, Nashville, and Las Vegas.[10] Agricultural labor markets in Florida, Georgia, North Carolina, and other states in the Southeast had for some time attracted Mexican workers.[11] In this economically dynamic region Mexicans found their way to a variety of urban industries, some of which, like poultry production, seafood processing, and furniture and carpet manufacturing had undergone dramatic restructuring and growth.[12] The large and medium-sized cities of the Southeast drew new waves of Mexican immigrants to work in construction, services, and labor-intensive manufacturing.

Many of the above-mentioned industries have resorted to the formal and informal recruitment of workers. The poultry- and seafood-processing industries, for instance, have used recruiters and official temporary work visa programs to draw workers to uncharted destinations in the Southeast. Recruitment in construction and poultry played a fundamental role in bringing a small group of Mexican immigrant pioneers to Dalton in the 1970s that formed the first Mexican settlement in this city. In the early 1990s carpet industrialists briefly resorted to recruitment of Mexicans and Mexican-Americans in South Texas. By the mid- to late 1990s Dalton was a regular destination point on bus routes shuttling migrants from Monterrey and other places in Mexico's interior to hubs such as Houston, Texas, and onward to cities and towns in Georgia and North Carolina.[13]

Social networks soon assumed the role of recruiters and fostered the exponential growth of the Mexican population in Dalton and other new destinations. Immigrant networks provided the infrastructure to continue channeling Mexicans from historical destinations like Los Angeles, Chicago, and Houston to the Southeast in what represented an internal secondary migration for these international migrants.[14] Asked about the number of kin and friends who had used him as a contact and resource in order to migrate from Southern California to Georgia, a seasoned Mexican immigrant and former resident of Los Angeles was able to identify more than a hundred people. At the same time, these social networks also fostered fresh flows from Mexico, composed of substantial numbers of women and children. According to our survey of Latino immigrant parents, women had come to make up the majority of new arrivals in Dalton in the 1993–97 period, showing a clear trend toward family reunification (table 3.1). Mexicans had arrived in Dalton both directly from Mexico (table 3.2) and from U.S. states that have been historical gateways for this flow (principally California, Texas, and Florida). Most of the Mexican immigrants in Dalton in the late 1990s were from Mexico's historical region of out-migration (table 3.3). The states in western and north-central Mexico, namely Jalisco, Michoacán, Zacatecas, Guanajuato, San Luis Potosí, Durango, Nayarit, Colima, and Aguascalientes, have provided most of the migration to the United States since the early twentieth century.[15]

Mexican Immigration and the Transformation of Southern Communities

REPOSITIONING OF LOCAL ACTORS

In this section we examine community-level changes produced by immigration to Dalton and northwestern Georgia, focusing on changes that have occurred in the social and political positioning of key local actors, the social and

Table 3.1 Period of Arrival to Dalton, Georgia

	Men (n=359)	*Women (n=366)*	*Total (n=725)*
Pre-IRCA* (1965–86)	5.8%	2.4%	4.1% (30)
First Post-IRCA (1987–92)	29.2%	18.6%	23.9% (173)
Second Post-IRCA (1993–98)	64.9%	79.0%	72.0% (522)

* IRCA = Immigration Reform and Control Act (1986)

Source: Survey of Hispanic families in Dalton, 1997–98

Table 3.2 Place of Residence before Moving to Dalton, Georgia

	Men (n=396)	*Women (n=411)*	*Total (n=807)*
Mexico	37.9%	49.6%	43.9% (354)
California	16.4%	14.8%	15.6% (126)
Texas	12.9%	10.2%	11.5% (93)
Florida	10.1%	5.6%	7.8% (63)
Georgia (other cities)	4.5%	4.6%	4.6% (37)
Illinois	4.0%	1.9%	2.9% (24)
Other U.S. States	14.1%	13.1%	13.6% (110)

Source: Survey of Hispanic families in Dalton, 1997–98

Table 3.3 Top Ten States of Birth of Mexican Men and Women in Dalton, Georgia

	Men (n=389)	*Women (n=404)*	*Total (n=793)*
Guanajuato	28.3%	22.5%	27.6% (201)
Zacatecas	14.1%	15.6%	14.9% (118)
Michoacán	9.8%	8.9%	0.9% (74)
Jalisco	7.5%	8.4%	0.8% (63)
Guerrero	7.7%	7.4%	0.8% (60)
San Luis Potosí	7.2%	7.9%	0.8% (60)
Durango	6.9%	8.2%	0.8% (60)
Chihuahua	5.1%	6.7%	0.6% (48)
Tamaulipas	3.6%	4.2%	0.4% (31)
Distrito Federal	1.3%	2.0%	0.2% (13)
Total from Top Ten States	91.5%	91.8%	92.0% (728)

Source: Survey of Hispanic families in Dalton, 1997–98

spatial boundaries in the urban landscape, and the cultural images and narratives associated with Dalton and its history.[16] Mexican immigration has fostered a fundamental repositioning of local actors in this small city. During the late 1990s carpet industrialists "broke" with anti-immigrant and nativist groups to endorse the presence of Mexican and other Latinos in Dalton's mills and public schools. In so doing, these industrialists reopened the old fault lines that separated blue-collar Daltonians from the local elite, but also appeared to side with a nonwhite ethnic group.[17] In a region where whiteness had historically assured working-class whites certain privileges, including access to industrial jobs to the exclusion of blacks, the elites' self-interested embrace of Dalton's new ethnic-racial minority has had an array of consequences.

Certainly the civil rights movement of the 1960s seriously challenged white privilege in the South, including whites' hold on industrial jobs. However, this was not the case in the Dalton area, a center of textile production for most of the twentieth century and where the mass production of carpeting began in the 1950s and 1960s. The barring of African Americans from mill jobs was systematic even after the 1960s; they were relegated to lower-paying cleaning jobs and domestic services. Local industrialists developed a system of corporate paternalism that included a kind of intraethnic pact with white workers to preserve their privileged access to industrial jobs.[18] The exclusion of African Americans from industrial work helps explain the decline of the black population in Whitfield County: the percentage of African Americans in the total population dropped from 15 percent in 1890 to 6.6 percent in 1930 and then to 3.8 percent in 2000.[19] The intraethnic pact was broken during the 1990s when Mexican and other Latino workers were hired in high numbers by almost every company in the region. Local entrepreneurs became the source of a new arrangement whereby part of the local white population lost its traditional privileges in the industrial sector. Beginning in the 1990s entrepreneurs welcomed Mexican migrant workers and the ethnic diversity they brought to what had been a predominantly white community.

A number of other social and institutional actors have adopted new roles and positions as a result of Latino immigration to the region. Teachers and public school officials are now discussing the merits of bilingual education and multicultural curricula. Over the last ten years more than a hundred teachers working in Whitfield County, Murray County, Calhoun City, Colquitt County, and Dalton City public schools have participated in the summer institute for teachers at the University of Monterrey in order to learn Spanish and better understand their students' cultural background. As one participant in the 2006 summer institute wrote in her application form: "I would hope that what I learn about culture and the people of Mexico would enhance my teaching. I am fascinated with other cultures and I know that the little things I do or do not do are important in making a bridge between the two worlds that my students live in."[20]

Moreover, about eighty Mexican bilingual teachers have been hired in these school districts to help principals and teachers address the growing Latino school enrollment. The schools in the area, especially in Dalton and Whitfield County, are beginning to resemble the schools along the U.S.-Mexican border. As of 2006, 64 percent of the students in Dalton Public Schools and 32 percent in Whitfield County Schools are Latino. Some Georgia teachers are learning Spanish, placing symbols of Mexican culture in the classrooms, and sending official letters in Spanish to Latino parents.

Political, civic, and business leaders have responded in different ways to the immigrant newcomers in Dalton and northern Georgia. Some of them feel nostalgic about the past and hope that one day things will return to the way they were before the immigrants arrived. Others are deeply disturbed by the demographic revolution and think that these "illegal aliens" should be compelled to leave. And still others have formed task force groups, nonprofit associations, and business organizations that welcome immigrants, perhaps because they derive benefits from Mexican immigrant labor or because they see the benefits of living in a more diverse society. Protestant religious leaders are trying to recruit Spanish-speaking worshipers and to make sense of Roman Catholicism in their region. Local journalists, educators and social service providers are seeking to expand their understanding of the Latino immigrant population.

The local newspaper represents an important case in point. In less than ten years, Dalton's *Daily Citizen* changed from being a platform for mostly anti-immigrant voices to a newspaper that provided fair coverage of and service to the Latino immigrant population. Needless to say, this was not a seamless process. In the mid-1990s the opinion and letters-to-the-editor sections of the newspaper were the venue of a heated debate about the pros and cons of immigration, a debate in which long-term residents of Dalton were the sole participants. At that time, the only systematic reporting on Latino immigrants in the newspaper was found in the police pages. By the end of the decade, however, the *Daily Citizen* was publishing a separate weekly publication in Spanish that was distributed without charge in Latino stores. The regular English daily had expanded its coverage of Latino immigrants and their concerns, including information about successful Mexican entrepreneurs and striving immigrant students. Mexican-owned businesses began to advertise in the newspaper, while American-owned businesses altered their advertisements in an effort to attract Spanish-speaking customers.

The repositioning of key local actors in response to immigration has also entailed the rise of new institutional actors like the Georgia Project. Shortly after its formation in 1996, the nonprofit organization became the institutional voice of Latino immigrants in the city.[21] The Georgia Project has also functioned as a conduit to channel Mexican and other Latino newcomers who are members of its board to work with other agencies and organizations, such as the chamber of commerce, the administration of the local shopping mall, the boards of parent-teacher associations, newspapers and radio stations, and political campaigns.

CHANGING SOCIAL AND SPATIAL BOUNDARIES

Immigration has also transformed Dalton's social and spatial boundaries, a process researchers have referred to as "debordering-rebordering." When boundaries do not move, members of a community have the impression that everything, every person or event, is in its proper place; for example, that separate restrooms for girls and boys in schools maintain an appropriate gender boundary. The stability of boundaries is in fact the best definition of social "normality." Debordering-rebordering means the transformation and renegotiation of established boundaries. As David Spener and Kathleen Staudt (1998) state: "By rebordering, we mean processes that involve the reassertion or rearticulation of socially constructed boundaries, both territorial and nonterritorial. The dialectical cycle the debordering-rebordering antimony implies is one in which an existing boundary is challenged and penetrated (debordered), only to be reestablished, repositioned, or reconfigured in a new guise in response to a competing set of interests (rebordered)."[22]

The most visible aspect of the debordering-rebordering process in Dalton is the transformation of the city's physical environment with the emergence of Mexican businesses, institutions, and cultural symbols. Mexican immigration has transformed not only the workplaces but also the urban and rural landscapes of Dalton and its surroundings. Mexican restaurants, taco stands, grocery stores, butcher shops, tortillas factories, churches, *cantinas*, religious images, and soccer fields are now ubiquitous in northwestern Georgia. One would expect to find ethnic merchandise in small, ethnic-owned stores, but when Wal-Mart managers discovered the potential of Mexican purchasing power, they added aisles with Mexican products and began announcing special sales over the store's public-address system in Spanish as well as English. By 2000 Mexican families made up a substantial number of the shoppers in Wal-Mart. Similar changes have taken place in local and regional supermarket chains that used to cater primarily to the white population. Still, some local businesses have resisted change by discouraging Latino shoppers and maintaining their identity as businesses for white customers, exemplifying another side of the rebordering process: the movement toward boundary maintenance.

Another example of the debordering process may be found in one of the largest restaurants in the city, owned by a naturalized citizen of Mexican origin. The restaurant is decorated with colorful murals that display motifs of Mexican history and culture, from the ancient pyramids of Tenochtitlán to the modern stock exchange in Mexico City. Popular among Latino immigrants and native Georgians alike, the place is typically crowded at lunch and dinner. The restaurant, with its murals, is fast becoming a cultural landmark in the city. The owner challenged established symbolic boundaries by inserting visual representations of Mexico in the urban landscape and repositioned these boundaries by inviting his customers to feel as if they are experiencing a part of Mexico in Dalton.

The debordering and rebordering process can also be observed in the transformation of key social categories in the host community as a result of large-scale immigration. Institutionalized labels that delineate boundaries between social classes, ethnic groups, and religious groups are in a process of redefinition because of the new demographic and social realities in Dalton. A case in point is the social category "carpet mill worker." Heirs to the Jim Crow era when textile mill jobs were the exclusive realm of Appalachian workers, whites long remained the dominant group of workers in the carpet industry. Until the late 1980s, the image of the carpet mill worker was intimately associated with white Appalachian workers, whose virtues were praised by local industrialists.[23] Today, the content and the boundaries of this social category have been redefined as thousands of Mexicans and other Latino immigrants work in the carpet mills. Echoing the sentiments of other business leaders, George Woodward, the president of the Dalton-Whitfield Chamber of Commerce, has remarked about Mexican immigrants: "In general, these are people with strong family values—red, white and blue values; people who are buying homes, setting roots and becoming part of the community."[24] The access to these mill jobs is no longer determined by white privilege but by membership in the networks that channel coethnics from Los Angeles or the towns of western and north-central Mexico to Dalton, Georgia.

A NEW IMAGINED COMMUNITY

In a process closely connected with the redefinition of social and spatial boundaries, Mexican immigration has also produced changes in the cultural symbols and narratives associated with Dalton among its citizens and leaders. Today local officials still attend reenactments of Civil War battles that took place in the vicinity, but they also participate in the annual parade celebrating Mexico's independence on September 16. In this traditionally anti-Catholic area, large

Roman Catholic churches have sprung up and Catholic priests now join Baptist and other Protestant pastors as important religious leaders representing the community.

Significant holidays recognized in Dalton now include Mexican and Catholic as well as American and Protestant celebrations. As early as 1996 the holiday newsletter for the ConAgra poultry-processing plant, which was published in English and Spanish, acknowledged the cultural and religious celebrations of both its immigrant and American workers: "As we gather with our families and friends for Thanksgiving Day, we share a tradition we look forward to throughout the year. . . . During the winter of 1621, half of the 102 Mayflower passengers who settled in Plymouth, Massachusetts, died."[25] In the same issue an article on the Christmas holidays explained that the December celebrations begin with "the arrival of Mary and Jose at the Inn" and then on December 12 there is "a birthday party for the Virgen [de] Guadalupe. . . . On December 24th and 25th we celebrate the birth of the baby Jesus. Then we get together and have a big party where we have *tamales, buñuelos, ponches, atole, envoltorios*, etc."[26]

On a different cultural front, industrialists and city officials have sponsored the construction of soccer fields in order to satisfy the sports and leisure preferences of immigrant workers and their children. Football and baseball, long the dominant sports in the region, now face a new competitor on the sports scene. New soccer fields built in the late 1990s under the auspices of the third-largest carpet corporation in town literally and symbolically moved the sport and its fans from the periphery of the city, where it used to be played, to a more central location.

Other symbolic events in Dalton are changing in meaning as a result of immigration from Mexico and Latin America. In June 2004 a Mexican U.S. marine from Dalton died in combat in Ramadi, west of Baghdad, Iraq. Having migrated from Guanajuato to Dalton as teenager, Juan López graduated from a local high school, then joined the U.S. Marine Corps. After his burial in his hometown of San Luis de la Paz, Guanajuato, an editorial of the *Daily Citizen* stated that "in his far-too-short life, Marine Corps Lance Cpl. Juan Lopez made two towns very proud."[27] This event showed Dalton residents how intermingled the recent histories and fates of the two towns are while subverting notions of community self-perception and patriotism: a patriotic son of Dalton was not born in Dalton but in Guanajuato, Mexico.

The new symbols have not been established without contestation from white and African American Daltonians. Even though Spanish is used in many quarters—partly to attract Latinos as customers to stores, banks, and doctor's offices—some social actors still actively resist it. Many of these expressions of resistance occur in the realm of private and relatively intimate spaces, where individuals feel that others share their sentiment, but they also occur in an indirect way in public arenas, when white residents produce nostalgic accounts of Dalton's recent history and when white parents transfer their children from public schools into private Christian academies.[28]

Resistance to the changing cultural images associated with Dalton has also taken the form of public debate. In 1997 Dalton's oldest radio station, WDAL-1430 AM, began broadcasting only in Spanish in response to the growing market for Mexican musical programming. The decision prompted a number of English-speaking listeners to contact the management of the station and send letters to the local newspaper protesting the change. In the end the owners decided to return WDAL-1430 to English and start a new radio station for Spanish-language listeners, thus avoiding the highly charged issue of converting Dalton's pioneer radio station into a Mexican station.

The Anti-Immigrant Backlash in Georgia: What about Dalton?

As the current wave of documented and undocumented immigration has gathered momentum in the United States, so has the backlash against newcomers. Although the backlash can be seen in the formation and activism of nativist and anti-immigrant groups, it is also evident in the passage of state laws and local ordinances aimed specifically at the unauthorized population. Across the country, state legislatures and city councils have approved new measures to recapture health, public safety, and education expenses incurred by local governments as a result of the influx of undocumented immigrants. These measures also seek to make local environments less hospitable to immigrants by denying them opportunities to rent and by turning local policing into a tool of immigration control. Scholarly analyses and journalistic reports show that these kinds of measures partly deflect migratory flows away from the localities in question to places that are still tolerant of immigrants and their socioeconomic strategies.[29]

Georgia has not been an exception to this pattern. In the spring of 2006 the state senate passed the Georgia Security and Immigration Compliance Act (Ga. SB 529), a bill that denies state welfare benefits to undocumented immigrants; deters the employment of unauthorized workers, especially in businesses with public contracts; instructs local law-enforcement officials to collaborate with immigration authorities; and increases penalties for human trafficking. Anecdotal and journalistic evidence suggests that the approved bill is already having the same chilling effect that accompanies and often precedes deflection. Latino immigrants in Georgia are choosing to postpone large and long-term expenditures, such as purchasing a home, in anticipation of potential dislocation.[30]

How has the anti-immigrant backlash unfolded in Dalton so far? Not surprisingly, Dalton has not experienced the overt anti-immigrant sentiment found elsewhere in Georgia. In this regard Dalton's response to immigration differs greatly from that of Gainesville, a poultry-processing center in northeastern Georgia that has one of the largest concentrations of Mexican immigrants in the state. Gainesville is a regular host to anti-immigrant demonstrations, many of them organized by right-wing nativist and racist groups but also attended by average residents with less extreme views. When the U.S. House of Representatives organized local hearings on immigrants' impact on the economy during the summer of 2006, similar anti-immigrant demonstrations welcomed the federal delegation to town.[31]

In contrast to Gainesville, the Carpet Capital has not witnessed such rallies in years, although, according to press reports, a small group protested when the congressional hearings came to Dalton in summer 2006, gathering in public and holding up signs advocating border security legislation.[32] At the same time, the local press in Dalton has refrained from publishing strongly anti-immigrant editorials and letters to the editor. While making sure it does not appear to embrace immigrants, the local press has continued to maintain the editorial position that newcomers are needed for economic reasons.

The question then becomes what accounts for Dalton's more tolerant response in comparison not only to Gainesville's but also to that of other towns and cities across the region and the country. The answer has to do with the nature of the Carpet Capital's urban regime, unquestionably led by the employers of Mexican immigrants. In contrast to many other localities where food processing and labor-intensive manufacturing have attracted thousands of Mexicans, Dalton's carpet mills have been owned by local industrialists who have also played a direct role in the governance of the city and the surrounding county. As we have argued elsewhere, carpet industrialists and their political allies have signaled their distaste for overt anti-immigrant movements, effectively discouraging them, and have given their blessings to initiatives such as the Georgia Project and the building of a new Roman Catholic church.[33] In doing so, the carpet industry has not only exerted its influence in a way that the poultry industry has not in Gainesville, it has also continued with Dalton's long tradition as a company town in which local industrialists play a central role in the political and social affairs of the community.[34] The large and ubiquitous multinational corporations that have made Gainesville the poultry capital of the world can recruit immigrants without having to deal directly with the local consequences of their actions. In contrast, the owners of carpet manufacturing corporations with deep roots in northwestern Georgia have to face the day-to-day consequences of the arrival of their new preferred source of labor.[35]

Still, the social and political control that a powerful social actor can exercise has its limits. In neighboring Calhoun, a town twenty-two miles south of Dalton and part of the four-county region of northwestern Georgia where the industry as a whole is clustered, a group of native workers sued Mohawk, one of the largest carpet manufacturers in the country, also headquartered in Dalton. Filed in 2004, the class action suit accuses Mohawk of recruiting undocumented workers with the purpose of lowering wages. The plaintiffs have apparently received the advice of law firms and activists advocating for immigration control. As part of their legal maneuvers the plaintiffs' side tried to convince the courts to use antiracketeering laws against Mohawk, arguing that in recruiting undocumented workers the company's managers behaved like an illegal enterprise, engaging in a conspiracy with the purpose of criminal intent. Notably, this aspect of the suit made it all the way to the U.S. Supreme Court in 2006. The class action suit was still under litigation at the time of this writing.[36]

In 2008 the Whitfield County sheriff's office joined the Immigration and Customs Enforcement (ICE) 287(g) program, in which sheriff's officers are trained and deputized to screen for the legal status of immigrants detained on criminal charges in the county jail. The program allows local law enforcement officers access to a national database, to hold detainees on immigration-related violations, and to transfer them to the custody of federal agents. Needless to say, it is too soon to assess fully the consequences of this program in Whitfield and Dalton. Still, we can envision that the collaboration between sheriff officers and ICE agents is likely to put more undocumented immigrants, whether they are charged with criminal violations or not, into the hands of immigration authorities. At the same time, we doubt that this collaboration can alter the fundamental process of social change that the carpet capital of the world has undergone.

In new areas of immigrant destination, like Dalton, the sudden arrival of Latino and Mexican newcomers has produced a range of community-level changes. The traditional local community order has been challenged and redefined by the newcomers. Old actors have been forced to play new roles and new actors have appeared on the scene. The urban and social landscapes of the city have changed as well as its main institutions: schools, churches, and community groups. New social boundaries and new visions of the community future have developed.

It is important to recognize that we have been documenting an emerging process. We have described the uncertainties, trials and errors, and multiple initiatives to address the ongoing challenges of migration within a specific southern community. We have sought to emphasize the significance of locality in analyses of international migration, arguing that in order to understand immigration-driven social change fully, scholars, policy makers, and activists need to comprehend not only the dynamics of globalization but also the particular mix of local actors at hand.

Notes

1. Jorge Durand, Douglas S. Massey, and Emilio Parrado, "The New Era of Mexican Migration to the United States," *Journal of American History* 86, no. 2 (1999): 518–36.

2. Rubén Hernández-León and Víctor Zúñiga, "'Making Carpet by the Mile': The Emergence of a Mexican Immigrant Community in an Industrial Region of the U.S. Historic South," *Social Science Quarterly* 81, no. 1 (2000): 49–66; U.S. Census Bureau, *American FactFinder*, 2004, http://factfinder.census.gov/, accessed 14 Sept. 2004.

3. Hernández-León and Zúñiga, "'Making Carpet by the Mile'"; Rubén Hernández-León and Víctor Zúñiga, "Appalachia Meets Aztlán: Mexican Immigration and Intergroup Relations in Dalton, Georgia," in *New Destinations: Mexican Immigration in the United States*, eds. Víctor Zúñiga and Rubén Hernández-León (New York: Russell Sage Foundation, 2005), 244–74; Víctor Zúñiga and Rubén Hernández-León, "A New Destination for an Old Migration: Origins, Trajectories, and Labor Market Incorporation of Latinos in Dalton, Georgia," in *Latino Workers in the Contemporary South*, eds. Arthur D. Murphy, Colleen Blanchard, and Jennifer A. Hill (Athens: University of Georgia Press, 2001), 126–35; Víctor Zúñiga, Rubén Hernández-León, Janna L. Shadduck-Hernández, and María Olivia Villarreal, "The New Paths of Mexican Immigrants in the United States: Challenges for Education and the Role of Mexican Universities," in *Education in the New Latino Diaspora: Policy and Politics of Identity*, eds. Stanton Wortham, Edmund Hamann, and Enrique Murillo Jr. (Westport, Conn.: Ablex Publishing, 2002), 99–116.

4. Zúñiga, Hernández-León, Shadduck-Hernández, and Villarreal, "New Paths of Mexican Immigrants."

5. Philip L. Martin and J. Edward Taylor, "Immigration Reform and Farm Labor Contracting in California," in *The Paper Curtain: Employer Sanctions' Implementation, Impact, and Reform*, ed. Michael Fix (Washington, D.C.: Urban Institute Press, 1991), 239–61.

6. Rubén Hernández-León, interview with Dámaso Pérez, n.d.

7. Jorge Durand, *Política, modelo y patrón migratorios* (San Luis Potosí, Mexico: Colegio de San Luis, 1998).

8. Jorge Durand, Douglas S. Massey, and Fernando Charvet, "The Changing Geography of Mexican Immigration to the United States: 1910–1996," *Social Science Quarterly* 81, no. 1 (2000): 1–15; Jorge Durand, Douglas S. Massey, and Chiara Capoferro, "The New Geography of Mexican Immigration," in Zúñiga and Hernández-León, *New Destinations*, 1–22.

9. Hernández-León and Zúñiga, "Appalachia Meets Aztlán."

10. Mark A. Grey and Anne C. Woodrick, "'Latinos Have Revitalized Our Community': Latino Migration and Anglo Responses in Marshalltown, Iowa," in Zúñiga and Hernández-León, *New Destinations*, 133–54; Martha W. Rees, "How Many Are There?

Ethnographic Estimates of Mexican Women in Atlanta, Georgia," in Murphy, Blanchard, and Hill, *Latino Workers in the Contemporary South*, 36–43; Hal Rothman, *Neon Metropolis: How Las Vegas Started the Twenty-first Century* (New York: Routledge, 2003); Jamie Winders, "What Difference Does Latino Migration Make? Race, Ethnicity, and Urban Politics in Nashville, Tennessee," paper presented to the Summer Institute on International Migration, University of California, Los Angeles, 21–26 June 2004.

11. Greig Guthey, "Mexican Places in Southern Spaces: Globalization, Work, and Daily Life in and around the North Georgia Poultry Industry," in Murphy, Blanchard, and Hill, *Latino Workers in the Contemporary South*, 57–67; David Griffith, Alex Stepick, Karen Richman, Guillermo Grenier, Ed Kissam, Allan Burns, and Jeronimo Camposeco, "Another Day in the Diaspora: Changing Ethnic Landscapes in South Florida," in Murphy, Blanchard, and Hill, *Latino Workers in the Contemporary South*, 82–92; Jack G. Dale, Susan Andreatta, and Elizabeth Freeman, "Language and the Migrant Worker Experience in Rural North Carolina Communities," in Murphy, Blanchard, and Hill, *Latino Workers in the Contemporary South*, 93–104.

12. David Griffith, "Rural Industry and Latino Immigration and Settlement in North Carolina," in Zúñiga and Hernández-León, *New Destinations*, 50–75; Hernández-León and Zúñiga, "'Making Carpet by the Mile'"; William Kandel and Emilio Parrado, "Industrial Transformation and Hispanic Migration to the American South," in *Hispanic Spaces, Latino Places: A Geography of Regional and Cultural Diversity*, ed. Daniel D. Arreola (Austin: University of Texas Press, 2004).

13. Hernández-León and Zúñiga, "Appalachia Meets Aztlán"; Rubén Hernández-León, "¿Prácticas transnacionales o industria de la migración? Una mirada alternativa al proceso social de la migración internacional," paper presented at the seminar "Cultura política, migración y procesos transnacionales," CRIM, UNAM, Mexico City, 2004.

14. Zúñiga and Hernández-León, "New Destination for an Old Migration."

15. Jorge Durand and Douglas S. Massey, *Clandestinos: Migración México–Estados Unidos en los albores del siglo 21* (Mexico City: UAZ-Porrúa, 2003).

16. Our findings bear similarities to those in studies conducted in North Carolina, Florida, Tennessee, Louisiana, and other regions of Georgia. See Guthey, "Mexican Places"; Griffith et al., "Another Day in the Diaspora"; Griffith, "Rural Industry and Latino Immigration"; John D. Studstill and Laura Nieto-Studstill, "Hospitality and Hostility: Latin Immigrants in Southern Georgia," in Murphy, Blanchard, and Hill, *Latino Workers in the Contemporary South*, 68–81; Katharine M. Donato, Melissa Stainback, and Carl L. Bankston III, "The Economic Incorporation of Mexican Immigrants in Southern Louisiana: A Tale of Two Cities," in Zúñiga and Hernández-León, *New Destinations*, 76–100.

17. Hernández-León and Zúñiga, "Appalachia Meets Aztlán."

18. Randall L. Patton, *Carpet Capital: The Rise of a New South Industry* (Athens: University of Georgia Press, 1999); Douglas Flamming, *Creating the Modern South: Millhands and Managers in Dalton, Georgia, 1884–1984* (Chapel Hill: University of North Carolina Press, 1992); Joseph A. McDonald and Donald A. Clelland, "Textile Workers and Union Sentiment," *Social Forces* 63, no. 2 (1984): 502–21.

19. Hernández-León and Zúñiga, "Appalachia Meets Aztlán."

20. Collette G. Fields, ESOL teacher, Whitfield County Schools, Georgia.

21. Edmund T. Hamann, *The Educational Welcome of Latinos in the New South* (Westport, Conn.: Praeger, 2003).

22. David Spener and Kathleen Staudt, eds., *The U.S.-Mexico Border: Transcending Divisions, Contesting Identities* (Boulder, Colo.: Lynne Rienner Publishers, 1998), 236.

23. James D. Engstrom, "Industry, Social Regulation, and Scale: The Carpet Manufacturing Complex of Dalton, Georgia," Ph.D. diss., Clark University, Worcester, Mass., 1998; Hamann, *Educational Welcome of Latinos.*

24. Jerry Grillo, "Carpet Maker to the World," *GeorgiaTrend.com*, 2006 http://www.georgiatrend.com/site/page8168.html, accessed 14 Aug. 2006.

25. ConAgra, *ConAgra Chick Chat* 32 (Dec. 1996): 2, Dalton, Georgia Division.

26. Ibid., 25.

27. "Lopez Service Deserved Better," *Dalton (Ga.) Daily Citizen*, 8 July 2004, www.daltondailycitizen.com/articles/2004/07/08/news/opinion/opinion02.txt, accessed 13 Sept. 2004.

28. Hernández-León and Zúñiga, "Appalachia Meets Aztlán."

29. Ivan Light, *Deflecting Immigration: Networks, Markets and Regulation in Los Angeles* (New York: Russell Sage Foundation, 2006); Elen Barry, "It's 'Get These People out of Town,'" *Los Angeles Times*, 16 Aug. 2006, 1A.

30. William E. Baker and Paul A. Harris, "Unwelcome Strangers to the New South: Georgia's Response to Undocumented Migration," in Sigrid Baringhorst, James F. Hollifield, and Uwe Hunger, eds., *Herausforderung Migration—Perspektiven der Vergleinchenden Politikwissenschaft: Festschrift für Dietrich Thränhardt* (Berlin: Lit Verlag, 2006); Jenny Jarvie, "Georgia Law Chills Latino Home-Buying Market," *Los Angeles Times*, 19 June 2006, http://www.latimes.com/news/nationworld/nation/la-na-housing19jun19,0,1948022.story?track=tothtml, accessed 19 June 2006.

31. "Hearing Takes Aim at Wage Provision," *Dalton (Ga.) Daily Citizen*, 15 Aug. 2006, 3A.

32. Karina Gonzalez, "House Panel Holds Dalton Hearing on Health Immigration," *Chattanooga Times Free Press*, 15 Aug. 2006, http://www.tfponline.com/absolutenm/templates/breaking.asp?articleid=3718&zoneid=41, accessed 16 Aug. 2006.

33. Hernández-León and Zúñiga, "Appalachia Meets Aztlán"; see also Hamann, *Educational Welcome of Latinos.*

34. Flamming, *Creating the Modern South*; Patton, *Carpet Capital.*

35. Hamann, *Educational Welcome of Latinos.*

36. Giovanna Dell'Orto, "Ga. Town at Center of Immigrant Labor Case," *Washington Post*, 22 April 2006, http://www.washingtonpost.com/wp-dyn/content/article/2006/04/21/AR2006042100973-pf.html, accessed 26 April 2006.

CHAPTER FOUR

Globalization and Latin American Immigration in Alabama

RAYMOND A. MOHL

In 1992 Felipe Patino settled in Russellville, Alabama, along with his wife Patricia and their children Juan and Alma. During the previous four years Felipe had traveled back and forth between Mexico and Florida to work, leaving his family behind in Mexico. Still earlier he had made numerous annual trips for seasonal jobs in California agriculture. In the early 1990s Patino was drawn to heavily rural, mostly white northwestern Alabama by the opportunity to work in the Gold Kist poultry plant in Russellville, where, he was told by fellow Mexicans, he could almost double the wages he earned as a migrant farmworker in Florida.

The Russellville poultry plant had opened in 1990, but Gold Kist managers had trouble securing a local, stable labor force. Gold Kist found in Latinos like Patino the reliable, low-cost workers they needed to maintain efficient production. In an effort to boost its labor force recruitment in the late 1990s, Gold Kist sponsored a huge billboard in Tijuana, Mexico, promising "Mucho Trabajo en Russellville, Alabama" and listing a local recruiter's telephone number. By the end of the decade the population of the Russellville area had become more than one-third Hispanic (3,500 of about 10,000 residents). By that time the Patino family had bought a home and enrolled their children in local schools. The Mexican community in Russellville was now large enough to provide many of the elements of "home": foods such as flat tacos, hot peppers, and goat meat; Mexican videos; Spanish-language soap operas on satellite television; weekend soccer leagues; Spanish-language church services on Sundays; Spanish-speaking workers in government agencies; and Latino clerks in local retail stores.

As the Patinos and other Mexican immigrants adapted to life in Russellville's Little Mexico, the town's white population was becoming increasingly uneasy about the ethnic changes that they perceived as a threat to the stability of small-town southern life. Initially (in the early to mid-1990s), newcomers from south of the U.S. South were received cautiously, but in generally positive ways. They worked hard and spent their money locally, boosting rental housing, retail stores, and the used-car market. They provided about one-third of the labor force in the Gold Kist plant and contributed to the economic turnaround of the local economy. By the late 1990s, however, Russellville locals had begun complaining about the newcomers' preference for the Spanish language and the rising costs for health care, social services, and schooling, which they blamed on the growing immigrant population. A few raised the disturbing specter of a rejuvenated Ku Klux Klan (KKK) that might scare off the Mexicans and restore the familiar whiteness of the past. Yet discontented whites had little appreciable effect in stemming the flow of new immigrants to the area. Despite rising ethnic tensions in Russellville and elsewhere in Alabama, the Patinos and other newcomers seemed permanently settled.[1]

The scene is much the same in northeastern Alabama, where tens of thousands of Latinos have settled. Near Gadsden, in the small town of Attalla, Raul and Guadalupe Cantellano live in a small, ramshackle house with fifteen other family members, including six children, three of them married with children of their own. After several years as a migrant farmworker in the East Coast migrant stream, Raul brought his family to settle in Alabama in 1994, finding work at the Cagle poultry plant in nearby Collinsville. Over time, Cantellano's three adult sons and their wives also began to work at the plant, in which Latinos comprised 63 percent of the workforce by 1999. Guadalupe Cantellano works at home, caring for younger children, cooking great quantities of tortillas a day, and raising chickens in the backyard. Raul and Guadalupe's adult sons, who received little education in Mexico, hope that educational opportunities in the United States will enable their children and grandchildren to break the cycle of poverty and low-skill, low-pay work that characterizes the lives of most Latinos in the U.S. Southeast.[2]

In Birmingham the critical role that social networks play in the migration process is evident. Birmingham is now home to some six thousand Mexicans from the *municipio* of Acambay in the south-central state of Mexico. The few Mexican unskilled workers who arrived from Acambay in the late 1980s relayed news of good-paying work in Birmingham, resulting in the migration of many others from Acambay, a process often referred to as "chain migration." Some Acambay transplants, like Matias Pérez, are day laborers who send remittances to their wives and children back in Mexico; others, like Gregorio Roque, are small business owners.[3] Roque, who became a legal U.S. resident as a result of the 1986 Immigration Reform and Control Act (IRCA)—and later a U.S. citizen—is now a successful middle-class entrepreneur, who nevertheless is building a new home in Acambay and hopes to return some day to the village of Dongu where other family members still reside. As a successful businessman his story contrasts with that of most other Mexican immigrants in Alabama, but it suggests the diversity of the Latino migration patterns and the economic opportunity that many newcomers find in the United States.[4]

Latinos in Alabama

As these immigrant stories suggest—and there are many thousands of similar stories—Dixie is experiencing a dramatic demographic, economic, and cultural transformation. As noted in the introduction to this book, these changes are linked to global and regional economic shifts, and to changes in U.S. immigration policies. New immigration has fueled the South's changing economy and altered its system of racial relations. Black and white once defined the racial landscape of the American South, but multicultural and multiethnic rather than biracial now describe society in many southern places. As one Alabama editorialist noted in 2000, "Life in the South used to be defined in shades of black and white. But a growing wave of Hispanic immigrants is adding brown to that color scheme."[5]

Alabama became an important destination for Mexican and Central American immigrants in the 1990s. According to the U.S. Census Bureau the number of Hispanics in the state increased from 25,000 in 1990 to 76,000 in 2000, a growth rate of 208 percent. The Hispanic population has continued to grow at a rapid pace since 2000; 2006 census estimates placed the Hispanic population at 114,000 in the state and at 33,728 for the seven-county Birmingham metro area. Those who work with the Latino communities—social workers, public health professionals, church people, teachers and education administrators, and police officials—suggest that census reporting, and especially the agency's statistical sampling methods, have not kept pace with the continuing migration. State and local officials have routinely disparaged the census statistics because of the recognizably large undercount of immigrants. According to some, the true number of Hispanics in Alabama ranges between 150,000 and 200,000, possibly more.

The 2007 American Community Survey data also provided a proportionate breakdown of Hispanics from diverse national backgrounds as of summer 2006. According to that survey Mexicans made up 64 percent of Alabama Hispanics, while about 24 percent came from other Central and South American countries. Alabama had few Puerto Ricans or Cubans in 2006, roughly 8 and 5 percent, respectively. This proportional breakdown, only marginally different from 2000 census data, was almost certainly more accurate than the statistics on the total number of Hispanics or Latinos in the state.[6]

The newcomers have spread throughout Alabama to both rural and urban areas. Besides metro Birmingham, the state's other major metro areas—Montgomery, Mobile, and Huntsville—each have sizable Latino communities, almost certainly more than the 5,000 (Montgomery) to 14,000 (Huntsville) indicated by the 2005 census estimates (last available data). Locals suggest that doubling the census statistics for those three metros would provide a more accurate reflection of the Latino communities there. In northern Alabama, where the poultry and garment industries are concentrated, small cities and towns such as Gadsden, Cullman, Decatur, Russellville, Albertville, Collinsville, Oneonta, and a few others also have substantial numbers of Latino newcomers. "Little Mexicos" have sprouted in northern Alabama neighborhoods, trailer parks, and apartment complexes.[7]

Jobs and economic opportunity have provided the magnetic pull attracting Mexicans and others to Alabama. The booming U.S. economy of the 1990s, with the lowest unemployment rates in decades, created a demand for cheap, reliable, nonunion labor. Universally praised for their strong work ethic, Mexican workers found themselves in demand for many factory, farming, forestry, construction, landscaping, and service jobs. The poultry-processing industry, in particular, played a major role in drawing Latino workers to Alabama. Several scholars have documented the strategic decision of meatpackers and poultry companies in the 1980s and 1990s to shift their processing plants to southern and midwestern small towns and rural areas, where unions had little influence. These areas generally were losing population to larger urban areas, but the companies recognized that low-wage immigrant workers, especially Mexicans, could be recruited to fill their labor needs. Poultry and farm work in Alabama provided important initial enticement for Latino immigrants and internal migrants, but an ongoing economic crisis in Mexico through the 1980s and 1990s supplied an important push factor as well. Many labor migrants came directly from rural and small-town Mexico, where unemployment and poverty were rife, but many others, such as Felipe Patino, Raul Cantellano, and Matias Pérez, had already worked in Texas, Florida, California, Oregon, or other U.S. states before arriving in Alabama.[8]

Big business in the United States—big agriculture, big manufacturers, big food processors, and the like—played an important role in this migration process as well, often directly recruiting undocumented, low-wage workers in Mexican border areas for jobs in Alabama. The Gold Kist billboard in Tijuana, mentioned earlier, and similar billboards all over Mexico advertised work in the U.S. South, as did newspaper and radio ads. Interviewed in April 2005, a Latino activist in Albertville, Alabama, recounted that in the 1990s labor recruiters for northern Alabama poultry companies regularly signed up Mexican workers. They put the recruits on old school buses with blackened windows and drove them from Texas directly to chicken plant jobs in Alabama. Los Angeles journalist Hector Tobar wrote about a similar journey in his book, *Translation Nation* (2005). Tobar went undercover as a migrant worker, signed up with a manpower recruiter in McAllen, Texas, and received a free bus ticket to Ashland, Alabama, where he worked the night shift at the Tyson's poultry plant and lived in a run-down mobile-home park with several other workers. Tyson's required a drug test, but no one seemed concerned about his documents.[9]

The new Latino labor force has become an important ingredient in Alabama's rural and urban economies. In small northern Alabama towns Latinos work on chicken farms and in poultry-processing plants, and in hosiery, garment, textile, carpet, furniture, and plastics manufacturing. They work extensively in agriculture, where they pick and pack tomatoes, peaches, strawberries, potatoes, cucumbers, and watermelons. Throughout the American South, farm labor has been transformed in the past two decades, as Latino workers now make up a huge percentage of the farm labor force, as much as 90 percent or more in some states. Notably, former migrant agricultural workers are also settling permanently in northern Alabama towns, many moving into factory jobs and chicken plants. This pattern of "settling out" of the migrant stream is common in other states as well. Latinos are fewer in number but still very much in evidence in southern Alabama, where they provide migrant agricultural labor, grow peaches, plant sod, replant timber land, process poultry and seafood, and work on dairy farms, truck farms, in saw mills, and in nurseries. With the expansion of poultry plants in Clayton and Barbour Counties after 2000, southern Alabama's Latino labor force grew rapidly to fill the new jobs. As one business leader in Barbour County noted, "the Hispanic labor force follows poultry operations."[10]

In metropolitan areas such as Birmingham, Mexican newcomers work in restaurants, landscaping, roofing, construction, car washes, and warehousing. They clean rooms and make beds in Birmingham area hotels. A major portion of the janitorial work in downtown and suburban Birmingham office buildings is done by Latino service workers. Throughout the 1990s employers found in Latinos a cheap, reliable, and nonunionized labor force at a time when national labor markets were very tight. During the economic downturn that began in 2000, employers continued to seek out Latino workers because they represented lower wage costs and brought higher levels of efficiency to the workplace than the workers they replaced. The Latino immigrants, in turn, found numerous ethnic niches in the U.S. economy—niches where even low wages represented a huge premium over wage rates in Mexico or Central America.[11]

Mirroring immigrant waves of past eras, the initial Latino newcomers were primarily young, single men who shared cramped housing, worked in teams or crews, and sent earnings to families back home. News of job opportunities in Alabama spread quickly to the sending villages and towns in Mexico and elsewhere. Industrial recruiters or independent labor contractors in poultry, agriculture, construction, and forestry have provided an important mechanism through which Mexicans became part of the Alabama labor force. For example, researchers have documented the role of labor contracting firms in legally recruiting guest workers on H-2B contracts for work in the south Alabama forest industry. These forestry workers entered the state legally, but many others have not. Through a familiar process of chain migration, homeland relatives, friends, and neighbors joined *compadres* in certain Alabama towns and workplaces. In a pattern reminiscent of employment practices in the industrial era, Alabama plants and firms have come to rely on their Latino workforce as a recruitment mechanism. Mexicans returned home often, eventually bringing wives, children, and even aging parents to the United States. Over time Mexicans and other Latinos began putting down roots, sending children to U.S. schools, and buying homes and property.[12]

A substantial number of Latinos have started their own businesses, with restaurants, groceries, and landscaping and construction companies the most common form of immigrant entrepreneurialism. According to U.S. Census data the Birmingham area had 629 Hispanic-owned businesses in 1997, an increase of 180 percent over 1992. Of other midsized southern cities, only Knoxville had a faster growth rate of Hispanic-owned businesses. By 2002 Latinos had established over 2,500 businesses throughout Alabama, with total sales of $741 million. Small construction companies comprised some 25 percent of Alabama's Hispanic businesses in 2002.[13] Moreover, the 2002 U.S. agricultural census reported some 450 Hispanic farm owners and operators in Alabama.[14] The rising number of Latino business people has paralleled the growth of the Latino population in Alabama. At the same time, Latino buying power in Alabama rose dramatically to almost $2.5 billion in 2007, still small compared to that of African Americans at more than $20 billion, but sufficient to persuade big companies such as Wal-Mart, as well as supermarkets and banks to cater to Latino consumers by carrying Latino products and hiring Spanish-speaking workers. Reflecting these changes, the Birmingham Regional Chamber of Commerce and the Latino Business Council have been conducting diversity workshops for business people in metro Birmingham. At least one staffing company has been established in Birmingham to assist area companies seeking Latino workers. Another Birmingham company provides translation services for schools, hospitals, and businesses, while still another firm trains executives and managers to communicate and work more effectively with Latino and other minority workers. Similar endeavors are underway throughout Alabama. Latinos have become an integral part of the state's economy.[15]

Immigration Controversies in Alabama

A large but unknown number of Latino workers in Alabama are undocumented immigrants. Beginning in 1986 IRCA required that employees provide documentation proving eligibility to work in the United States, but the legislation did not require employers to verify the accuracy of such documentation. Thus in urban and rural Alabama an underground labor market built on unauthorized immigrant workers and often functioning with the complicity of employers thrives without much regulation or control. Until 2000 Alabama had only two permanent Immigration and Naturalization Service (INS, now Immigration and Customs Enforcement or ICE) agents, both stationed in Birmingham, and six U.S. Border Patrol agents, all assigned to Mobile. Consequently, enforcement efforts have been relatively weak. Once they navigate the border crossing, undocumented workers easily enter the state on bus and commercial van routes that traverse the interstate highways. As one of the state's few border patrol agents noted in the late 1990s, "I couldn't tell you a corner of the state of Alabama that doesn't have some illegal immigrant population."[16] Little has changed since then.

The sense that immigration has been "out of control" has helped to fuel hostility toward Latino newcomers in parts of Alabama. In 1990 Alabama voters overwhelmingly supported an amendment to the state constitution that would make English the official language of the state. The measure had initially been sponsored by state Representative Euclid Rains of Albertville, who complained in legislative debate in 1989 that "the Spanish are creeping in."[17] In fact Rains's district in DeKalb and Marshall Counties soon became a center of growth for Alabama's Spanish-speaking population. Language controversies periodically flared throughout the 1990s, an issue kept alive by the Alabama English Committee and its supporters. On matters ranging from Spanish-language driver's license tests to applications for homestead exemptions to Spanish television ads, language usage became a matter of heated debate. The language controversies, a *Washington Post* reporter noted in 2000, suggested that "many in the Birmingham area are uncomfortable with the notion that their city could take on the characteristics of a Miami."[18]

In the 1990s more overt expressions of anti-immigrant sentiment surfaced in Oneonta and Cullman, two small towns north of Birmingham. In 1997 in Oneonta a white supremacist group affiliated with the America First Committee and headed by a Ku Klux Klansman demonstrated against what they called the "Mexican invasion." William Riccio, the demonstration's organizer, contended that Oneonta's new immigrants were "illegal," that they were "creating a tremendous drain on the economy," and that they were "holding jobs that should go to white residents." Continued Latino immigration, Riccio asserted, threatened to make Blount County the "little Miami north of Birmingham."[19] For some in Alabama, multicultural Miami had come to symbolize an unwanted, potentially dangerous, and nonwhite future. In 1998 in Cullman after an immigration protest meeting organized by the KKK and white militia leaders, three men were arrested for burning the Mexican flag. James Floyd, leader of the Stand Up for Cullman protest, argued for a permanent halt to Latino immigration, which, he believed, would ultimately challenge Cullman's white majority population. "I like my own people more than others," Floyd later asserted, "and I'm not ready for a world without borders."[20]

These anti-immigrant sentiments emerged again in 2004 during a mayoral election campaign in Hoover, a Birmingham suburb where Latinos have clustered in moderately priced apartment complexes. Both mayoral candidates made the subject of illegal immigration a key issue, and they threatened to close down a local multicultural immigrant service center run by Catholic Family Services. Staffed by volunteers from local churches and charities, the Multicultural Resource Center provided English-language classes, family counseling, and other services to Latinos and other immigrants from over fifty countries. After the election the Hoover city government established a municipal Department of Homeland Security and Immigration, the only such agency in the state. The one-person department seemed primarily interested in monitoring and harassing Latinos who gathered at the center for day-labor pickup. After the city ousted the center from a city-owned building in 2005, the multicultural agency found a new home in a donated building, though it lacked the space for day-labor pickup. Ironically, Tony Fletcher, the mayor who turned immigration into a local political issue, owned a general contracting company that relied on subcontractors to provide Latino workers.[21]

The Hoover immigration controversy anticipated the subsequent resurgence of anti-immigrant sentiment in Alabama. Beginning in 2005 the U.S. Congress and the national media heatedly debated new federal immigration legislation. A house bill passed in December 2005 focused exclusively on tougher border controls, but many in the Senate argued for a guest-worker program and a path to legal residency for the millions of undocumented immigrants who met certain conditions. In a reprise of the immigration policy battles of the mid-1980s, many legislators rejected guest worker provisions and what they called "amnesty," favoring a crack-down on unauthorized immigrants already in the country. Sensing an issue that resonated with their Alabama constituents, U.S. Senators Jeff Sessions and Richard Shelby, along with Governor Bob Riley, advocated beefed-up border security and a tougher approach to unauthorized immigrants.[22]

In Alabama some state legislators sought to cut government services such as schooling, welfare, and health care to undocumented residents, although such bills died in legislative committee. State troopers received special training in enforcing federal immigration laws, making Alabama the first state to dedicate resources to arresting and deporting undocumented immigrants. Language purists went to court to limit Alabama driver's license exams to English only. Politicians in Huntsville proposed a city ordinance to punish employers who hired undocumented immigrants, while in Hoover, Pelham, and Alabaster municipal authorities considered zoning ordinances to limit Latinos living in large groups in single-family residences. In Birmingham a Jefferson County judge created a controversy when he ordered eleven undocumented Latino men who had been arrested for minor traffic offenses deported from the United States. Citizens poured out their complaints about immigration in letters to local newspapers and in town-hall type forums around the state.[23]

The anti-immigrant backlash in Alabama drew an unexpected response from the immigrants themselves. In April and May 2006 Latinos, energized by similar events across the United States, mobilized in their own defense by participating in marches, rallies, demonstrations, and boycotts around the state. In April some five thousand people, mostly Latinos, marched for immigrant rights in Albertville, while another three thousand jammed downtown streets in Birmingham. In May 2006 Latino immigrants in Alabama participated in the one-day national economic boycott and work stoppage—an effort to demonstrate the significance of immigrant workers in local economies. In Huntsville, Albertville, Russellville, Decatur, Birmingham, Tuscaloosa, and Dothan, the boycott shut down poultry plants, construction sites, and other workplaces, as Latinos sought to "flex fiscal muscle."[24]

The Latino demonstrations and boycotts intensified anti-immigrant activity in Alabama. Counter demonstrations and "procitizenship" rallies around the state protested calls for amnesty and urged a crackdown on "illegal" immigrants. In Decatur, Cullman, and Montgomery, Alabamians complained about the Latinos' impact on local job markets; demonstrators carried signs that read "Close Our Borders" and "Remember the Alamo." Hate groups such as the KKK jumped into the anti-immigrant fray as well, tapping into partially hidden ethnic and racial concerns about Latino immigration.[25]

Latino immigrants had their defenders, however. Agricultural, construction, and other business interests that rely on Latino workers were quick to point out the essential labor provided by newcomers from Mexico and Central America. Alabama farmers warned that tougher immigration laws would have a devastating economic impact on their industry. One poultry farmer posed the question, "If we didn't have guest workers, who would catch my chickens?" This sentiment was shared by many other farmers across the state. Spokespeople for the Associated Builders and Contractors of Alabama aired worries that new immigration and employment verification provisions would leave local builders without 40 percent or more of their construction workers. Poultry processors, production companies, landscapers, retailers, and apartment owners, among others, heavily depend on Latino immigrants as workers and consumers. As the immigration wars heated up in Alabama, Latinos found themselves at the center of divisive debates over immigration policy, law enforcement, language usage, citizenship, and Americanization.[26]

Immigration and Job Competition

Recent immigration debates have captured attention statewide, but another dispute has been simmering below the surface since the mid-1990s. The surge of Mexican and other Latino workers to Alabama has produced new tensions in neighborhoods and workplaces. In Birmingham and elsewhere in Alabama, Latinos have been settling in traditionally black neighborhoods, where rents are often more reasonable. Latino migration has also placed wage and job competition issues in the spotlight. Latinos have already supplanted blacks and low-income whites in many areas of employment, such as food processing, janitorial work, landscaping, construction, forestry, farm labor, and service work. Some have argued that Latinos have not only displaced black workers but have also kept wages low for all low-skill and semiskilled workers. The seeming preference of employers for Latino workers, who are often praised as being more compliant and having a strong work ethic, has rankled black communities across the South.[27]

These tensions surfaced in the 1990s at a Tyson's poultry plant in Ashland, Alabama, where African Americans formed a large part of the workforce at the time. Journalist Roy Beck, in congressional testimony and his book, *The Case against Immigration* (1996), noted the distressingly low wages and dangerous working conditions at the plant, but black workers had few other job prospects in the Ashland area. In the mid-1990s when black workers flirted with unionism and "staged a couple of work slowdowns and walkouts to protest working conditions," the poultry company quickly bused in Latino workers to replace them. As Beck put it, "the corporation was using foreign workers to re-assert its dominance over those native workers." The lesson was clear, one Ashland worker concluded at the time: "The next time black workers walk out over a labor problem, they'll be replaced by Third World workers." Beck emphasized the ways in which uncontrolled immigration damaged the economic prospects of low-wage, low-skilled, and especially African American workers. Although by no means widespread in Alabama, black resentment about job competition and unwelcome neighbors has surfaced in some places.[28]

Many labor economists and immigration scholars reject the labor competition argument. They contend that the new Latino immigrants are filling jobs that no one else wants. Job turnover in the fields and in food-processing plants has been extremely high, they contend, as much as 100 percent or more a year in some industries. Moreover, they say, Latino workers are taking new jobs created in the 1990s by expanding urban and regional economies. In many lines of work Latinos are filling "replacement" jobs abandoned by black workers who have rejected low pay and excessively demanding work. Some labor researchers have described a pattern of ethnic succession in southern labor markets in which Latinos "are replacing African American or white workers who leave the worst jobs . . . [in textiles, furniture manufacturing, custodial services, and meat processing] rather than displacing them from the more desirable jobs in the industry."[29] A North Carolina sociologist echoed that view: "It looks like the whites are moving out, the blacks are moving up, and the Latinos are filling in at the bottom."[30]

Several studies of labor turnover in Alabama's forestry industry illustrate how the availability of low-wage immigrant labor affects regional labor markets. Alabama's forest production is concentrated in the sixteen-county Black Belt, a rural south Alabama region originally named for its dark, rich soil. The region is also marked by a high percentage of African American population and by high levels of poverty and unemployment. In recent decades, Black Belt cotton fields have been replaced by large pine plantations, as the nation's timber production has shifted from the U.S. West to the South. Despite the available black and white labor pool in the region, timber companies and plantation owners chose to use labor contractors to recruit H-2B guest workers from Mexico for unskilled jobs planting trees and applying herbicide. According to rural sociologist Vanessa Casanova, "timber companies, labor contractors, and forest landowners have turned to migrant workers to reduce labor costs at the bottom rungs of the industry's employment ladder."[31]

Keeping wages low for unskilled forestry work also reduced wage pressures for more skilled jobs, thus insuring industry profits at a time of global competition. Chain migration patterns and kinship-based recruitment almost certainly meant that over time guest workers would be followed by undocumented immigrants. American workers in the Black Belt rejected low-pay, low-skill, low-status jobs lacking opportunity for upward mobility. Not coincidentally, Black Belt counties have been losing population to other areas of the state with more attractive job markets. By driving down wage levels, the Black Belt forestry industry created a "racially based segmentation of labor markets," as Latinos came to hold virtually all the unskilled jobs in the forests and pulp and paper mills. Moreover, marginalizing wages across the board meant that a profitable industry that enjoyed major tax concessions was contributing little to the economic development of Alabama's poorest region. Similar economic outcomes can be found in many small southern towns where poultry processing and carpet manufacturing have become dominant local industries.[32]

Clearly, experts disagree over issues of job competition between African Americans and new Latino immigrants, and over the economic consequences of immigration in general. The latter issue has been hotly debated among economists and policy experts since the 1980s, with some emphasizing the positive benefits of immigration, while others cite economic costs as measured in job losses and wage cuts among U.S. citizens. Whatever the reality, blacks and Latinos have been at odds over jobs, neighborhoods, and cultural differences since the 1990s. These troublesome issues have added a new component to the black and white binary that has shaped the South for most of its history. Consequently, new patterns of racial and ethnic tension linger unresolved in Alabama and throughout the region.

Immigrant Advocacy and Service

The Latino influx to Alabama has produced an anti-immigrant backlash in some quarters, but it has also unleashed an avalanche of advocacy and service activities. In Birmingham and elsewhere in Alabama, civic leaders, union organizers, and advocacy groups have sought to mediate emerging ethnic and racial conflicts. Both the Birmingham Civil Rights Institute and Operation New Birmingham have engaged in this effort. In Montgomery the National Association for the Advancement of Colored People (NAACP) has developed alliances with Latino organizations in pursuing goals common to both groups. In many places churches, schools, and public agencies have responded in positive ways to the new immigrants. The Roman Catholic Church and numerous Protestant denominations have embraced the newcomers, offering Spanish-language religious services, English classes, and varied social services. The Roman Catholic Diocese of Birmingham ministers to tens of thousands of Latinos in thirty-nine northern Alabama counties. The Catholic Hispanic Ministry of

Mobile conducts similar religious and social service programs in south Alabama. Spanish-language Masses provide a comforting and familiar haven for new immigrants still adjusting to life in the United States. Protestant churches have also engaged in religious, educational, and social service work with Latino immigrants. Baptist churches are heavily involved in this sort of work, and Latinos have become missionary targets of traditional Protestant denominations, as well as for some evangelical churches.[33]

Public schools in small towns and large cities are struggling to provide English-as-a-second-language (ESL) classes to a growing number of Latino children. In Shelby County public schools, for instance, 391 students needed special English-language instruction in 2001, but by 2006 that number had increased fourfold, to 1,550. Public health agencies also provide a range of services, despite the problems of serving a new population without proper immunizations and mostly without health insurance. Police and emergency management personnel are receiving Spanish-language instruction geared to providing more effective services.[34]

Throughout the state, public agencies and private organizations have emerged that serve and advocate for the Latino newcomers. For example, Project Aprende works with migrant farmworkers in several northern Alabama counties, providing information on health care and environmental safety, as well as promoting the importance of schooling for migrant children. Nursing students from Birmingham's Samford University staff a medical clinic for migrant agricultural workers at the Mexican Cultural Center in Steele, Alabama. In Hoover the Multicultural Resource Center sponsored by Catholic Family Services works cooperatively with government, church, and community organizations in providing assistance to new immigrants. The Hispanic Interest Coalition of Alabama, established in Birmingham in 1999, coordinates the work of numerous public and private agencies that serve and advocate for Latinos. In Huntsville the North Alabama Hispanic Association is doing similar work, although the preservation of Hispanic culture shares equal billing with housing, education, and legal services. Several agencies in Russellville, including the Franklin County Coalition for the Hispanic Community, provide social services, health care, and practical advice for newcomers. In Baldwin County volunteers from the San Pedro United Methodist Church staff the Clinica Migrante, which serves migrant agricultural workers in southern Alabama. The Barbour County Hispanic/Latino Coalition in Eufaula provides social services and help with finding housing, schooling, and medical services. Many such organizations in Alabama have rejected the nativist response and work instead to serve, to protect, and to ease the adjustment process for Latino newcomers.[35]

Building a New Life

Mexican immigrants and migrants have begun putting down roots and building new communities in Alabama and elsewhere across the American South. Like immigrants to the United States in earlier times, they have found strength in their communal activities and cultural heritage. They quickly created a vibrant cultural life based on homeland food ways, kinship activities, and festive and musical traditions. In Alabama these cultural activities centered not just in the home but in hundreds of restaurants, grocery stores, music and dance clubs, and traditional holiday festivals. For example, Mexican groceries, retail stores, and many restaurants supply not only familiar food but also Spanish-language newspapers, Latino movie videos, music tapes and CDs, religious icons, traditional clothing (from white baptism dresses to cowboy boots and hats), and check-cashing and money-wiring services. Mexican national holidays and important religious events such as the feast of the Virgin of Guadalupe, the Día de los Muertos, Cinco de Mayo, and Christmas become occasions to celebrate ethnic culture. Customary religious practice, such as universal veneration of the Mexican national patron saint, the Virgin of Guadalupe, has sustained cultural persistence. Language and culture have been essential ingredients in the Latino struggle to adapt without losing identity and tradition in the new land.[36]

On dusty fields near the trailer parks of northern Alabama's "Little Mexicos," young men and boys pursue the national sport of their homelands—soccer. A network of soccer leagues in northern Alabama and in the Birmingham metropolitan area provides leisure time activities for young men and Sunday outings for entire families, smoothing the transition to life in America. In October 2000 the Latin American Soccer League of Birmingham organized with sixteen teams from the Birmingham metro area, complete with colorful uniforms and sponsors. In less than a year the league had expanded to thirty-two teams, and by 2006 to sixty teams in four divisions. Smaller soccer leagues emerged in Russellville, Decatur, and Anniston in northern Alabama. Latino high-school students have come to dominate soccer teams in northern Alabama public schools. Soccer is dominant, but Birmingham Latinos have also organized a Latino Baseball League. Some play baseball on Saturday and soccer on Sunday. For Hernán Prado, an Ecuadorian immigrant and businessman who coached soccer in Collinsville, traditional sports helped young Latinos "to maintain their culture while learning the ways of their new country."[37]

An emerging Spanish-language media serves similar cultural functions. *El Reportero*, a bilingual newspaper published in Huntsville since October 1999, currently has a twenty-five-county circulation of sixty thousand. Two additional Latino newspapers, *Latino*, published in Gadsden, and *La Voz Latina*, published in Birmingham, reach tens of thousands of Latino newcomers. These papers contain news of homeland politics and sports, as well as job ads and information designed to ease adaptation to life in the United States. Latino radio stations broadcasting music and Spanish talk radio can be found in Birmingham, Huntsville, Decatur, and Oneonta, providing cultural sustenance for new arrivals. In Hoover a local movie theater began showing Spanish-language films in 2004.[38] Often isolated from mainstream America in work and residence, Alabama Latinos have found comfort in their own Spanish-language media, which contribute in important ways to the maintenance of language, culture, and tradition.

To conclude, the convergence of globalization and U.S. immigration policy has brought a transnational, low-wage, mostly Mexican labor force to Alabama and, more generally, to the land of Dixie. This new human migration has produced substantial cultural and demographic change in a region where change has always been slow and received with skepticism, if not hostility. Early in the twenty-first century this process of southern ethnic and cultural change has been intensifying. Farms and factories and employers of all kinds now seek out Latino workers for their work ethic and their willingness to work for low pay. Southerners have now come to recognize the ethnic change spreading across the land, but they still seem surprised by it. Ethnic and linguistic change has ignited new forms of nativism and stoked concerns about the social and economic costs of immigration. Many African Americans believe that Latinos have taken jobs and depressed wages, but there are also signs of interracial activism and alliance among the two groups. In addition, the new migration has spawned a myriad of helping agencies that serve Latino migrants and immigrants with care and respect. The newcomers themselves have been adapting to life in a new land, while also building new communities based on common culture and tradition. This is the *nuevo* New South. Ready or not, Dixie appears to be on the cusp of a long-term process of Latinization, mirroring what has already happened in other parts of the United States.

Notes

1. For the Patino story see Rose Livingston, "A New Home," *Birmingham News*, 21 Sept. 1997; Rose Livingston, "Russellville Blends Hispanic Flavor," *Birmingham News*, 5 Oct. 1997; Rose Livingston, "Hispanic Families Seek Better Life Here," *Birmingham News*, 5 Oct. 1997; telephone interview with Neil Taylor, immigration attorney in Russellville, Ala., Dec. 2002.

2. On the Cantellano family see Rose Livingston, "Settlers Build a Lifestyle," *Birmingham News*, 18 Sept. 2000.

3. Daniel Connolly, "Seeking a Better Life: Thousands Leave Acambay, Mexico, for Birmingham Area," *Birmingham Post-Herald*, 26 July 2004.

4. Daniel Connolly, "Sweet Success," *Birmingham Post-Herald*, 29 July 2004.

5. "Folks Very Much Like Us," *Huntsville Times*, 25 Feb. 2000.

6. Jeremy Gray, "Area Hispanic Population Up by 50% Since 2000, Data Say," *Birmingham News*, 4 Aug. 2006; Suevon Lee, "Hispanic Immigration Comes to Alabama," *Florence Times Daily*, 18 Aug. 2006; Ben Evans, "South Leads in Immigrant Influx," *Mobile Press-Register*, 20 Aug. 2006; U.S. Bureau of the Census, 2007 American Community Survey.

7. U.S. Census, 2006 American Community Survey; Daniel Connolly, "Albertville: Little Mexico," *Birmingham Post-Herald*, 28 July 2004; Raymond A. Mohl, "Latinization in the Heart of Dixie: Hispanics in Late Twentieth-Century Alabama," *Alabama Review* 55 (Oct. 2002): 243–74.

8. Dell Champlin and Eric Hake, "Immigration as Industrial Strategy in American Meatpacking," *Review of Political Economy* 18 (Jan. 2006): 49–69; David Griffith, "*Hay trabajo*: Poultry Processing, Rural Industrialization, and the Latinization of Low-Wage Labor," in *Any Way You Cut It: Meat Processing and Small-Town America*, ed. Donald D. Stull, Michael J. Broadway, and David Griffith (Lawrence: University Press of Kansas, 1995), 129–51; Nestor Rodriguez, "'Workers Wanted': Employer Recruitment of Immigrant Labor," *Work and Occupations* 31 (Nov. 2004): 453–73.

9. Interview with Rose Boman, Hispanic American Society of Marshall County, 19 April 2005; Karen D. Johnson-Webb, *Recruiting Hispanic Labor: Immigrants in Non-Traditional Areas* (New York: LFB Scholarly Publishing, 2003); Hector Tobar, *Translation Nation: Defining a New American Identity in the Spanish-Speaking United States* (New York: Riverhead Books, 2005), 77–102.

10. Jack Smith, "Minorities Now Majority in County," *Eufaula Tribune*, 5 Oct. 2004; Randy E. Ilg, "The Changing Face of Farm Employment," *Monthly Labor Review* 118 (April 1995): 2–12; Manuel Torres, "The Latinization of the South," *Mobile Register*, 28 June 1999; Connie Baggett, "Changing Work Force," *Mobile Register*, 8 Aug. 2000; Steve Mayo, "Migrant Work Force Declining," *Mobile Register*, 19 Nov. 2000; Brett Clanton, "Pay Lures Workers to Tough Jobs," *Montgomery Advertiser*, 10 Feb. 2003; Daniel Connolly, "Sueño de Alabama," *Birmingham Post-Herald*, 24–30 July 2004; Kelli Hewett Taylor, Jeff Hansen, and Mike Cason, "El corazón de Dixie," *Birmingham News*, 6–8 Nov. 2005.

11. Dale Short, "Mexico in the Heart of Dixie," *UAB Magazine* 21 (summer 2001): 2–9; Bill Caton, Niki Sepsas, and Chianti Glegett, "Searching for Magic: Hispanics in the City," *Birmingham Magazine* 41 (May 2001): 100–107; Jennifer Edmondson, "Willing to Work—Anywhere," *Birmingham Post-Herald*, 27 July 2001; Roy Williams, "Employers Say Immigrants Ease Critical Worker Shortage in Area," *Birmingham News*, 9 Sept. 2001; Guy Busby, "The New Alabamians," *Mobile Press-Register*, 4 June 2006.

12. Vanessa Casanova and Josh McDaniel, "'No sobra y no falta': Recruitment Networks and Guest Workers in Southeastern U.S. Forest Industries," *Urban Anthropology* 34 (spring 2005): 45–84. For an illuminating report on chain migration patterns from

Mexico to the Atlanta area see Mark Bixler, "The Latino Network," *Atlanta Journal-Constitution*, 15 April 2001.

13. Michael Shattuck, "Metro Birmingham Rapidly Becoming Alabama's Hispanic Population and Business Center," press release, Birmingham Regional Chamber of Commerce, 10 Sept. 2001.

14. "Ag Census Reveals Alabama Trends," *Southeast Farm Press*, 3 March 2004.

15. *The Multicultural Economy 2007*, Selig Center, University of Georgia, 2007; Roy L. Williams, "Hispanics Growing Economic Force in State, Says Georgia Researcher," *Birmingham News*, 17 Nov. 2004; Roy L. Williams, "Diversity Summit a Step for City in Reaching Out," *Birmingham News*, 9 Nov. 2004; Kelli Hewitt Taylor, "Boom Fuels Hispanic Enterprises," *Birmingham News*, 22 March 2006.

16. Manuel Torres, "The Latinization of the South," *Mobile Register*, 28 June 1999; Rose Livingston, "INS Agent Shortage Called 'Dangerous' for Alabama," *Birmingham News*, 16 March 2000; Todd Kleffman, "Immigration Agency Barely Visible in Alabama," *Montgomery Advertiser*, 10 Feb. 2003; Daniel Connolly, "Immigration Enforcement Lax," *Birmingham Post-Herald*, 28 July 2004; James Goldsborough, "Out-of-Control Immigration," *Foreign Affairs* 79 (Sept./Oct. 2000): 89–101; Angie C. Marek, "Border Wars," *U.S. News and World Report*, 28 Nov. 2005, 46–56.

17. *Birmingham News*, 27 April 1989.

18. "English Now Official State Tongue," *Birmingham News*, 6 June 1990; Marcos McPeek Villatoro, "Mexican in Alabama," *Southern Exposure* 22 (fall 1994): 26–27; Dave Bryan, "Hispanics Make Headway in Old South," *Washington Post*, 10 Oct. 2000; Mohl, "Latinization in the Heart of Dixie," 264–66.

19. Suzy Lowry, "White Supremacists Plan Oneonta March," *Blount Countian*, 21 May 1997.

20. Gita M. Smith, "Klan Targets Hispanics Welcome in Alabama," *Atlanta Journal-Constitution*, 17 June 1997; Beth Lakey, "Three Arrested at Protest," *Cullman Times*, 18 Jan. 1998; Manuel Torres, "The Latinization of the South," *Mobile Register*, 28 June 1999.

21. Daniel Connolly, "Issue: Illegal Immigrants," *Birmingham Post-Herald*, 9 Sept. 2004; Rosa Ramirez, "Hoover's Security," *Birmingham Post-Herald*, 7 May 2005; Dawn Kent, "Hoover Cultural Center Feels Community Heat," *Birmingham News*, 24 July 2005; Dawn Kent, "Hoover to Close Hispanic Center," *Birmingham News*, 2 Aug. 2005; Elaine Witt, "Regarding Immigrants, the Problem Is Us," *Birmingham Post-Herald*, 6 Aug. 2005.

22. Mary Orndorff, "Sessions Wants to Fence Off Mexico," *Birmingham News*, 19 Nov. 2005; Holly Hollman, "Shelby Backs Tough Stance on Illegals," *Decatur Daily News*, 7 Feb. 2006.

23. David White, "Committee Calls for Limiting Services to Illegal Immigrants," *Birmingham News*, 24 Feb. 2005; Mike Linn, "Alabama Could Join States That Require Drivers to Know English," *USA Today*, 29 Dec. 2005; Jeff Hansen, Kelli Hewitt Taylor, and Dawn Kent, "Banished" *Birmingham News*, 19 March 2006; Brian Lyman, "Immigration Hot Politically in Alabama Despite the Facts," *Anniston Star*, 9 June 2006; Lee Ropp, "Passions Flare Up during City Forum on Immigration," *Huntsville Times*, 11 July 2006.

24. Kelli Hewitt Taylor, "3,000 March Downtown for Immigration Reform," *Birmingham News*, 10 April 2006; "Thousands March in Albertville for 'Immigrant Justice,'" *Decatur Daily News*, 11 April 2006; Kent Faulk and Kelli Hewitt Taylor, "Hispanics Seek to Flex Fiscal Muscle," *Birmingham News*, 30 April 2006; Kent Faulk and Kelli Hewitt Taylor, "Hundreds of Hispanics in Alabama Add Their Voices to a Chorus of Protestations," *Birmingham News*, 2 May 2006; Eric Fleischauer, "Immigrant Uprising," *Decatur Daily News*, 2 May 2006.

25. "Cullman Rally Protests Alien Amnesty Call," *Huntsville Times*, 16 April 2006; April Wortham, "Businesses Close, Hispanics March in Alabama Protests," *Tuscaloosa News*, 2 May 2006; Kelli Hewitt Taylor, "Capital Protest Targets Illegal Immigration," *Birmingham News*, 6 May 2006; Kent Fault, "Franklin Klan Rally Targets Immigrants," *Birmingham News*, 7 May 2006; Ronnie Thomas, "Some Speak Mind on Illegal Immigration," *Decatur Daily News*, 14 May 2006; Kent Faulk, "Immigration Issues Get Hateful," *Birmingham News*, 30 May 2006.

26. Mary Orndorff, "State's Farmers Split with Sessions on Immigration," *Birmingham News*, 16 March 2006; Kelli Hewitt Taylor, "ABC Pledges to Support Its Hispanic Workers," *Birmingham News*, 29 March 2006; Sherri C. Goodman, "Local Companies Pinched by Latino Walkout," *Birmingham News*, 3 May 2006; Roy L. Williams, "Campaign to Tout Role of Hispanic Workers," *Birmingham News*, 2 Aug. 2006.

27. "Alabamians Still Need to Work on Tolerance," *Huntsville Times*, 27 June 1999; Cynthia Tucker, "Latino Growth a Wake-up Call for Black Folks," *Atlanta Journal-Constitution*, 18 March 2001; Dahleen Glanton, "Hispanic Influx in Deep South Causes Tensions—with Blacks," *Chicago Tribune*, 19 March 2001; Barbara Ellen Smith, "The Postmodern South: Racial Transformations and the Global Economy," in *Cultural Diversity in the U.S. South: Anthropological Contributions to a Region in Transition*, ed. Carole E. Hill and Patricia D. Beaver (Athens: University of Georgia Press, 1998), 164–78; Raymond A. Mohl, "Blacks and Hispanics in the Modern South," in *Migration and the Transformation of the Southern Workplace Since 1945*, ed. Robert Cassanello and Colin Davis (Gainesville: University Press of Florida, forthcoming). More generally see Steven Shulman, ed., *The Impact of Immigration on African Americans* (New Brunswick, N.J.: Transaction Publishers, 2004).

28. Roy Beck, "Testimony before the U.S. House Subcommittee on Immigration and Claims," 13 May 1997, at http://judiciary.house.gov/Legacy/681.htm; Roy Beck, *The Case against Immigration* (New York: W. W. Norton, 1996), 21–22, 176–202, 248. On black and Latino interaction involving unionization in the poultry industry see also Charlie LeDuff, "At a Slaughterhouse, Some Things Never Change," *New York Times*, 16 June 2000; Leon Fink, *The Maya of Morganton: Work and Community in the Nuevo New South* (Chapel Hill: University of North Carolina Press, 2003).

29. Sheryl Skaggs, Donald Tomaskovic-Devy, and Jeffrey Leiter, "Latino/a Employment Growth in North Carolina: Ethnic Displacement or Replacement?" Research report, North Carolina State University, 2000, at http://sasw.chass.ncsu.edu/jeff/latinos/eeoc.pdf.

30. Ned Glascock, "Latinos Now Filling Bottom-Rung Jobs," *Raleigh News and Observer*, 29 Oct. 2000.

31. Casanova and McDaniel, "'No sobra y no falta,'" 54.

32. Josh McDaniel and Vanessa Casanova, "Pines in Lines: Tree Planting, H2B Guest Workers, and Rural Poverty in Alabama," *Southern Rural Sociology* 19, no. 1 (2003): 73–96, quotation on 79; Tom Gordon, "Hispanic Population Grows in Black Belt," *Birmingham News*, 13 Aug. 2006. On guest workers generally see Philip L. Martin and Michael S. Teitelbaum, "The Mirage of Mexican Guest Workers," *Foreign Affairs* 80 (Nov./Dec. 2001): 117–31.

33. Community Forum of Greater Birmingham, *Birmingham, a City of Roots and Wings: A Special Report on Race Relations and Diversity Survey* (Birmingham, Ala.: Community Foundation of Greater Birmingham, 2003); James D. Ross, "Hispanics Gain Influence in Central Alabama," *Montgomery Advertiser*, 9 Feb. 2003; "Church Adapts to Hispanic Immigrants," *Huntsville El Reportero*, 16 July 2000; "Alabama Protestants Develop Ministries for Catholic Hispanics," Associated Press, 9 May 2005; Greg Garrison, "Iglesia de Cristo," *Birmingham News*, 4 Feb. 2005; Jannell McGrew, "Faith, Traditions Anchor Life," *Montgomery Advertiser*, 11 Feb. 2003.

34. Ken L. Spear, "Schools Bridge Learning Barrier," *Montgomery Advertiser*, 11 Feb. 2003; Marie Leech, "Shelby ESL Program Grows with Immigrant Population," *Birmingham News*, 27 May 2005; Carol Ann Dagostin et al., *Hispanic Health Profile, Alabama 2003* (Montgomery: Alabama Department of Public Health, 2005).

35. Interview with Rose Bowman, 19 April 2005; Rose Livingston, "Meeting Needs of New Residents," *Birmingham News*, 21 Sept. 1997; "Hispanic Association Formed in Huntsville," *Huntsville El Reportero*, Nov. 1999; Jamie Kizzire, "Hispanics' Clout Rising in Alabama," *Birmingham News*, 22 June 2000; Rose Livingston, "Samford Program Gives Migrant Workers Medical Help," *Birmingham News*, 19 July 2000; Glenny Brock, "Service Stronghold," *Birmingham Weekly*, 3 July 2003; Jack Smith, "Minorities Now Majority in County," *Eufaula Tribune*, 5 Oct. 2004; Guy Busby, "Clinic Numbers on Rise," *Mobile Press-Register*, 14 May 2006.

36. Anne Ruisi, "Hispanic Culture Honored," *Birmingham News*, 16 Sept. 2002; Jannell McGrew, "Area Lacks Cultural Connections," *Montgomery Advertiser*, 11 Feb. 2003; Greg Garrison, "Hispanics Laud 'Our Lady,'" *Birmingham News*, 16 Dec. 2005; Eric Velasco, "Latino Pig Roast Fires Cultural Unity," *Birmingham News*, 8 Jan. 2006; Guy Busby, "The New Alabamians," *Mobile Press-Register*, 4 June 2006.

37. Solomon Crenshaw Jr., "Hispanic Leagues Expand Beyond Sundays," *Birmingham News*, 23 Aug. 2006; Rose Livingston, "Leaping a Language Barrier," *Birmingham News*, 5 Dec. 1997; Scott Adamson, "Bridging the Gap," *Birmingham Post-Herald*, 22 May 2004.

38. "Latin Rhythms from Huntsville and for All of North Alabama," *Huntsville El Reportero*, Dec. 1999; Joe Distelheim, "The Challenge in Reaching Newcomers," *Huntsville Times*, 21 Jan. 2001; Jeff Hansen, "'La Voz' of Oneonta," *Birmingham News*, 16 Feb. 2005.

CHAPTER FIVE

Hispanic Newcomers to North Carolina

Demographic Characteristics and Economic Impact

JAMES H. JOHNSON JR. AND
JOHN D. KASARDA

The state of North Carolina is undergoing a dramatic demographic transformation. Paralleling national trends, immigration from Mexico, other parts of Latin America, and Asia is changing the size, composition, and geographical distribution of the state's population as well as its economic landscape.[1] In this chapter we examine the nature, magnitude, and geographical manifestations of Hispanic population change in the state and attempt to measure the economic costs and benefits associated with this population influx.[2] We conclude with an overall assessment of the growing presence of Hispanics in the state of North Carolina.

To achieve these goals we utilize data from a broad spectrum of public and proprietary sources. We also rely on key informant interviews with a host of academic experts, applied researchers, policy analysts, and practitioners in a wide array of fields including immigration studies, demographic forecasting, international trade and commerce, workforce development, and public administration and social services.[3]

North Carolina as a Hispanic Migration Magnet

Among the new Hispanic magnet states, North Carolina led the nation in terms of relative Hispanic population change during the 1990s.[4] The state's Hispanic population grew by 393 percent—from 76,700 in 1990 to 378,963 in 2000—a net absolute increase of 302,000.[5] By 2004 according to the American Community Survey the North Carolina Hispanic population had increased to 506,206. Many believe that this number significantly underestimates the actual number of Hispanics in North Carolina. Our research supports this contention.[6] We estimate that a total of 600,913 Hispanics resided in the state in 2004.[7] According to our calculations Hispanics accounted for 27.5 percent of the state's population growth between 1990 and 2004. They made up 7.0 percent of the state's residents in 2004, up from 1.1 percent in 1990.

Hispanics have increasingly concentrated in a set of metropolitan counties along the state's urban crescent or I-40/I-85 corridor, which extends through the center of the state from Wake County in the east to Mecklenburg County in the southwest (fig. 5.1). Until recently Hispanics were also highly concentrated within the vicinity of military bases in Cumberland and Onslow Counties. But these two counties lost Hispanic population (–7.9 percent and –8.3 percent, respectively) between 2000 and 2004—in all likelihood coincident with the deployment of U.S. troops to Afghanistan and Iraq.[8] Only about 30 percent of the state's Hispanic population resides in nonmetropolitan or rural counties, and their numbers are relatively small in most of these counties. But there are four rural counties in which the Hispanic share of the total population exceeds 10 percent: Duplin (18.2 percent), Sampson (14.3 percent), Lee (13.4 percent), and Montgomery (13.3 percent). Specialty industries that rely heavily on Hispanic labor (e.g., meat and poultry processing) are largely responsible for the high concentration of Hispanics in these counties.[9]

By virtue of either having been born in North Carolina (20.7 percent) or in another U.S. jurisdiction (20.7 percent), 41.3 percent of the state's Hispanics are U.S. citizens. The remaining 58.7 percent of the state's Hispanic population are foreign born and either have become naturalized citizens, obtained a visa, or have migrated to North Carolina without legal authorization.

Due to the clandestine nature of entry, the unauthorized proportion of the foreign-born Hispanic population is difficult to enumerate. Our estimate was derived by matching Hispanic movers from abroad to North Carolina between 1995 and 2004 with Immigration and Naturalization Service (INS) data on those receiving formal authorization during this period. Of the 196,449 Hispanics who immigrated to North Carolina between 1995 and 2004, 47,390 received some form of authorized documentation. Thus we estimate that 76 percent of Hispanic immigrants to the state over the past ten years were unauthorized. When calculated on the basis of all Hispanic residents of North Carolina (including those born in the state and other U.S. jurisdictions), the unauthorized constitute 45 percent of North Carolina's Hispanic population.

For the most part Hispanic migration to North Carolina is a form of labor migration.[10] Despite massive losses of textile jobs, North Carolina has been a magnet for employment growth for much of the past quarter century and especially during the 1990s. Much of this employment growth was driven by the heightened demand for housing, schools, and other public infrastructure, as

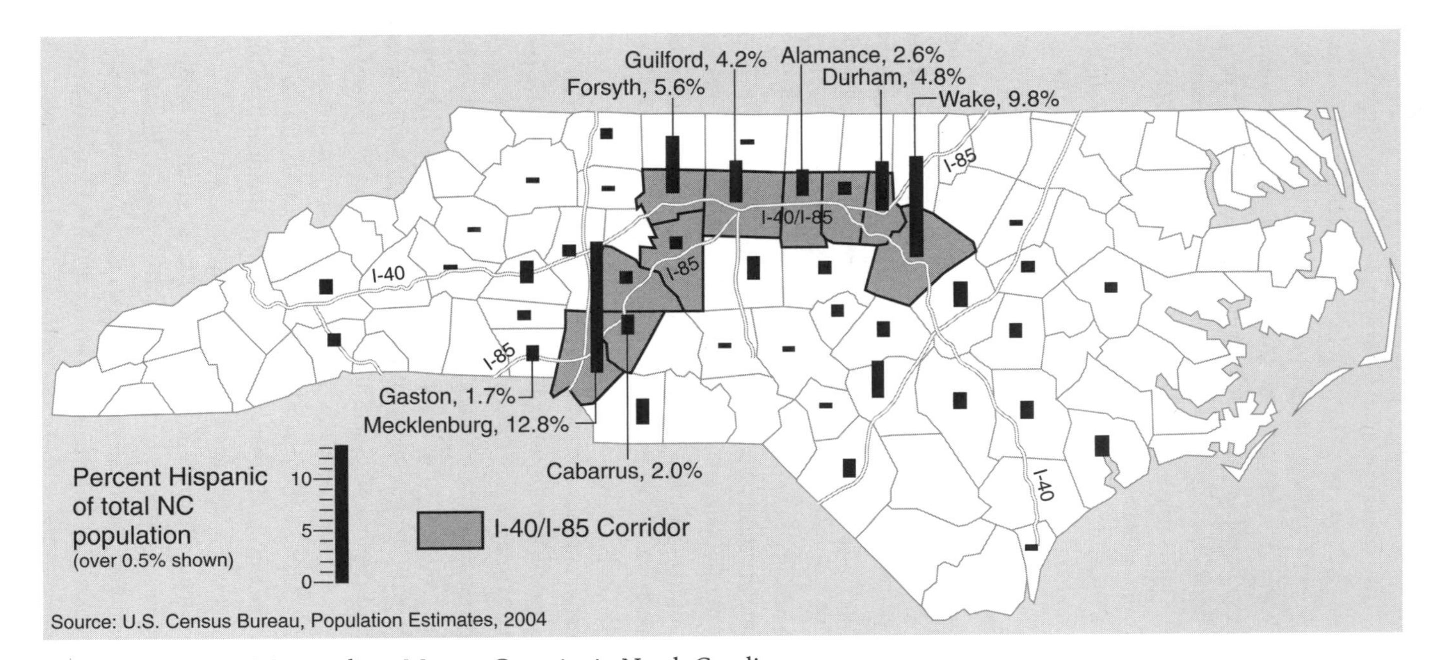

Figure 5.1. Hispanic Metropolitan Magnet Counties in North Carolina, 2004.

well as other services associated with the rapid growth of the North Carolina population during this period. It was also driven by the maturation of the Research Triangle Park as a high-technology hub and the Charlotte region as a major financial services center during this period.

Annual unemployment statistics for the decade of the 1990s underscore the demand for workers created by these developments. Throughout the 1990s North Carolina's unemployment rate was consistently below the national average, and during the late 1990s it was at or below 4 percent, a rate that economists consider to be indicative of a tight labor market, one in which there are far more jobs than there are people to fill them. Throughout the decade a strong demand existed for workers to fill unskilled and low-skills jobs in the North Carolina economy.

Given this state of affairs North Carolina employers began to recruit Hispanic labor both domestically and abroad. They used a number of recruitment strategies, including advertising in Spanish-language and mainstream media outlets (newspapers, radio, and TV) in immigrant gateway communities, hiring Hispanic labor recruitment intermediaries, and establishing referral networks with local Hispanic nonprofit and government organizations, including the Mexican consulate.[11]

The demand for Hispanic labor in North Carolina has continued unabated despite the economic downturn following September 11, 2001.[12] This is especially true in employment sectors where non-Hispanic workers are less inclined to seek employment because of the working conditions or the wages or both. As we show, Hispanic workers, in contrast to non-Hispanics workers, have displayed a willingness to work in these sectors of the North Carolina economy. Between 1995 and 2005 North Carolina added 687,579 workers, a 22.1 percent increase, to its labor force. During this same period North Carolina's Hispanic workforce expanded by 241,602, a 431 percent increase. Hispanics thus accounted for 35.1 percent of the state's overall workforce increase between 1995 and 2005. North Carolina's construction industry absorbed the largest increase of Hispanic workers (111,630), followed by retail and wholesale trade (26,769). Hispanics today account for nearly a third of all construction workers in the state.

The number of Hispanic workers grew across virtually all North Carolina industries, even those hard hit by increased global competition. For example, while North Carolina's manufacturers shed 327,470 workers between 1995 and 2005, the number of Hispanics employed by North Carolina manufacturing firms actually expanded by 14,786.

In 2005 nearly three-fourths of all Hispanics in North Carolina were employed in four industries: construction (42.2 percent), wholesale and retail trade (11.5 percent), manufacturing (10.7 percent), and agriculture, forestry, fishing, and hunting (9.2 percent). Although education and health services is the top employment sector in North Carolina (20 percent of the workforce), it employs only 4.4 percent of the state's Hispanics. Within North Carolina industries Hispanics are concentrated mainly in blue-collar occupations in the construction trades, agriculture, trucking, and janitorial and maid services. There is a definite gender division of labor within the blue-collar workforce. Hispanic males are concentrated in construction occupations as laborers, painters, roofers, carpenters, brick masons, and stonemasons, whereas Hispanic females are concentrated in maid and janitorial services, food processing, retail sales, dry cleaning, and secretarial support occupations (table 5.1).

Nevertheless, Hispanics are beginning to make significant headway into white-collar occupations. Between 1995 and 2005 Hispanics added almost as many North Carolina workers in office and administrative support occupations (15,164) as in farming, fishing, and forestry (20,102). Hispanics employed in management, business, and financial occupations increased by 8,908 in the same decade, while those employed in professional and related occupations increased by 8,073. Hispanics have thus become interwoven into the overall economic fabric of North Carolina and are critical to a number of the state's most important sectors.

Some Hispanics are using self-employment as a path to upward mobility and integration into the North Carolina economy. This should not be surprising given the general tendency for immigrants to be more entrepreneurial than native-born populations.[13] Although the absolute numbers are much smaller, the percent increase in self-employment was much greater among North Carolina's Hispanics (426 percent) than non-Hispanics (9.8 percent) between 1995 and 2005. More than three-fourths (76 percent) of the Hispanic self-employment growth was concentrated in the professional and business services (+4,284) and construction (+4,284) industries.

Despite recent inroads into white-collar occupations, Hispanics do not have the same level of formal education as non-Hispanics (median of 7.5 versus 12.0 years of school completed). In part as a function of lower education levels, Hispanic households earn about $32,000 annually, or about $8,649 per capita, while non-Hispanic households earn about $45,700 annually, or $15,480 per capita. Owing to these disparities in household and per capita income, poverty rates are higher among Hispanics (26.3 percent) than non-Hispanics (14.5 percent) in North Carolina.[14]

Table 5.1 Top Ten Occupations for North Carolina Hispanics by Gender, 2005

	Occupation	*Number of Workers*
Male Hispanics		
	Construction laborers	51,931
	Painters, construction, and maintenance	21,400
	Miscellaneous agricultural workers	15,998
	Roofers	13,900
	Carpenters	13,120
	Industrial truck and tractor operators	13,112
	Brick masons, block masons, and stonemasons	9,816
	Retail salespersons	6,203
	Janitor and building cleaners	5,853
	Food preparation workers	5,627
Female Hispanics		
	Maid and household cleaners	7,986
	Janitors and building cleaners	4,825
	Butchers and other meat-, poultry-, and fish-processing workers	4,748
	Cashiers	4,112
	Retail salespersons	3,800
	Pressers, textile, garment, and related materials	3,206
	Packers and packagers, hand	3,084
	Secretaries and administrative assistants	2,697
	Cooks	2,424
	Miscellaneous agricultural workers	2,413

Source: U.S. Bureau of Labor Statistics, Current Population Survey, Annual Social and Economic Supplement, 2005

Assessing the Economic Impact of Hispanic Newcomers

To assess the economic impact of Hispanic newcomers on North Carolina, we address four key issues:

- The impact of Hispanic consumer spending on the state and its communities.
- The net balance of the Hispanic population's contributions and costs on the state budget.
- The effect of Hispanic workers on the total economic output and competitiveness of the state.
- The potential business opportunities North Carolina's expanding Hispanic presence provides.

Figure 5.2 depicts our conceptual framework for assessing the overall economic impact of Hispanics on North Carolina. On the contributions side we focus largely on those that accrue to the state from the following factors:

Consumer Spending. This is the total Hispanic after-tax personal income available for local spending on goods and services. Such spending has both direct and indirect effects on North Carolina business revenues and employment. Hispanic purchases also contribute to a host of state and local taxes including, among others, sales tax, highway-use tax, motor fuel tax, alcohol tax, and cigarette tax.

Payroll and Property Taxes. Hispanics directly contribute to North Carolina's revenue base through taxes on their earnings and property.[15]

Industry Competitiveness. Hispanic workers benefit North Carolina industries by augmenting the labor supply and economic output at competitive wages and salaries.

On the cost side we estimate the financial impact of Hispanics on three major public costs that are typically considered in immigrant impact studies: K–12 education, health-service delivery, and corrections.[16] For much of our analysis we utilized an input-output model known as IMPLAN. This model is based on interindustry purchasing patterns, consumption patterns, and local production, retail, and service availability. IMPLAN traces consumer spending through over five hundred sectors of North Carolina's economy to generate a variety of economic impacts at the state, metropolitan area, and county levels.[17]

Buying power data for North Carolina Hispanic residents were the primary inputs to the IMPLAN model.[18] Generally such income is spent locally. However, North Carolina's Hispanics, especially those who are more recent immigrants,

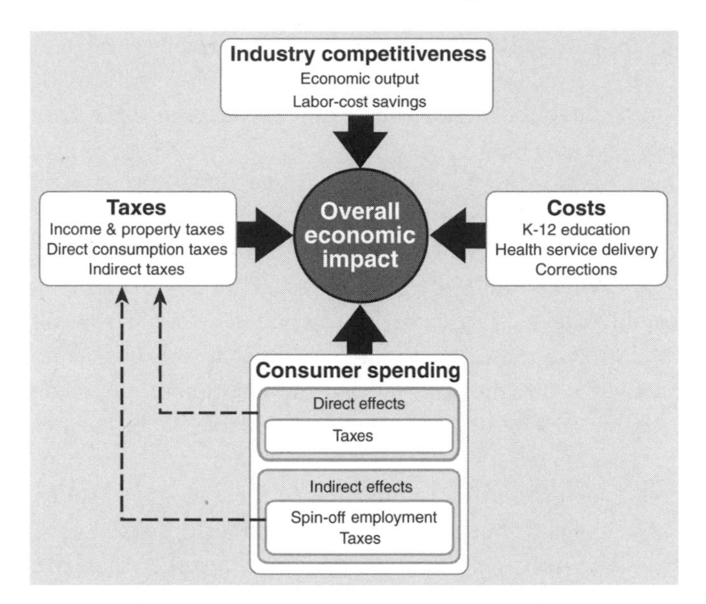

Figure 5.2. Conceptual Framework for Assessing the Economic Impact of Hispanics in North Carolina.

typically remit substantial portions of their income back to their country of origin.[19] Based on recent research on Hispanic immigrants in North Carolina and other states, we deflated Hispanic buying power by 20 percent before beginning our analysis.[20] This reduction takes into account not only remittances but also savings and interest payments that also reduce local spending.[21] Methods and data used to estimate Hispanic tax contributions, labor output, and wage savings to North Carolina's industries, as well as Hispanic public costs, are described separately.

Estimated Impact of Hispanic Spending on the State

North Carolina's Hispanics had an estimated $8.35 billion in buying power (after-tax income) in 2004. Even after discounting their buying power by 20 percent to account for remittances, savings, and interest payments, Hispanic purchases rippled through the state's economy, creating an overall economic impact of $9.19 billion—roughly $15,030 per Hispanic resident—in 2004. The indirect effects of Hispanic spending in North Carolina include 89,600 spin-off jobs and $2.41 billion in additional labor income in 2004. Hispanic spending also was responsible for $455 million in additional state tax receipts and $661 million in federal taxes, of which some of the latter eventually flows back to the state. As table 5.2 shows, these contributions have increased considerably since 2000, and monumentally since 1990.

Hispanic spending had the greatest direct and indirect economic impacts on five metropolitan areas along the I-40/I-85 corridor: Charlotte, Raleigh, Durham, Greensboro, and Winston-Salem. For example, in addition to generating $2 billion in business revenues and 16,900 spin-off jobs, Hispanic spending in the Charlotte metropolitan area catalyzed over half a billion dollars in spin-off labor income for area workers and nearly $93 million in additional state tax receipts. Hispanics residing in the combined Raleigh and Durham metropolitan areas generated nearly the same business revenues, spin-off jobs, labor income, and additional state tax receipts.[22]

Paralleling Hispanic population concentration along the I-40/I-85 corridor, the top five counties in Hispanic buying power and economic impact in 2004 were Mecklenburg, Wake, Durham, Forsyth, and Guilford. Together, these five counties accounted for 43.7 percent of the total buying power and 40.8 percent the total economic impact of the state's Hispanics. These same counties account for over half of the $6.6 billion in economic impact that is concentrated in metropolitan counties. Hispanic residents of Mecklenburg County, for instance, had a local economic impact that exceeded $1.3 billion in 2004. In that year Wake County Hispanics had an economic impact of almost $950 million, while in Durham and Forsyth Counties the Hispanic impact exceeded $500 million and in Guilford County over $380 million.

The economic impact of Hispanic spending in North Carolina's nonmetropolitan counties collectively was $1.6 billion in 2004—just above that of Hispanics in Mecklenburg County alone. Over 40 percent of the nonmetro Hispanic impact is concentrated in seven counties: Duplin, Robeson, Lee, Sampson, Wilson, Iredell, and Surry. Most of these counties, as noted previously, host specialty industries that employ large numbers of Hispanics.[23]

Major Public Costs of Hispanics to North Carolina

In estimating the costs to the state of the Hispanic population, we focused on three of the major and most often discussed public sectors in immigrant studies: K–12 public education, health-service delivery, and corrections.[24] There are no doubt other significant costs, but these three are generally agreed to be the primary ways to measure the impact of an immigrant group on state budgets. After subtracting federal transfers, North Carolina spent $10.1 billion

Table 5.2 Economic Impact of Hispanic Spending in North Carolina, 1990–2004

	1990	*2000*	*2004*
Direct impact of purchases	$928,144*	$5,290,094	$9,188,380
Spin-off labor income†	$243,921	$1,390,263	$2,414,752
Spin-off state taxes	$45,960	$261,953	$454,987
Spin-off federal taxes	$66,793	$380,696	$661,231
Total	$1,284,818	$7,323,006	$12,719,350

* All figures are given in thousands of dollars.

† The number of spin-off jobs was 9,000 in 1990, 51,500 in 2000, and 89,600 in 2004.

Source: Kenan Institute of Private Enterprise, 2005

on education in 2004. Approximately 61 percent of this amount was spent on K–12 education. For our K–12 educational cost estimates, we assumed that the percentage of expenditures attributable to Hispanics was proportional to their representation in the student population (7.5 percent). This amount in 2004 was estimated to exceed $466.8 million.[25]

To calculate net health-care delivery costs to the state, we used our estimate of the state's Hispanic population, the Medical Expenditure Panel Survey (MEPS) health service expenditure data, and the Centers for Medicare and Medicaid Services (CMMS) information on costs and sources of payments by race/ethnicity.[26] These data show that Hispanics use health-care services less frequently than most other major racial and ethnic groups and, when they do, incur relatively lower costs. This may reflect their younger age distribution and, despite their low average income, a propensity to self-pay at least a portion of their costs, which significantly reduces their cost to the state. Our estimate of the net cost (after payments) to the state for health services to Hispanics in 2004 is nearly $299 million.

For our estimate of costs to the state correctional system, we began with the total expenditures in the state budget.[27] The North Carolina Department of Corrections supplied the data on the total number of individuals in the system, whether in prison, on parole, or on probation, and the number of Hispanics as well. We then calculated the percentage of expenditures on Hispanics based on their percentage in the prison, parole, and probation populations in the state. That percentage is 5.2 percent, less than their share of North Carolina's total population (7.0 percent). The resulting estimated cost of Hispanics in 2004 to North Carolina's corrections system is more than $50.7 million.

Direct and Indirect Hispanic Tax Contributions to the State

We considered three different categories of taxes accruing to the state government as a result of Hispanics' presence in North Carolina in 2004; the figures cited throughout this section are given in table 5.3. The taxes on income and property are not considered disposable income and thus do not enter into the accounting of Hispanic buying power discussed above. State payroll tax contributions were calculated by computing the tax owed by the average Hispanic household, multiplying that amount by the estimated number of Hispanic households, and then adjusting that figure by a tax compliance rate of 65 percent.[28] The total annual amount of personal income tax paid by North Carolina Hispanics in 2004 is estimated to be more than $145 million.

An estimate of business tax owed by Hispanic-owned small businesses in the state was calculated from information on the number of businesses, their average earnings, and the effective tax rate. The total annual amount of small-business tax paid by North Carolina Hispanics in 2004 is estimated to be just under $86 million.

Separate property tax calculations were estimated for Hispanic homeowners and renters. In both cases, estimates of the average tax owed were calculated using information about home value and rent paid, average effective North Carolina tax rates, and the number of households in each tenure category. A similar procedure was used to calculate non–real estate property tax. The total annual amount of property tax paid by North Carolina Hispanics is estimated to be nearly $62.8 million. The three subcategories (personal income, small-business income, and personal property taxes) total nearly $293.8 million.

Hispanics also pay taxes on their consumer spending. These were calculated by using information on Hispanic household spending patterns derived from national data and multiplying average spending by North Carolina's tax rates, with the two major categories being the state sales tax and the motor vehicle use tax.[29] Together these total an estimated $114 million paid by North Carolina's Hispanics in 2004.

The final and largest tax contribution category includes all state and local taxes generated as an indirect result of Hispanic consumer spending. These include the estimated $221.5 million additional income and property taxes paid by businesses as a result of their operation, and the estimated $126.1 million additional income, property, and consumer taxes paid by their employees. Calculated using the input-output model described above, these total an estimated $347.7 million.

Collectively, Hispanic residents in 2004 were responsible for an estimated $293.8 million in personal current taxes, over $114 million in sales and other

Table 5.3 North Carolina State Tax Impact Estimates, 2004

	Direct Contributions	*Indirect Contributions*		*Total Contributions*
		From Business	*From Persons*	
Personal income tax	$145,082*		$67,802	$212,884
Property tax	$62,772	$115,483	$769	$179,024
Small-business tax	$85,920	$17,225		$103,145
subtotal	$293,774	$132,708	$68,571	$495,053
Highway tax	$9,176	$3,914	$3,914	$17,004
Sales and use tax	$102,592	$51,369	$51,369	$205,330
subtotal	$114,062	$88,828	$57,577	$260,467
Other taxes	$2,294	$33,545	$2,294	$38,133
Total	$407,836	$221,536	$126,148	$755,520

* All figures are given in thousands of dollars.

consumption taxes, and nearly $347.7 million in taxes on the increased business and earnings resulting from Hispanic spending. This totals over $755.5 million in North Carolina state and local taxes paid by North Carolina Hispanics in 2004.

Net Effect of Hispanics on the State Budget

Determining the net cost or benefit of Hispanics to the state budget is a multifaceted and complex effort. It also is fraught with potential oversights and sometimes questionable assumptions. Studies conducted elsewhere of net public costs or benefits of Hispanics on states have often resulted in conflicting analyses, depending on the assumptions and models used.[30] Given these strong caveats, we developed a series of reasonable estimates of the primary direct and indirect contributions and costs of North Carolina's Hispanics to state and local budgets in 2004.

Our model is illustrated in figure 5.3. We begin, on the left side of the figure, with the state's Hispanic population as tax contributors. Hispanic earnings are reduced by remittances, which leave the state's economy, and by taxes on income and property (sometimes termed "personal current taxes" or "statutory taxes"), which go directly into state and local coffers. Hispanic spending generates direct and indirect business revenue and employment, which generates three types of taxes: direct sales taxes, indirect business taxes, and indirect personal taxes. Altogether, as noted above, these totaled to an estimated $756 million.

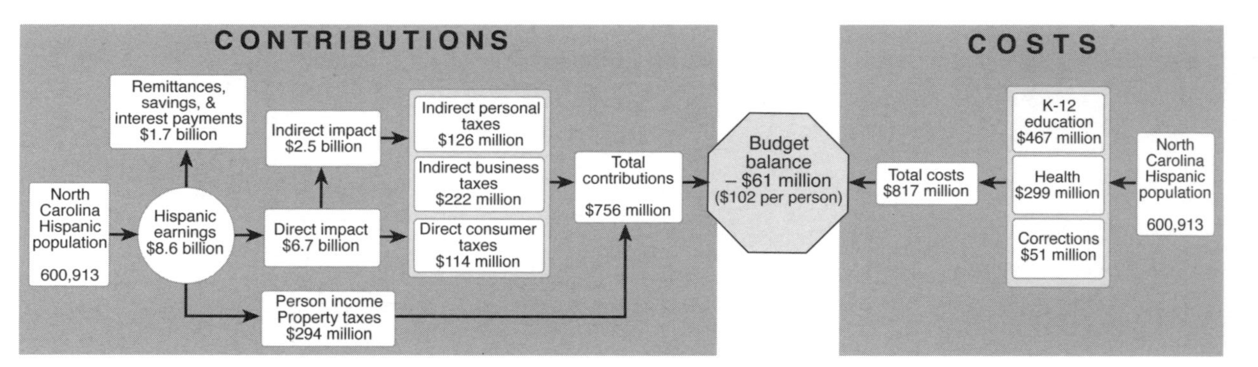

Figure 5.3. Framework for Assessing the Hispanic Impact on the State Budget.

On the right side of figure 5.3 we consider the state's Hispanic population as consumers of state services. As noted above, North Carolina's Hispanic population is responsible for an estimated $816.6 million in state public costs for K–12 education, health-service delivery, and corrections. The difference in 2004 between Hispanics' estimated major tax contributions of $756 million and their estimated major public costs of $817 million results in a net cost to the state of just over $61 million, or approximately $102 per Hispanic resident.

Hispanic Contributions to North Carolina Economic Output

We need to view the estimated net cost to the state within the broader context of the overall benefits Hispanics bring to the state's economy. Hispanics comprise 7 percent of North Carolina's overall workforce and considerably more in certain key sectors. This labor has allowed the state's economic output to expand. In its absence, a substantial portion of North Carolina's economic vitality would likely disappear. Determining the net effects of a withdrawal of Hispanic immigrant workers on North Carolina industries is virtually impossible. For illustration purposes, however, we looked at North Carolina's construction industry. Throughout North Carolina this industry has become heavily dependent on Hispanic workers, who make up 29 percent of the state's construction workforce.

Ignoring labor substitution effects, construction work could be cut by up to 29 percent if Hispanic workers were withdrawn. The hypothetical impact in 2004 would have been the loss of up to $10 billion in value of construction done in the state, including: a revenue loss of up to $2.7 billion for companies supplying construction materials and supplies; a loss of up to $149 million in revenue for companies renting buildings, machinery and equipment; and up to 27,000 houses not being built.

A withdrawal of Hispanic construction workers would also mean up to a 29 percent reduction in nonbuilding construction, including the installation of guardrails and signs, bridge construction, paving, and water and sewer construction. Even if the net effect were a fraction of the above upper-limit estimates—which, again, do not take labor substitution effects into account—there would be a dramatic impact on North Carolina's construction sector (and other sectors, such as banking, through ripple effects) if Hispanics were to substantially withdraw from the state's workforce.

Another way to look at the impact of Hispanic workers on North Carolina's industries is in terms of wage savings, costs to consumers, and overall competitiveness of the industries. Hispanics have added substantially to North Carolina's supply of cost-effective labor. This has resulted in an estimated statewide wage savings of almost $1.9 billion (1.4 percent of the total wage bill).[31] The benefits are enjoyed by every county and virtually all industries that export from the state and by many firms that serve local needs. In many cases labor-cost savings are passed on to local consumers.

The Hispanic wage advantage is concentrated in two industries, agriculture and construction, in which Hispanics comprise 31 and 29 percent of the labor force, resulting in savings of $147 million (6.6 percent) and $980 million (7.4 percent), respectively. Hispanics thus benefit the state by making an important rural export industry more competitive (agriculture) and by substantially reducing costs in an industry that fuels metropolitan area growth (construction).

On the other hand, it has been argued that Hispanic immigrants often depress wage levels of non-Hispanics, especially in lower-wage, labor-intensive sectors.[32] Given the downward pressure that less-educated Hispanics place on wages in these sectors, not everyone in North Carolina benefits from the influx of Hispanic workers.

Local Business Opportunities to Serve Hispanics

In a substantial number of nonmetropolitan counties, and even some metropolitan counties, the buying power of Hispanic residents exceeds their economic impact. At least two factors account for this. First, we estimated that remittances, savings, and interest payments reduce local Hispanic buying power by 20 percent.[33] Second, insufficient retail and service facilities limit Hispanic (and other group) expenditures in these counties. The result is that Hispanic spending and its impact takes place outside these counties, often in a larger metropolitan area. This is commonly termed "leakage."

The fact that the retail, services, and employment structure of the county, which our input-output models take into account, does not meet local Hispanic buying power needs may provide an opportunity for appropriate businesses to fill that space profitably. We therefore developed a methodology to estimate both the absolute and relative size of the Hispanic business revenues leaked to other areas.[34]

Counties with the largest Hispanic buying power tend to have the largest absolute amount of Hispanic impact leakage. But, many smaller North Carolina counties have large absolute leakages (e.g., Duplin, Sampson, and Robeson). The relative leakage figures show that ten counties (Bertie, Bladen, Camden, Caswell, Gates, Graham, Greene, Jones, Northampton, and Tyrrell) are capturing only 70 percent or less of the expected economic impact (30 percent or more business-revenue leakage).

Conversely, seven counties (Buncombe, Durham, Forsyth, Guilford, Mecklenburg, New Hanover, and Wake) have less than 10 percent leakage rates. Their absolute amounts of leakage are large, though, given the scale of Hispanic purchasing power in these counties. Not all of the business revenue leakage can be captured, but our analyses suggest a significant potential for Hispanic-targeted business development in a substantial number of North Carolina counties.

The Hispanic presence in North Carolina is now large and widespread. Hispanics live in every one of the state's hundred counties and work in all sectors of the state's economy and have been responsible for almost 30 percent of the population increase since 1995. For the most part the growth of the Hispanic population in North Carolina has been a form of labor migration. Over the last decade the North Carolina labor force has increased by 22 percent. Hispanics accounted for 35 percent of that growth. In other words, one out of every three net new workers in the state is Hispanic. The construction industry and the agricultural industry have become particularly dependent upon Hispanic workers.

North Carolina Hispanics had an estimated total after-tax income of $8.3 billion in 2004. Approximately 20 percent of this was sent to families abroad, saved, or used for interest payments. The remaining spending had a total impact of $9.2 billion on the state, much of which was concentrated in the major metropolitan areas along the I-40/I-85 corridor but also supported businesses in every corner of the state.

The large and growing Hispanic population was reflected in a fiscal impact on the state budget with the costs of education, health services, and corrections totaling an estimated $817 million in 2004. Those costs were balanced to a large degree by direct and indirect tax contributions of $756 million, resulting in a net cost to the state budget of $61 million. It is important to view this estimated $61 million net cost to the state budget within the broader context of the aggregate benefits Hispanics bring to the state's economy. Along with directly and indirectly generating over $9 billion annually in North Carolina business revenues, Hispanic workers contribute immensely to the economic output of the state and to the cost competitiveness of a number of key industries. For example, our estimates indicate that, without Hispanic labor, the output of the state's construction industry would likely be considerably lower and the state's total private sector wage bill as much as $1.9 billion higher. Some of these labor-cost savings keep North Carolina's businesses competitive while others are passed on in the form of lower prices to North Carolina consumers.

On a per-capita basis Hispanics contributed about $15,130 to the state's economy through their consumer expenditures and tax contributions, while only costing the state $1,360 per person in essential services in 2004. The difference between per-capita contributions and per-capita costs yields a net benefit to the state of $13,770 per Hispanic resident. Thus, for every dollar spent on essential services for Hispanics (i.e., K–12 education, health-care services, and corrections), the state received a $10 return on its financial investment in 2004.

The total impact of Hispanic spending may increase substantially in the future if localities can figure out how to retain more of the Hispanic consumer dollar, that is, to forestall Hispanic business revenue leakage. Hispanic entrepreneurship and opportunities for recruiting Latin American investment to the state could also substantially boost North Carolina's jobs and tax revenues in the years ahead.

Notes

1. John D. Kasarda and James H. Johnson Jr., *The Economic Impact of the Hispanic Population on the State of North Carolina* (Chapel Hill, N.C.: Frank Hawkins Kenan Institute of Private Enterprise, 2006); James H. Johnson Jr., "Immigration Driven Population Change in North Carolina: Opportunities for the Banking Industry," *Carolina Banker* 83, no. 3 (fall 2004): 13–14.; K. D. Johnson-Webb and J. H. Johnson Jr., "North Carolina Communities in Transition: An Overview of Hispanic In-migration," *North Carolina Geographer* 5 (1996): 21; J. H. Johnson Jr., K. D. Johnson-Webb, and W. C. Farrell Jr., "A Profile of Hispanic Newcomers to North Carolina," *Popular Government* 65 (1999): 2–12; Malcolm T. Simpson et al., *Hispanic Economic Impact Study: An Eastern North Carolina Analysis* (Greenville, N.C.: Regional Development Institute, 1999); Mark R. Sills, *Hispanics in North Carolina: Introduction to Our New Neighbors* (Greensboro, N.C.: Faith in Action Institute, 1999); D. T. Stallings, *A Statistical Overview of Latino Achievement in North Carolina* (Durham, N.C.: Duke University, 2003).

2. The term *Hispanic* is used throughout this chapter because the analysis is based heavily on U.S. Census data, which uses the category *Hispanic*. See the introduction for a more detailed explanation of the terminology used in this book for Latin American immigrants and their descendants.

3. See Kasarda and Johnson, *Economic Impact of the Hispanic Population*, C-1.

4. See Johnson, "Immigration Driven Population Change in North Carolina"; M. S. C. George, "Isolation and Incorporation: The Lives of Hispanic Immigrants in Asheville, North Carolina," M.A. thesis, Warren Wilson College, 2005; Sills, 1999.

5. Georgia, Arkansas, and Tennessee are the other three southern states that experienced Hispanic population growth above the national average between 1990 and 2000. Many of the other states experiencing rapid Hispanic population growth are in the U.S. Heartland (e.g., Iowa, Kansas, Minnesota, and Nebraska), the Mountain region (e.g., Utah and Colorado), and the Pacific Northwest (Oregon and Washington).

6. Kasarda and Johnson, *Economic Impact of the Hispanic Population*.

7. To arrive at our estimate of the Hispanic population in North Carolina we began by looking at public school enrollment figures—an actual count of the Hispanic school-attendee population (102,174). We then built in additions to the base number using several assumptions from the 2000 census: private school-attendees are 6.2 percent of the school-age population (6,335); school-aged dropouts are 45 percent of ages 15–19 (12,194); and idle and working teens are 23 percent of ages 15–19 (6,340). Taking these numbers into account, our adjusted number for Hispanic school-aged children is 127,043. Next, we applied a ratio, from the 2000 census, of 3.73 non-school-aged Hispanic persons for every school-aged Hispanic person. Multiplying 127,043 by 3.73 equals 473,870. Adding 473,870 to 127,043 brings us to our total estimate of the state's Hispanic population of 600,913.

8. Puerto Rican families with members in the U.S. military made up a significant percentage of the Hispanic population in these areas.

9. K. D. Johnson-Webb, *Recruiting Hispanic Labor: Immigrants in Non-Traditional Areas* (New York: LFB Scholarly Publishing, 2003).

10. Ibid.

11. Ibid.

12. During the second half of the 1990s North Carolina reportedly lost an estimated 57,000 blue-collar jobs due to globalization or foreign competition. See "North Carolina Manufacturing Job Losses Top Other States," *Wilmington Morning Star*, 9 Feb. 2001. And since January 2001 North Carolina has lost 148,400 manufacturing jobs—more than either Michigan (130,200 loss) or New York (131,600 loss), which have larger manufacturing workforces. See Democratic State of the Union Response Center, "Manufacturing Jobs Lost Since the Beginning of the Bush Administration," 2004, at http://democrats.senate.gov, accessed 23 Dec. 2005; Michael Steinberg, "North Carolina Among the Hardest Hit by NAFTA Job Loss," Asheville Global Report, 14–20 June 2001, at http://www.stoptheinvasion.com/nafta2.html, accessed 23 Dec. 2005; Willie Green, "North Carolina Manufacturing Continues to Bleed Jobs," *Charlotte Observer*, 5 Feb. 2004, at http://209.157.64.200/focus/f_news/1072114/posts, accessed June 2008.

13. See, for example, B. J. Robles and H. Cordero-Guzmán, "Latino Self-Employment and Entrepreneurship in the United States: An Overview of the Literature and Data Sources," *Annals of the American Academy of Political and Social Science* 613 (2007): 18–31; M. Lofstrom and C. Wang, "Mexican-Hispanic Self-Employment Entry: The Role of Business Start-Up Constraints," *Annals of the American Academy of Political and Social Science* 613 (2007): 32–46.

14. J. H. Johnson Jr., "The Changing Face of Poverty in North Carolina, 1970–2001," *Popular Government* 68 (2003): 14–24.

15. The state and its localities also receive revenues from flow-backs of portions of federal income taxes paid by Hispanics, but these are not considered in our technical analysis.

16. Rebecca L. Clark et al., *Fiscal Impact of Undocumented Aliens: Selected Estimates for Seven States* (Washington, D.C.: Urban Institute, 1994); R. L. Clark and Jeffrey Passel,

"How Much Do Immigrants Pay in Taxes? Evidence from Los Angeles County" (Washington, D.C.: Program for Research on Immigration Policy, Population Studies Center, Urban Institute, 1993); Jeronimo Cortina et al., *The Economic Impact of the Mexico-California Relationship* (Los Angeles: Tomás Rivera Policy Institute, 2005); Hank H. Fishkind, *Regional Economic Impact Research: Hispanic Communities of Central Florida* (Orlando: Fishkind & Associates, 2005); Simpson et al., *Hispanic Economic Impact Study*; Thunderbird School of Global Management, *Economic Impact of the Mexico-Arizona Relationship* (Glendale, Ariz.: Thunderbird School of Global Management, 2003); Douglas P. Woodward, "The Economic and Business Impact of Hispanics (Latinos)," unpublished presentation, (Columbia, S.C.: University of South Carolina, 2005); Steven A. Camarota, *The High Cost of Cheap Labor: Illegal Immigration and the Federal Budget* (Washington, D.C.: Center for Immigration Studies, 2005).

17. According to Stephen J. Appold: "The IMPLAN model is broadly used in economic impact analyses. It uses data provided by the U.S. Bureau of Economic Analysis, the Bureau of Labor Statistics, and various state and federal agencies. The model generates, among other results, the number of jobs, labor income, and taxes created by a specified input. It also generates economic output, roughly equated to business revenue, resulting from a group's direct, indirect, and induced economic impacts. The IMPLAN software can combine any number of counties into one study area. Computations were done by the Kenan Institute's Carolina Center for Competitive Economies" (Testimony of Stephen J. Appold to the U.S. House of Representatives' Judiciary Committee's Subcommittee on Immigration, Citizenship, Refugees, Border Security, and International Law, Thursday, 17 May 2007, p. 3, n.2, at http://www.aila.org/content/fileviewer.aspx?docid=22935&linkid=163687, accessed July 2008).

18. Jeffrey M. Humphreys, *The Multicultural Economy* (Athens, Ga.: Selig Center for Economic Growth, 2004); J. Humphreys and DeShelia S. Hall, *African American, Asian, Hispanic, and Native American Buying Power in North Carolina: Estimates for 1990–2004 and Projection through 2009* (Durham: North Carolina Institute of Minority Economic Development, 2004).

19. R. Suro, "Latino Remittances Swell Despite US Economic Slump," Migration Policy Institute, http://www.migrationinformation.org/feature/display.cfm?ID=89.

20. Pedro De Vasconcelos, *Sending Money Home: Remittances to Latin America from the United States* (Washington, D.C.: Inter-American Development Bank, 2001).

21. We further reduced the buying power and economic impact estimates by 5.6 percent to account for the fact that our estimate of the state's Hispanic population in 2004 was 5.6 percent less than that used by our data source for buying power.

22. Kasarda and Johnson (2006) document the economic effects of the rise in Hispanic spending since 1990 on North Carolina's metropolitan statistical areas (MSAs) in appendix tables B4 through B8 of their recent study. These tables represent the direct and indirect effects Hispanic spending on the state's metropolitan areas in 1990, 2000, and 2004, including spin-off employment, labor income, and state and federal taxes.

23. Johnson-Webb, *Recruiting Hispanic Labor*.

24. Camarota, *High Cost of Cheap Labor*; Clark et al., *Fiscal Impact of Undocumented Aliens*; Clark and Passel, "How Much Do Immigrants Pay in Taxes?"; Cortina et al., *Economic Impact of the Mexico-California Relationship*; Fishkind, *Regional Economic Impact Research*; Simpson et al., *Hispanic Economic Impact Study*; Thunderbird School of Management, *Economic Impact of the Mexico-Arizona Relationship*; Woodward, "Economic and Business Impact of Hispanics."

25. We note that the large majority of Hispanic schoolchildren are citizens of the United States, even if their parents are not.

26. Agency for Health Care Research and Quality, *Total Health Services-Mean and Median Expenses per Person with Expenses and Distribution of Expenses by Source of Payment* (Rockville, Md.: Agency for Healthcare Research and Quality, U.S. Department of Health and Human Services, Dec. 2005, at http://www.ahrq.gov/qual/nhqr05/nhqr05.pdf); Centers for Medicare and Medicaid Services, "National Health Expenditures Tables," Office of the Actuary, National Health Statistics Group, http://www.cms.hhs.gov/statistics/nhe/historical/t3.asp, accessed 5 Oct. 2005.

27. North Carolina Department of Revenue, *North Carolina: State and Local Taxes* (Raleigh, N.C.: Department of Revenue, Tax Research Division, 2004); David T. McCoy, *Post-Legislative Budget Summary, 2004–2005* (Raleigh: North Carolina Office of State Budget and Management, 2004).

28. In reviewing previous reports on taxes paid by undocumented Hispanics (e.g., Clark et al. 1994), most authors assumed a compliance rate of 55 to 60 percent, with the remainder being paid under the table. Our discussions with North Carolina Hispanics indicate that more workers are obtaining Social Security numbers and/or tax identification numbers, legally or illegally, to obtain jobs on the payroll. These workers are paying taxes, which leads us to assume a higher compliance rate.

29. Sarah Dougherty, "Riding the Rising Wave of Hispanic Buying Power," *EconSouth* (1st quarter 2005), at http://www.frbatlanta.org, accessed June 2008; Brian Grow et al., "Hispanic Nation," *Business Week*, 15 March 2004, at http://www.businessweek.com, accessed June 2008; Suro, "Latino Remittances Swell Despite US Economic Slump."

30. Clark et al., *Fiscal Impact of Undocumented Aliens*; Clark and Passel, "How Much Do Immigrants Pay in Taxes?"; Cortina et al., *Economic Impact of the Mexico-California Relationship*; Fishkind, *Regional Economic Impact*; Simpson et al., *Hispanic Economic Impact Study*; Woodward, "Economic and Business Impact of Hispanics."

31. Using data from the March 2005 Current Population Survey, we estimated the total wage bill for the state by multiplying the number of Hispanics and non-Hispanics with low levels of education (less than a high-school diploma) and high levels of education (a high-school diploma or higher) in each industry by their respective average hourly wage rates and mean number of hours worked over the previous year. We then repeated the calculation using the average non-Hispanic hourly wage for each industry-education category to estimate what the total wage bill would be without the immigrant wage advantage. Capital substitution and labor shortage effects were not taken into account.

32. See George Borjas, "Immigrants, Minorities, and Labor Market Competition," in NBER working paper 2028; G. Borjas, "The Labor Demand Curve Is Downward Sloping: Reexamining the Impact of Immigration on the Labor Market," in *Quarterly Journal of Economics* 118 (2003): 1335–74; G. Borjas, "Increasing the Supply of Labor through Immigration: Measuring the Impact on Native Workers" (Washington, D.C.: Center for Immigration Studies, 2004); Randy Capps and Michael Fix, *Trends in the Low-Wage Immigrant Labor Force, 2000–2005* (Washington, D.C.: Urban Institute, 2007); Daniel S. Hammermesh and Frank D. Bean, *Help or Hindrance: The Economic Implication of Immigration for African Americans* (New York: Russell Sage Foundation, 1998); Andrew Sum, Paul Harrington, and Ishwar Khatiwada, *The Impact of New Immigrants on Young Native-Born Workers, 2000–2005* (Washington, D.C.: Center for Immigration Studies, 2006).

33. De Vasconcelos, *Sending Money Home*; Dougherty, "Riding the Rising Wave"; Humphreys, *Multicultural Economy*; Humphreys and Hall, *African American, Asian, Hispanic, and Native American.*

34. This methodology began by computing a net impact ratio for the state as a whole. This is a simple ratio of estimated state Hispanic buying power to calculated Hispanic total state economic impact. The ratio was 1.101 in 2004 (including the 20 percent buying power reduction for remittances, etc.). We then multiplied the buying power of each county by this ratio to simulate what the Hispanic economic impact on the county would be if it followed Hispanic state buying power multipliers. The difference between the potential impact and the IMPLAN software calculated economic impact is the estimated total economic impact (business revenues) leakage.

CHAPTER SIX

Race, Migration, and Labor Control

Neoliberal Challenges to Organizing Mississippi's Poultry Workers

ANGELA C. STUESSE

Severiano, a twenty-two-year-old Tzotzil speaker from Chiapas, spends his days hanging live chickens by their feet on a conveyor belt in a poultry-processing plant in rural Mississippi. In 2003 he paid a "coyote" two thousand U.S. dollars to bring him from Tamaulipas, Mexico, and today he hangs a staggering fifty birds per minute. He sends 85 percent of his earnings home, where he says he will start a small business when he returns to his rancho. *Less than a minute down the line from him in the plant, Lillie, a single African American mother in her thirties, separates livers from gizzards of the same birds as she wipes the sweat from her forehead and tries to ignore the dull pain in her forearms that worsens by the day. She glances at the brown men all around her, speaking a language she doesn't understand, and she wonders what brought them here. Still farther down the line stands forty-seven-year-old Ernesto, who was a bank teller in Argentina. Now in the United States, he shares a dilapidated trailer with his wife, their two children, and three coworkers from South America. He works in 40-degree temperatures deboning chicken breasts for $6.25 an hour. His tourist visa expired a few years ago, but no one seems to care. If he's lucky, he says, he'll never go back; Mississippi is home now.*

Race, Migration, and the Transformation of the Rural South

The poultry-processing industry in the United States, located predominantly in the South, has gone through a radical transformation in recent decades.[1] Today Americans eat almost twice as much chicken per capita (89.1 pounds annually) than they did in 1980 (48.0 pounds), and as consumption skyrocketed the industry began massive recruitment of foreign-born labor.[2] Whereas traditionally local whites and (later) African Americans supplied the industry's labor power, in many areas today Latino migrants constitute the majority of workers.[3] As of 2000, Latinos represented 29 percent of all meat-processing workers, in comparison to only 9 percent twenty years prior, and 82 percent of these "Hispanic" laborers are foreign born.[4] In fact, over 50 percent of the nation's quarter-million poultry workers are now immigrants.[5] This phenomenon has stimulated dramatic social and cultural changes in rural communities across the South, which are just beginning to be examined by academics, organizers, and policy makers alike.

Although immigration is not new to the South or even to Mississippi, the intensity and breadth of recent transnational migrant flows is novel. The historically rooted Black-white racial binary continues to frame social relations in this region, and the recent arrival of Latinos to rural areas complicates traditional hierarchies. Most rural southern communities have limited infrastructure to support the integration of new migrants, and many residents know little about newcomers' cultures and reasons for migrating. Similarly, the migrant pool itself is heterogeneous, and migrants are often unaware of the particular histories and identities of their coworkers from other parts of Latin America. Many also lack knowledge of the social and political histories of the South and often find it difficult to empathize with the life experiences of their coworkers and neighbors who are often African American. A great need exists for anthropological research that investigates the transnationalization of this region, its relationship to capital and labor, and this phenomenon's human implications for established southern communities as well as new immigrant groups.

Mississippi is both the poorest state in the nation and one of the world's leading producers of chicken, selling more than $2.2 billion in poultry products annually.[6] It is also the most recent southern state to feel the effects of the poultry industry's recruitment of transnational labor, as busloads of Latinos began arriving only ten years ago, in the mid-1990s. Scott County is the principal poultry-producing area in Mississippi, with eleven processing plants there and in surrounding counties as of 2005. Scott County is also home to the state's greatest concentration of Latinos, a demographic shift driven by a family-owned poultry plant that began recruiting workers through its institutionalized Hispanic Project in 1993.[7] The 2000 U.S. Census, which substantially undercounted immigrants in Mississippi, reported 1,643 people of Hispanic origin living in Scott County, as compared to only 141 people one decade before, representing an increase of over 1,000 percent.[8] In 2004 the census bureau counted 1,891 Hispanic residents in Scott County, or 6.6 percent of the county's total population, and the vast majority of these were foreign born.[9] In contrast, over two-thirds of Mississippi's counties reported that Hispanics comprised 1.5

percent of their population or less. As suggested by the epigraph at the head of this chapter, Scott County's Latino population is exceptionally diverse, representing over a dozen countries. The largest groups come from Mexico (almost exclusively from the new sending regions of southeastern Mexico), Guatemala (predominantly the department of San Marcos), Argentina, and Peru.[10] The diversity of Mississippi's foreign born goes beyond questions of nationality, as ethnic, racial, linguistic, gender, class, and educational differences also create divisions and tensions within and between migrant groups.

Although obstacles such as pervasive poverty, institutionalized racism, legislation that favors corporations, and the undocumented legal status of many in the workforce discourage workers from claiming and exercising their rights in the contemporary South, Mississippi is an important case study because it possesses a rich history of community organizing, particularly during, but not limited to, the African American freedom struggle of the 1950s and 1960s.[11] More recently, there has been limited but significant labor-organizing activity within the state's poultry-producing region. Ongoing poultry worker justice efforts there include those of the Mississippi Immigrants' Rights Alliance (MIRA) and MPOWER (formerly the Mississippi Poultry Workers' Center), both of which have identified the importance of cultivating relationships between workers of different backgrounds, specifically among African Americans and new immigrants, in order to achieve greater power and voice within the industry.[12]

In this chapter I examine how different groups' discourses about race and national origin create obstacles to collective movements for change within the Mississippi poultry industry. These discourses depend largely on stereotypes promoted by state, corporate, and other social actors and nourished by the lack of communication and mutual understanding that plagues Mississippi's poultry workers. They are also rationalized by the everyday lived experience of working in poultry plants, which often separate workers along these very lines of difference into distinct departments, lines, and shifts. Beliefs about difference based on race and national origin—which function to differentiate one's own group from the cultural Other—are increasingly being manipulated by the industry to keep the workforce divided.[13] This case illustrates the complex ways in which the exploitation of discourses that perpetuate racial stereotypes is a conscious and deliberate practice of corporations used to control, fragment, and divide working people along lines of difference for the benefit of corporate profit. Indeed, it has become an essential part of the cultural logic of neoliberalism—"a programme of the methodical destruction of collectives."[14] Interrogating how these racialized discourses are wielded through the practices of Mississippi's poultry industry and through the subjectivities of workers of diverse backgrounds provides a window of understanding into the workings of neoliberal globalization and its consequences for the collective power of working people in the twenty-first century.

The principal research methods employed for this chapter were participant observation, interviews, and focus groups. Rooted in the school of activist anthropology and emerging from my critical alignment with an explicit political project, my qualitative methods are designed to dovetail with my various collaborators' goals so as to educate, strengthen networks, and build local capacities at the same time they produce data for social analysis.[15] One way I have done this in my research has been to carry out small-group discussions with different contingencies of workers. These focus groups were held separately with Mexican and Central American workers, South American workers, and African American workers, and provided a space for workers of similar backgrounds to discuss pressing workplace concerns, share their experiences and frustrations with one another, talk openly about conceptions of race, national origin, and gender, and brainstorm ways that MPOWER might help them address some of these issues. Many of the insights presented in this chapter surrounding workers' perceptions of one another were shaped through dialogue with the participants of these focus groups.

Neoliberal Globalization and the Restructuring of the Poultry Industry

Since Upton Sinclair's acclaimed *The Jungle* detailed the dangerous and unjust practices of Chicago's meatpacking industry a century ago, little has been written on the social impact of the meat-processing industries.[16] Literature specific to the U.S. poultry industry is even harder to obtain, although some information can be obtained from periodical articles, memoirs, popular literature, legal proceedings, and policy reports.[17] Few social scientists have published research analyzing the intersections of culture with political economy in this industry.[18]

Globalization theorists today identify qualitative differences in the ways in which the world economy operates, and they have labeled this phenomenon "globalization."[19] Whether it is conceptualized as a "speeding up" or a "stretching out," globalization theory understands time and space as having been reconfigured through the conditions of postmodernity.[20] Social and cultural relations are fundamentally disembedded from traditional spatially bound contexts and reinscribed in specific locales across the globe.[21] These locales are determined by the routes of transnational capital, as people and ideas are deterritorialized and reterritorialized.[22] Today's migrants are more than laborers; they are social actors that maintain economic, social, and political relationships in both their home countries and their countries of settlement.[23]

In this transnational present, the hypermobility of capital and labor provide new opportunities for capitalist exploitation and regulation of low-income communities and individuals.[24] Like classic liberalism, the neoliberalism of the current moment suggests that the state should interfere as little as possible with the market, allowing its "invisible hand" to guide economic, political, and social relationships.[25] However, unlike the liberalism of the earlier twentieth century, today's economic, cultural and political logic is fuelled by the transnational processes described above, suggesting that the term "neoliberal globalization" may more accurately describe the dynamics currently at play.

Although the neoliberal paradigm indicates that the state should not impede the market flows of advanced capitalism, I am not suggesting that the state is not a key actor within neoliberal globalization. On the contrary, the state clearly wields its regulation powers in order to allow capitalist logic to govern society.[26] At the federal, state, and local levels the state both sets policy and controls enforcement related to two realms of governance directly affecting poultry workers in Mississippi: labor and immigration (in addition to commerce, taxation, housing, education, health care, public benefits, infrastructure, and a myriad of other policy areas that affect both U.S.- and foreign-born working people). Transnational migrants' abilities to come to the United States and get hired to work in low-wage manufacturing and service sectors, two critical factors in the poultry industry's (and the nation's) prosperity in the twenty-first century, are a direct result of the state's strategic passage and enforcement of legislation that governs these social realms. In addition, the state intervenes through free trade and structural adjustment policies that have flourished in the age of neoliberal globalization and have had irreversible effects on countries throughout Latin America, pushing small farmers and working people to migrate to the United States in search of economic survival.[27] The state's actions and inactions, through its neoliberal policies and strategic wielding of law enforcement, clearly benefit corporations at the expense of low-wage workers, thus allowing the "invisible hand" to tighten its grip on social relations.

The U.S. poultry industry is a critical site for studying the changing effects of neoliberal globalization on local subjectivities because its innovative labor control practices are increasingly embraced as a model by other industries aiming to boost profits in the economy of advanced capitalism.[28] Neoliberal globalization has played a fundamental role in the restructuring of industry from a Fordist regime to a post-Fordist model of "flexible accumulation," in which corporate strategies such as outsourcing, contracting, part-time employment, and recruitment of migrant workers allow for greater capital accumulation.[29] Its mark on the poultry industry is perhaps most evident in corporations' abilities to harness labor market flexibility and control, readily available through the technologies of postmodernity's "time-space compression" and embodied in the immigrant workers now living throughout rural Mississippi.[30] Whereas in the past an individual might spend the majority of his or her working years with one company, gradually accruing seniority, benefits, and company loyalty over time, today's poultry industry displays little concern for worker retention.

Native and immigrant workers alike complain of a myriad of unjust practices in the poultry industry, including unpaid wages, denial of bathroom breaks, dangerous conditions that cause chronic injuries and illnesses, unauthorized paycheck deductions, abuse by plant supervisors and management, deceptive use of labor contractors, discrimination, and sexual harassment.[31] Jobs have been "deskilled" and production has been accelerated through massive technological advances, so that the average worker now repeats the same monotonous—and often dangerous—movement up to 30,000 times per day. As a direct result, repetitive-motion injuries now plague the workforce. Plants are often out of compliance with federal safety and health regulations, and the government agency charged with oversight of these laws, the Occupational Safety and Health Administration (OSHA), is appallingly underresourced and, consequently, largely ineffective.[32] Management frequently discourages workers from seeing doctors or filing workers' compensation claims for on-the-job injuries.[33] In addition, in a recent national survey the U.S. Department of Labor found violations of federal minimum wage laws in 100 percent of poultry plants, while the industry's corporate earnings have risen more than 300 percent since 1987.[34] It is not surprising then that annual turnover of workers is as high as 300 percent annually in some locations. Aside from their claim to being the only major employer in many rural towns, poultry companies give their workers virtually no incentive to stay.

Such incentives, however, are unnecessary in the age of neoliberal globalization, where workers, recruited from across the world, are literally expendable and infinitely replaceable. "Workforce flexibility" is secured through the use of transnational workers, a strategy employed to weaken the potential for collective bargaining with an organized labor force, put downward pressure on wages, maximize profits, and show local (often Black) workers the "meaning of a 'work ethic.'" Labor scholar David Griffith points out that

> low wage labor forces in the U.S. do not just emerge, naturally, as responses to market conditions. Instead, they are constructed, reorganized, and maintained by means of a few common practices. . . . Each of these practices also

> depends on the development and use of myths about specific kinds of workers as compared to others, particularly myths about "the work ethic." By looking at these processes of constructing labor forces, we can more fully understand how low-wage industries come to use new immigrants, minorities, and other workers considered "marginal."[35]

The industry's increasing reliance on the most marginal of workers—recent immigrants—demonstrates its shrewd understanding of the workings of our globalized, neoliberal present.

Challenges to Organizing Mississippi's Poultry Workers across Difference

Bobby Robertson, an African American former poultry worker and leader at one union local that represents poultry workers in processing plants in Central Mississippi, has witnessed the rapid Latinization of his surroundings.[36] Except for his brief time in the military, which allowed him to travel the world and witness different ways of life, Robertson has been in Mississippi since he was a teenager. He had worked in a poultry-processing plant for many years when, in the mid-1990s, his coworkers began to organize for their workplace rights and sought to find union representation. Robertson joined in the campaign, became an active union member, and eventually became business manager of the union local. He recalls, after a long uphill battle, when the plants began to heavily recruit immigrant workers—an industry tactic that he says displaced Black workers and significantly weakened the union's membership and bargaining power. Robertson's initial response was to organize an intense union campaign to force the plant's management to stop hiring foreign-born labor. He soon realized, however, that while he might succeed in getting one migrant fired, another person, speaking a language he didn't understand, would soon be standing in that worker's place. Over time Robertson eventually acknowledged that he and his mostly African American coworkers could do very little to keep new migrants from arriving. He recognized that if the labor movement in Central Mississippi were to survive, it would have to embrace new strategies of organizing to defend the rights of *all* poultry workers.

The task Robertson set for himself was challenging, not only because of the lack of local understanding about immigration and immigrants, but also because he was unable to communicate with these new potential union members. When he acknowledged that he "needed somebody who could speak Mexican," his union's international office responded by sending a bilingual organizer to work with him for a few weeks. The knowledge gained from being able to communicate with immigrant workers, albeit briefly, convinced Robertson that his organizing efforts must work to bridge differences of race, language, and national origin. Robertson's union and other workers' rights organizations in Mississippi have taken up this objective in recent years and have begun looking for ways to increase worker unity across difference.

Supporting local leaders like Robertson in the struggle to bring together immigrant and nonimmigrant poultry workers in defense of their rights are MIRA and MPOWER. MIRA is a statewide coalition of immigrant and civil rights advocates that works closely with progressive elected officials to encourage the legislature and other state institutions to adopt immigrant-friendly policies. MIRA's founders emphasize the importance of bringing organized labor and progressive churches—always a crucial partnership for organizing in the South—together in the struggle for social justice, and the organization maintains strong ideological links between its work today and the efforts of Mississippi's civil rights workers of the 1960s. African Americans, particularly in the state legislature, have been key participants in MIRA's campaigns and are central to the struggle for immigrant rights in Mississippi.[37] MPOWER is "a collaboration among poultry workers of diverse backgrounds, civil rights and immigrants' rights organizations, religious leaders, labor unions, employment justice groups, and other community partners." It "aims to increase workers' and advocates' abilities to ensure equity and justice on the job and in our communities by developing leadership among workers, strengthening [their] capacity to organize collectively, enhancing our access to knowledge, skills and resources, [and] building relationships across differences of race, culture, gender, language and religious affiliation."[38] The goals of bridging differences in ideology, strategy, and identity in the fight for worker justice are explicit in MPOWER's mission statement and exhibited through the intentional relationship and leadership building that has taken place there in recent years.

The principles espoused by Bobby Robertson, MIRA, and MPOWER suggest that the debate between theorists who sustain that collective organizing is best achieved through the classic Marxist approach that foregrounds socioeconomic class and those who argue for a politics of identity, which valorizes cultural differences such as race, ethnicity, and gender is no longer relevant.[39] Class is but one of a number of intersecting and ever-shifting axes of identity formation, and identities are multiply constituted and should be understood as such when theorizing collective political mobilization.[40] Communities live both in accommodation with and antagonism to the effects of capitalism, at times maintaining hegemonic discourses and at times resisting them. The collective actions and rights claims of new social movements reflect these contradictions as their struggles play out within the fissures in the system.

"Hispanics": Perceptions of Differences and Similarities among Latino Workers

As indicated at the outset of this chapter, the Latino population in Central Mississippi is tremendously diverse. The largest transnational group hails from Mexico's states of Veracruz, Chiapas, and Oaxaca.[41] Mostly men between the ages of fifteen and forty, these individuals send high percentages of their earnings home to wives, children, and parents and plan to return to Mexico after a few years in the United States. They are highly mobile, moving regularly between Mississippi and agriculture or construction jobs elsewhere in the United States and Mexico, and often participate in circular migratory patterns.[42]

Another contingent of workers comes from Central America, mainly Guatemala. They tend to be single indigenous men (and increasingly women) in their teens and early twenties from one particular *municipio* in the highlands. More and more have found partners and had children in Mississippi. Although when asked most say they will return to Guatemala in five years or so, only a handful have yet done so.[43] While they come mainly in search of economic opportunity, the political situation in Guatemala and other Central American countries is an additional incentive to migrate north. Because these migrants are almost exclusively indigenous, many arrive in Mississippi already multilingual, speaking both their native Mayan language, Mam, and Spanish. Because of their experience as second-language learners, they tend to pick up English quickly, providing them greater opportunities for upward mobility in the poultry plants.

There are also significant numbers of poultry workers in Mississippi from Argentina and Peru. A good portion of these men and women were blue- and white-collar professionals in their countries, and most brought their families with them to the United States. They arrived by air on tourist visas during the first years of the twenty-first century and stayed because of growing economic crises in their home countries. Nearly all first lived in Miami before being recruited to Mississippi by the poultry companies. Back home some of these workers have significant experience with labor unions, providing them with valuable knowledge and experience in organizing. Few South American migrants plan to return home, however, at least in the short to medium term. They often say Mississippi is a safe, quiet place to raise a family, and some have even purchased homes and established relationships within the local white community.

While these are just some of the many differences among Latinos of diverse backgrounds, native Mississippians tend to lump them all into one category, that of "Hispanic." When asked their thoughts on the term during focus group discussions, different groups of Latino poultry workers have very different reactions. In a discussion held with Mexican and Central American migrants, participants generally found the "Hispanic" classification useful, observing that all immigrant workers face similar problems in the poultry plants and thus can justly be considered one group. "I think it's a good term because it gives us a bigger group, and there is strength in numbers," stated one participant.[44] Another commented, "If we all work together, we can't be singled out for defending ourselves." This group reached a general consensus that it doesn't matter what they're called, as long as all Latino workers are united. "After all," one Guatemalan youth pointed out, "the *morenos* [Blacks] and the *bolillos* [whites] think we're all Mexican anyway."

South American focus group participants share very different views about being thought of as one homogeneous group. Although they recognize similarities in their experiences in the plants, they adamantly argue against being thought of as the same as Mexican and Central American migrants. Participants compared Mexicans and Central Americans to "machines" and "gypsies." "They are more humble and submissive [than we are]. They do what they are told without arguing," explained a middle-aged man from Argentina. Racial stereotypes inform much of what South Americans in Mississippi think about their Central American coworkers, and in this focus group, comments about lack of education and illiteracy quickly escalated to assumptions about the inherent gratification of physical labor and accusations of "ignorance."

Whereas this discourse linking race and nationality with social Darwinist ideas about submission and work leads some—typically light-skinned South American workers—to distance themselves from their Central American colleagues, other focus group participants highlighted the structural, as opposed to genetic or biological, nature of the differences between these groups: "Because they plan to go home," a younger Peruvian man reasoned, "they are more likely to work hard and complain less. They know their situation is temporary, which makes it easier to put up with abuse." Despite being quick to identify these differences, South Americans also recognize similarities they hold with Central American and Mexican coworkers, particularly their inability to communicate with English speakers, their vulnerability as undocumented workers, and the exploitation suffered in working the most dangerous and lowest-paid jobs.

African American Workers' Discourse about Their "Hispanic" Coworkers

Ironically, many African Americans in this study hold beliefs about Hispanics as a whole that are not unlike many South Americans' portrayals of Mexicans and Central Americans: "Hispanics are too willing to work for nothing," one often hears, "and they're taking our jobs and forcing us to work even harder."

Comments such as this are valid assessments of many workers' lived realities, yet they fall short of recognizing the complex social and economic realities faced by a transnational workforce. They do not illuminate, for example, the fact that many migrants work to support their families and send substantial sums of money back home. Through this practice low wages by U.S. standards translate into relatively high wages for the social reproduction of families in "sending communities." As David Griffith writes, "a black American's definition of subsistence and consequent wage needs are likely to be qualitatively and quantitatively distinct from a new immigrant Mexican's or an Indian fleeing the Central American ethnic wars."[45]

Comments that blame immigrant workers for the increased exploitation of native minorities also obscure the role of the state—through restrictive yet poorly enforced U.S. immigration policies, nearly nonexistent worker protections, multinational structural adjustment programs across the "developing" world, and the expansion of advanced capitalism across the globe—in stimulating a continued flow of undocumented transnational migrants to the United States to provide a virtually limitless supply of cheap labor that benefits the interests of corporations. Without this political analysis critics inaccurately place the responsibility for neoliberal exploitation on workers instead of on corporations and governments. With or without structural explanations, however, material realities indicate that in much of Mississippi's poultry industry Black workers *are* being indirectly displaced by immigrant laborers, who, in large part, are inclined to work hard and keep quiet because of their vulnerable status as undocumented workers and the "bootstrap" ideology that immigrants often espouse.[46]

Poultry plant executives are exploiting immigrant vulnerability and encouraging competition with locally born and mostly African American workers by employing a number of increasingly pervasive industry practices. Most notably they are recruiting more and more of their workforce through transnational social and familial networks, decreasing the need to depend on local labor. Network recruitment has been studied in depth by labor scholars and is one main vehicle for cultivating a fragmented workforce.[47] Both industry and the state depend on these networks to supplement the costs of maintaining and reproducing labor power by requiring migrant workers to "self-subsidize" through overcrowded housing and other cost-sharing strategies.[48]

The increasing use of labor contractors is another growing industry practice that segments the workforce, weakens the power of Black workers, and enables poultry plants to manipulate and evade government regulations to their advantage. In Mississippi some plants use contractors to hire large portions of their undocumented workforce. By claiming not to be these workers' employers plants can, at least superficially, insulate themselves from state sanctions for illegal employment practices.[49] The use of contractors also gives rise to higher turnover rates, further depresses workers' wages and working conditions, and weakens unions because contract workers—often those most in need of workplace protections—are typically not included in the collective bargaining unit.

When Black workers complain that "Hispanics" are overly docile, eager to please, and too willing to work for low wages, their concerns reflect an acute awareness that whites' descriptions of immigrants as "hard workers" are often accompanied by references to African American workers as "lazy" or lacking a strong "work ethic." Indeed, in research conducted in Scott County by historian Laura E. Helton, one white woman asserted, "[The immigrants] have been so much more workable and willing than blacks. They are much more humble and don't feel like the world owes them something." A Black elected official also pointed out to Helton: "[Immigrants] were brought in for cheap labor, not a shortage [as the industry claims]. . . . The labor's here but the jobs don't want to pay."[50] According to this alternative discourse, the hiring of immigrant labor is not simply a race-neutral labor practice to fill "empty" plant positions, but instead serves to put downward pressure on native workers' salaries and weaken attempts at organizing around workplace issues. Some Black workers, instead of blaming migrants for these conditions, empathize with them, reasoning, as one aging woman did, "They's where we was at fifty years ago before we even knew our rights." Even sympathetic analyses that draw parallels between the conditions that gave rise to the Civil Rights Movement and the problems faced by today's migrants are rarely linked to a broader understanding of advanced capitalism's impact on other locales across the globe. This void, accompanied by most Mississippians' inability to communicate in Spanish and limited knowledge about Latin America and its transnational migrants, hinders Black workers from building meaningful relationships with foreign-born coworkers.

Latino Workers' Discourse about Black Coworkers

Most Latinos in Mississippi are new to the United States and know very little about the histories of racial oppression and economic exclusion faced by people of color in this country. Just as their African American coworkers often lack an understanding of the structural causes of their presence, they, too, frequently fail to link local processes to larger social and political formations. Although migrants in Mississippi witness firsthand that most of their African American neighbors are poor, most typically accept the dominant discourse espoused by popular culture and neoliberal policy that blames poor Black communities for their socioeconomic condition. In my research I have come across very few migrants who recognize that Blacks in the United States and beyond live with an ongoing legacy of institutional racism, particularly in housing, education, and employment.[51] Without a solid analysis of the structural constraints impeding the progress of working people of color in the United States, Latino poultry workers often find it difficult to empathize with Black workers' complaints and responses to workplace problems.

U.S.-born workers' everyday forms of resistance, such as production slowdowns, the taking of long breaks, or even spitting on the processing line—all commonplace forms of covert resistance among workers—are usually misinterpreted by immigrants in Mississippi's poultry plants.[52] Similarly, expressions of apathy among African Americans are read out of context. The educational, employment, and justice systems in the United States continue to fail people of color, leading critical race scholars to suggest that, because of shrinking job opportunities, African Americans are becoming increasingly pessimistic about social justice issues.[53] Without this analysis, however, both resistance and apathy are misinterpreted by new migrants—as well as by plant management and dominant society—as laziness, poor manners, and lack of education.[54]

Throughout my research I have been troubled to find that deeply ingrained anti-Black and anti-indigenous racism among Latinos of diverse backgrounds seriously challenge efforts at crossracial organizing. During focus group discussions, for example, Latino workers were asked to identify similarities between the problems they have at work and those experienced by African Americans in the plants. Surprisingly, participants responded by suggesting that Black workers have no workplace complaints: "Most Blacks like how things are," "Blacks have no problem with discrimination," and "We are living in different worlds" were just a few of the comments offered. These comments suggest that Latino workers see themselves as the authentic exploited class of workers, incomparable to the presumed more privileged African Americans in the plants.

This discourse, like that of Black workers about immigrant workers, is promoted by industry practices that harness racial stereotypes so as to divide the workforce along lines of race and nationality and to obscure workers' abilities to find linkages in common experiences. These procedures are illustrated by comments heard regularly throughout my research, such as: "Supervisors are more lenient with Blacks than with us—they're allowed to wear jewelry, for example"; "Blacks can take long breaks and are not disciplined when they come to work late"; "Some workers are permitted to use the bathroom when needed, where others are denied bathroom breaks"; "Blacks are allowed to complain directly to management, and we're expected to go through plant translators and our supervisors"; and "A supervisor told me that Blacks don't like Hispanics." Although some of these differential forms of treatment may be implemented by abusive supervisors acting independently, this double standard—in which certain groups of workers are permitted, even encouraged, to abuse privileges—has become commonplace in the poultry industry across the South in order to alienate one group of disenfranchised workers from another.[55] In the "Right-to-Work" South, where new immigrant workers are less likely to know their rights, more likely to be employed through a labor contractor, and unquestionably vulnerable, this tactic has worked remarkably well.

Conclusions, Promises, and Prospects for Change

In recent decades the poultry industry has increasingly become vertically integrated, whereby a few giant producers now oversee every step of the production process, "from fertilization of the eggs through hatching through 'grow-out' to market weight and on through slaughter and processing."[56] Offsetting the possibilities of increased class solidarity that might be expected to accompany this shift, the industry has also begun massive network recruitment of foreign-born workers and is escalating and perfecting its labor control strategies. From utilizing third-party labor contractors to selectively rationing bathroom breaks to prohibiting talking on the production line, poultry plants are taking advantage of the realities of Mississippi's transnational present in order to intensify disparities and encourage competing discourses between African American and Latino workers, and even among Latinos of different national and ethnic origins. The framework of neoliberal globalization helps to better appreciate how such industrial restructuring exploits racialized practices and discourses in order to mold local subjectivities, and ethnographic analysis of poultry workers' perceptions and lived realities involving racial stereotypes gives us a deeper understanding of how advanced capitalism is affecting social relations and workers' potential to organize in Mississippi's poultry region today.

Recent contributions of critical race and social movement theorists point toward approaches that might begin to overcome some of the divisions among poultry workers outlined in this chapter. Scholarship that helps us better understand these challenges is an important first step in building long-term coalitions that respect, not erase, our differences. Both MPOWER and MIRA assert that, despite industry efforts to divide workers along lines of difference, people of all backgrounds hold basic employment, civil, and human rights. They not only recognize the abuse of these rights as the basis for coalition building, they also respect that poultry workers experience and interpret these abuses in unique ways depending on their identities, experiences, and goals. Moving beyond strictly class-based politics as well as past any exclusionary interpretations of the politics of identity, these groups seek to build alliances among different marginalized groups in hopes that they might gain the knowledge and power to demand social and economic justice.

Despite operating within racialized discourses that discourage communication, mutual understanding, and structural analysis, many poultry workers are eager to get to know each other better. In focus group discussions, workers of all backgrounds were receptive when facilitators dispelled some of the myths leading to misunderstandings, saying, for example, "oh, you mean *they* have problems too?" Participants often offered ideas for how MPOWER could help them begin to bridge cultural and racial differences.[57] They suggested that MPOWER could simply be a safe space in which workers of different backgrounds would be welcome to find information, share experiences, and get to know one another. This is a critical contribution in the South, where virtually no public gathering spaces exist outside of churches. Gatherings could be held, participants explained, in which Latino and African American workers could share each others' food and music and communicate via simultaneous interpreters to learn more about each others' lives, families, problems, and dreams.

In 2005 MPOWER (then the Mississippi Poultry Workers' Center) began to turn these suggestions into realities, creating a diverse worker-led Leadership Council, building programs around issues concerning workers of all backgrounds (such as its Workplace Injury Project), and developing popular education curricula that tie local experiences to global processes. It piloted Power and Oppression workshops to teach participants about their own and other groups' social and political histories and help them build an analysis of their common struggles and shared vision for the future. It also began offering English and Spanish classes with a focus on poultry workers' rights, thus beginning to bridge communication barriers while building a common language for collective mobilization. Although MPOWER is still young and political change happens gradually, perhaps one day in the not-too-distant future poultry workers in Mississippi might be able to smile when they recount the story of one organizer's uneasy plea, once upon a time, for someone who could help him "speak Mexican."

Notes

Earlier versions of this chapter have been published in Spanish and English. See Angela C. Stuesse, "Hablando 'mexicano': La restructuración industrial y los desafíos para la organización a través de la diferencia en un Mississippi transnacional," *Estudios migratorios latinoamericanos* 17, no. 52 (2003): 603–26; and Angela C. Stuesse, "Poultry Processing, People's Politics: Industrial Restructuring and Organizing across Difference in a Transnational Mississippi," in *Mexican Immigration to the U.S. Southeast: Impact and*

Challenges. Proceedings, Symposium on Mexican Immigration to the U.S. Southeast, Mary Odem and Elaine Lacy, eds. (Atlanta: Instituto de México, 2005).

1. Eight of the top ten poultry-producing states in the United States are located in the region traditionally referred to as the South. The top four—Georgia, Arkansas, Alabama, and Mississippi—all form part of the geographical, cultural, and historical subregion known as the Deep South.

2. Delmarva Poultry Industry, "Per Capita Consumption of Poultry and Livestock, 1960–2001," Delmarva Poultry Industry, n.d., at http://www.dpichicken.org/index.cfm?content=facts; USDA Economic Research Service, "Chicken Consumption Continues Longrun Rise," *Amber Waves*, at http://www.ers.usda.gov/AmberWaves/April06/Findings/Chicken.htm.

3. Laura E. Helton and Angela C. Stuesse, "Race, Low-Wage Legacies and the Politics of Poultry Processing: Intersections of Contemporary Immigration and African American Labor Histories in Central Mississippi," paper presented at the Southern Labor Studies Conference, Moving Workers: Migration and the South, Birmingham, Alabama, 2004.

4. William Kandell, "Meat-Processing Firms Attract Hispanic Works to Rural America," *Amber Waves*, June 2006, at http:www.ers.usda.gov/AmberWaves/June06/prf/MeatProcessingFeatureJune06.pdf.

5. Christopher D. Cook, "Fowl Trouble: In the Nation's Poultry Plants, Brutality to Worker as Well as to Bird," *Harper's Magazine* 299 (1999): 78–9. Although immigrant poultry workers in Mississippi are to date almost exclusively Latin American, in other states immigrant poultry workers also come from the Marshall Islands, Laos, Vietnam, and Korea, among other countries. See David C. Griffith, *Jones's Minimal: Low-Wage Labor in the United States* (Albany: State University of New York Press, 1993); and Steve Striffler, "Inside a Poultry Processing Plant: An Ethnographic Portrait," *Labor History* 43, no. 3 (2002): 305–313.

6. U.S. Bureau of the Census, "Personal Income Per Capita in Constant (2000) Dollars," in *State Rankings—Statistical Abstract of the United States* (2006), at http://www.census.gov/statab/ranks/rank29.html, accessed July 2008; Wallace G. Morgan and Steve Murray, "Economic Impact of the Mississippi Poultry Industry at the Year 2002," Mississippi Agricultural and Forestry Experiment Station, Mississippi State University, information bulletin 385, Jan. 2002, at http://msucares.com/pubs/infobulletins/ib385.pdf.

7. After Hurricane Katrina hit the Gulf Coast in 2006, many immigrant workers across Mississippi were recruited to the coast to do cleanup and reconstruction. Coupled with some area poultry companies' recent increased enforcement of federal labor and immigration laws, this demographic concentration may be shifting. See Angela Stuesse, "'Pienso que Dios me lo puso en el camino': The Industrial Logics and Migrant Recruitment that Transformed Mississippi Poultry," paper presented at the Latin American Studies Association Conference, Montreal, Canada, 2007.

8. U.S. Bureau of the Census, "Scott County, Mississippi, Census 2000 Population, Demographic, and Housing Information: General Demographic Characteristics: 2000";

U.S. Bureau of the Census, "Scott County, Mississippi, General Population and Housing Characteristics: 1990."

9. U.S. Bureau of the Census, "General Profile: Scott, MS," 2004.

10. Advocates report that in the late 1990s Scott County's immigrant population consisted of mostly Cubans, Dominicans, Nicaraguans, and Colombians. The national origin of Mississippi's immigrant poultry workers, then, is changing over time in relation to federal immigration policies, poultry plant labor control practices, and shifts in the local labor market.

11. Taylor Branch, *Parting the Waters: America in the King Years, 1954–63* (New York: Simon & Schuster, 1988); David Chalmers, "A Tremor in the Middle of the Iceberg—From a Stone that the Builders Rejected: Black and White in Mississippi," *Reviews in American History* 23, no. 3 (1995): 535–44; John Dittmer, *Local People: The Struggle for Civil Rights in Mississippi* (Urbana and Chicago: University of Illinois Press, 1994); Susie Erenrich, ed., *Freedom Is a Constant Struggle: An Anthology of the Mississippi Civil Rights Movement* (Washington, D.C.: Cultural Center for Social Change, 1999); Anne Moody, *Coming of Age in Mississippi* (New York: Dell Publishing Company, 1968); Charles M. Payne, *I've Got the Light of Freedom: The Organizing Tradition and the Mississippi Freedom Struggle* (Berkeley: University of California Press, 1997); Elizabeth Sutherland Martínez, ed., *Letters from Mississippi* (Brookline, Mass.: Zephyr Press, 2002).

12. MPOWER (Mississippi Poultry Workers for Equality and Respect) was originally the Mississippi Poultry Workers' Center (the Workers' Center), a project of the Equal Justice Center. Between 2002 and 2006 I conducted the bulk of my fieldwork in close collaboration with the Workers' Center. In late 2006 the Workers' Center spun off from the Equal Justice Center in the hopes of becoming a more locally run community-based nonprofit organization and changed its name to MPOWER. Throughout this chapter I refer to the organization using its current name, MPOWER, unless otherwise noted. MPOWER can be visited online at www.mpowercenter.org. The Mississippi Immigrants' Rights Alliance (MIRA) can be visited online at www.yourmira.org.

13. This argument is informed by labor scholars' "split labor market theory" (see Donald D. Stull et al., eds., *Any Way You Cut It: Meat Processing and Small-Town America* [Lawrence: University Press of Kansas, 1995]) and critical race theorists' "intersectionality" theory (Patricia Hill Collins, *Black Feminist Thought: Knowledge, Consciousness, and the Politics of Empowerment* [Boston and London: Unwin Hyman, 2000 (1990)]). See also Kimberlé Crenshaw, "Mapping the Margins: Intersectionality, Identity Politics, and Violence against Women of Color," *Stanford Law Review* 43, no. 6 (1991): 1,241–99.

14. Pierre Bourdieu, "A Reasoned Utopia and Economic Fatalism," *New Left Review* 227 (1998): 125–30.

15. Charles R. Hale, "What Is Activist Research?" *Items (Social Science Research Council)* 2, no. 2 (2001): 13–15; Nancy Scheper-Hughes, "The Primacy of the Ethical: Propositions for a Militant Anthropology," *Current Anthropology* 36, no. 3 (1995): 409–20.

16. Notable exceptions include: Deborah Fink, *Cutting into the Meatpacking Line: Workers and Change in the Rural Midwest* (Chapel Hill: University of North Carolina

Press,1998); Steve Striffler, *Chicken: The Dangerous Transformation of America's Favorite Food* (New Haven, Conn.: Yale University Press, 2005); Stull et al., *Any Way You Cut It.*

17. See, for example, Consumers Union, "Chicken: What You Don't Know Can Hurt You," *Consumer Reports* 63, no. 3 (1998): 12–18; Jesse Katz, "The Chicken Trail: How Migrant Latino Workers Put Food on America's Table," *Los Angeles Times*, 10 Nov. 1996; Cedric N. Chatterley et al., *I Was Content and Not Content: The Story of Linda Lord and the Closing of Penobscot Poultry* (Carbondale: Southern Illinois University Press, 2000); Cheri Register, *Packinghouse Daughter: A Memoir* (St. Paul: Minnesota Historical Society Press, 2000); Eric Schlosser, *Fast Food Nation: The Dark Side of the All-American Meal* (Boston: Houghton Mifflin, 2001); *M. H. Fox et al. v. Tyson Foods, Inc.*, U.S. District Court for the Northern District of Alabama Middle Division, 2001; U.S. Department of Labor, "Year 2000 Poultry Processing Compliance Report," 2000; Human Rights Watch, "Blood, Sweat, and Fear: Workers' Rights in U.S. Meat and Poultry Plants," 2004.

18. Notable exceptions include Griffith 1993, Striffler 2005, and Striffler 2002.

19. For an overview of the seminal literature on globalization theory, see Jonathan X. Inda and Renato Rosaldo, eds., *The Anthropology of Globalization: A Reader* (Malden and Oxford: Blackwell Publishers, 2002).

20. David Harvey, *The Condition of Postmodernity* (Ames, Iowa: Wiley-Blackwell, 1990); Anthony Giddens, *The Consequences of Modernity* (Stanford, Calif.: Stanford University Press, 1990).

21. Arjun Appadurai, *Modernity at Large: Cultural Dimensions of Globalization* (Minneapolis: University of Minnesota Press, 1996); Frederic Jameson, "Postmodernism, of the Cultural Logic of Late Capitalism," *New Left Review* 146 (1984): 53–92.

22. Akhil Gupta and James Ferguson, "Beyond 'Culture': Space, Identity, and the Politics of Difference," *Cultural Anthropology* 7, no. 1 (1992): 6–23; Anna Tsing, "The Global Situation," *Cultural Anthropology* 15, no. 3 (2000): 327–60.

23. Sonia E. Alvarez, Evelina Dagnino, and Arturo Escobar, eds., *Cultures of Politics, Politics of Cultures: Re-Visioning Latin American Social Movements* (Boulder, Colo.: Westview Press, 1998); Linda Basch, Nina Glick Schiller, and Cristina Szanton Blanc, *Nations Unbound: Transnational Projects, Postcolonial Predicaments, and Deterritorialized Nation-States* (Amsterdam, The Netherlands: Gordon & Breach, 1994); Leo R. Chavez, "The Power of the Imagined Community: The Settlement of Undocumented Mexicans and Central Americans in the United States," *American Anthropologist* 96, no. 1 (1994): 52–73; Leo R. Chavez, "Settlers and Sojourners: The Case of Mexicans in the United States," *Human Organization* 47, no. 2 (1988): 95–109; Michael Kearney, "Borders and Boundaries of State and Self at the End of Empire," *Journal of Historical Sociology* 4, no. 1 (1991): 52–74; Maxine L. Margolis, *An Invisible Minority: Brazilians in New York City* (Needham Heights, Mass.: Allyn & Bacon, 1997); Aihwa Ong, *Flexible Citizenship: The Cultural Logics of Transnationality* (Durham, N.C.: Duke University Press, 1999); Refael Pérez-Torres, "Nomads and Migrants: Negotiating a Multicultural Postmodernism," *Cultural Critique* 26 (1993–94): 161–89; Patricia R. Pessar, *A Visa for a Dream: Dominicans in the United States* (Needham Heights, Mass.: Allyn & Bacon, 1995); Alejandro Portes, ed., *The Economic Sociology of Immigration: Essays on Networks, Ethnicity and*

Entrepreneurship (New York: Russell Sage Foundation, 1998); Roger Rouse, "Mexican Migration and the Social Space of Postmodernism," *Diaspora* 1, no. 1 (1991): 8–23.

24. Ruth W. Gilmore, "Race and Globalization," in *Geographies of Global Change: Remapping the World*, R. J. Johnson et al., eds. (London: Blackwell, 2002), 261–74; R. B. Persaud and C. Lusane, "The New Economy, Globalisation and the Impact on African Americans," *Race and Class* 42, no. 1 (2000): 21–34.

25. Pierre Bourdieu, "The Essence of Neoliberalism: Utopia of Endless Exploitation," *Le Monde Diplomatique* (Dec. 1998), translated by Jeremy J. Shapiro, at http://mondediplo.com/1998/12/08bourdieu; Bourdieu, "A Reasoned Utopia and Economic Fatalism."

26. Neil Brenner, "State Theory in the Political Conjuncture: Henri Lefebvre's 'Comments on a New State Form,'" *Antipode* 33, no. 5 (2001): 783–808; J. Petras and H. Veltmeyer, *Globalization Unmasked: Imperialism in the 21st Century* (New York: Zed, 2001); Saskia Sassen, *Globalization and Its Discontents: Essays on the New Mobility of People and Money* (New York: New Press, 1998).

27. Grace Chang, *Disposable Domestics: Immigrant Women Workers in the Global Economy* (Cambridge, Mass.: South End Press, 2000); Joseph E. Stiglitz, *Globalization and Its Discontents* (New York: Norton, 2002).

28. William Boyd and Michael Watts, "Agro-Industrial Just-in-Time: The Chicken Industry and Postwar American Capitalism," in *Globalising Food: Agrarian Questions and Global Restructuring*, ed. David Goodman and Michael Watts (London: Routledge, 1997), 192–225; Griffith, *Jones's Minimal*.

29. Stuart Hall, "The Local and the Global: Globalization and Ethnicity," in *Culture, Globalization and the World System: Contemporary Conditions for the Representation of Identity*, ed. Anthony King (Binghamton: Dept. of Art History, State University of New York at Binghamton, 1991); David Harvey, "Class Relations, Social Justice and the Politics of Difference," in *Place and the Politics of Identity*, ed. M. Keith and S. Pile (New York: Routledge, 1990), 41–66.

30. Harvey, "Class Relations."

31. Data gathered through ethnographic research and collaboration with MPOWER from 2002 to the present.

32. Human Rights Watch, "Blood, Sweat, and Fear: Workers' Rights in U.S. Meat and Poultry Plants," New York, 2004, at www.hrw.org/reports/2005/usa0105.

33. Mississippi Poultry Workers' Center, "What You Need to Know If You Are Injured at Work," Morton, Miss., 2008.

34. United Food and Commercial Workers, "A Voice for Working America: Injury and Injustice—America's Poultry Industry," at http://www.ufcw.org/press_room/fact_sheets_and_backgrounder/poultryindustry_.cfm.

35. Griffith, *Jones's Minimal*.

36. Name and identifying information has been changed.

37. Since Hurricane Katrina devastated the Mississippi Gulf Coast in August 2005, MIRA's activities have shifted to focus heavily on this part of the state.

38. MPOWER, "Who We Are," MPOWER, 2008, at http://www.mpowercenter.org/about.

39. Marc Edelman, *Peasants against Globalization: Rural Social Movements in Costa Rica* (Stanford, Calif.: Stanford University Press, 1999); Harvey, "Class Relations, Social Justice and the Politics of Difference"; Teresa de Lauretis, "Eccentric Subjects: Feminist Theory and Historical Consciousness," *Feminist Studies* 16, no. 1 (1990): 115–50; Arturo Escobar, "Culture, Economics, and Politics in Latin American Social Movements Theory and Research," in *The Making of Social Movements in Latin America: Identity, Strategy, and Democracy*, ed. Arturo Escobar and Sonia E. Alvarez (Boulder, Colo.: Westview, 1992), 62–88; Ernesto Laclau and Chantal Mouffe, *Hegemony and Socialist Strategy: Towards a Radical Democratic Politics* (London: Verso, 1985).

40. Alvarez, Dagnino, and Escobar, *Cultures of Politics, Politics of Cultures*; Lisa Lowe and David Lloyd, eds., *The Politics of Culture in the Shadow of Capital* (Durham, N.C.: Duke University Press, 1997), 1–32; Barbara Smith, *The Truth That Never Hurts: Writings on Race, Gender, and Freedom* (New Brunswick, N.J.: Rutgers University Press, 2000); Julia Sudbury, *'Other Kinds of Dreams': Black Women's Organizations and the Politics of Transformation* (London: Routledge, 1998).

41. Angela C. Stuesse, "From One Southeast to Another: Experiences, Challenges, and Resources of Mexican Migrants in Mississippi," paper presented at the Symposium on Mexican Immigration to the U.S. Southeast: Impact and Challenges, sponsored by the Consulate General of Mexico in Atlanta, Instituto de México (Atlanta) Emory University, University of Georgia, Georgia State University, and Kennesaw State University, Atlanta, 2004.

42. Rouse, "Mexican Migration and the Social Space of Postmodernism." Due to federal policies over the last decade that have led to increased enforcement of the U.S.-Mexico border, however, migrants' visits to their home countries are becoming less frequent.

43. Those who have gone home talk regularly about wanting to return to the United States due to lack of economic opportunities in their hometowns.

44. All quotations from Spanish speakers have been translated into English by the author.

45. Griffith, *Jones's Minimal*, 199.

46. For an overview of the immigrant "bootstrap" ideology, see Juan F. Perea, ed., *Immigrants Out!: The New Nativism and the Anti-Immigrant Impulse in the United States* (New York: New York University Press, 1997).

47. Stull et al., *Any Way You Cut It*, 141.

48. Griffith, *Jones's Minimal*, 227.

49. In most cases in Mississippi's poultry plants, these contractors and the plants are legally considered "joint employers," and the plants would likely be found liable in a court of law.

50. Laura Helton, "Three Hundred Strangers Next Door: Native Mississippians Respond to Immigration," *Inter-American Policy Studies Occasional Paper No. 4* (Austin: University of Texas, 2003): 13–14.

51. For more on the contours of institutional racism in the United States, see Kimberlé Crenshaw et al., eds. *Critical Race Theory: The Key Writings That Formed the Movement*

(New York: New Press, 1995); George Lipsitz, *The Positive Investment in Whiteness: How White People Profit from Identity Politics* (Philadelphia: Temple University Press, 1998); Thomas Sugrue, *The Origins of the Urban Crisis: Race and Inequality in Postwar Detroit* (Princeton, N.J.: Princeton University Press, 1996).

52. María Patricia Fernández-Kelley, *For We Are Sold, I and My People: Women and Industry on Mexico's Frontier* (Albany: State University of New York Press, 1983); James Scott, *Weapons of the Weak: Everyday Forms of Peasant Resistance* (New Haven, Conn.: Yale University Press, 1985).

53. Crenshaw, "Mapping the Margins"; Collins, *Black Feminist Thought*, 59.

54. Helton and Stuesse, "Race, Low-Wage Legacies"; Arthur D. Murphy et al., eds., *Latino Workers in the Contemporary South* (Athens: University of Georgia Press, 2001).

55. Griffith, *Jones's Minimal*; Stull et al., *Any Way You Cut It*.

56. Stull et al., *Any Way You Cut It*, 55. Proponents of vertical integration argue that it is efficient and made the industry what it is today, but its critics argue that it effectively "placed a ninety million dollar industry in the hands of only five companies" (Chatterley et al., *I Was Content and Not Content*, 99). Family businesses were eventually bought out by corporations, and even "independent" farmers are heavily regulated and do not ever technically own the birds they raise.

57. Some focus groups were carried out in collaboration with Anita Grabowski and David Mandel-Anthony, students at the University of Texas at Austin. See Grabowski, "La Pollera," and David G. Mandel-Anthony, "From Comitancillo to Carthage, Mississippi: Activist Research, Transnationalism, and Racial Formation in a Community of Guatemalan Mam Poultry Workers," honor's thesis, University of Texas, 2005.

CHAPTER SEVEN

Latino Immigrants and the Politics of Space in Atlanta

MARY E. ODEM

In the fall of 1990 more than two hundred Latino immigrants, mostly Mexicans and Central Americans, gathered for Mass in the middle of New Peachtree Road in the Chamblee-Doraville area of Atlanta to protest the closing of a Catholic center that had served Latino immigrants for the previous two years. The crowd, which included men, women, and children, many of them undocumented immigrants, blocked traffic for an hour as they took part in the Mass led by a Colombian priest who worked for the Atlanta archdiocese. Over the next several weeks, the immigrant Mass moved from the street to a parking lot of an apartment complex, and when the cold weather came it moved inside, first to a local Mexican tortilla factory and then to a nearby Baptist church.

Immigrants continued to hold Mass and other church-related activities in streets, parking lots, and restaurants of the Chamblee-Doraville neighborhood for several months until the archdiocese agreed to provide funding for a new meeting place for the group. A prefabricated building formerly used as a warehouse was purchased and converted into a Latino Catholic mission and named La Misión Católica de Nuestra Señora de Las Américas in honor of Our Lady of Guadalupe. The Misión Católica quickly became a major religious and community center for thousands of Mexican and Central American immigrants in the Atlanta metropolitan area.[1]

The formation of the Misión Católica was an early sign of the major demographic transformation taking place in metropolitan Atlanta. By 1990 tens of thousands of Latin Americans had migrated to Atlanta to work in its thriving construction and service industries and in the nearby carpet and poultry-processing plants. Most of the early immigrants were young Mexican men who had moved from Texas, California, and northern Mexico. They were soon joined by migrants from other regions of Mexico and from Central American countries, principally Guatemala and El Salvador. At the same time, an increasing number of women and children joined male workers, resulting in a greater Latin American presence in schools, churches, and neighborhoods of the Atlanta area. During the 1990s the metropolitan region was one of the fastest growing Latino immigrant destinations in the country. Fueled primarily by foreign immigration, Atlanta's Latino population grew from 25,000 in 1980 to 57,000 in 1990 to nearly 270,000 in the year 2000, a growth rate of 370 percent in the decade from 1990 to 2000.[2]

The founding of the Misión Católica and its role among Latino newcomers in Atlanta draw our attention to the issue of social space in the process of immigration and settlement. Influenced by the work of cultural geographers and theorists, I pay particular attention to the spatial aspects of Latino immigrants' experiences in this southern metropolis. Henri Lefebvre, one of the first to develop a critical theory of space, holds that throughout history each society has produced a distinct social space that meets its demands for economic production and social reproduction. Particularly relevant to this chapter is his analysis of the space of social reproduction, the spaces created to perpetuate social and class relations, including housing, neighborhoods, schools, and the public spaces of the city.[3] In *The Power of Place* Delores Hayden uses Lefebvre's theoretical framework to explore the social and spatial history of the American urban landscape. Hayden proposes that we examine urban spaces as "political territories" where boundaries have been established to restrict marginal groups such as women, workers, and ethnic and racial minorities. "One of the consistent ways to limit the economic and political rights of groups," she argues, "has been to constrain social reproduction by limiting access to space."[4]

Drawing on the work of Hayden and Lefebvre, I suggest that a central form of regulation of Latino immigrants in U.S. urban areas occurs at the level of space. By restricting immigrants' movements within and excluding them from certain spaces (neighborhoods, roads, housing, etc.), authorities limit their ability to sustain social life in the new place of settlement. Mexican and Central American immigrants have struggled in various ways against these spatial barriers to appropriate the spaces they need to maintain families and communities in the face of discrimination and uncertain legal status.

I examine how this struggle was played out in Atlanta during the period of dramatic growth of the Latino immigrant population. A significant way that Latinos have claimed space in U.S. urban landscapes has been through religious practice and institution building. In Chamblee-Doraville immigrants created a Latino religious place that provided social and spiritual resources to help them deal with the hardships of migration and adaptation to life in the U.S.[5] I focus on the period 1988 to 2004, when the Misión Católica was located in the Chamblee-Doraville neighborhood. (In 2006, the Atlanta archdiocese moved the Misión ten miles to a new neighborhood in Gwinnett County, marking a new stage in its development.)

My analysis is based on varied sources: interviews with public officials and immigrant leaders and advocates in Atlanta; participant observation of religious and social activities in the Misión Católica; archival records of the Catholic Archdiocese of Atlanta; local newspapers (*Atlanta Journal-Constitution*, *Mundo Hispánico*, *Georgia Bulletin*); county and municipal records and reports; and U.S. census data for 1980, 1990, and 2000.

Latin American Settlement in Atlanta

One of the earliest and now most concentrated centers of immigrant settlement in metro Atlanta is in northern DeKalb County in the neighboring small cities of Chamblee and Doraville. Prior to 1970 the Chamblee-Doraville area was home to mostly white, blue-collar workers who labored in the factories nearby, including General Motors, Frito-Lay, Kodak, and General Electric. The economic slowdown of the 1970s resulted in factory closings and layoffs and the departure of many working-class residents from the area. As the number of housing and rental vacancies climbed, apartment managers began marketing to Vietnamese refugees and later to Chinese, Korean, and Latin American migrants.[6]

Immigrants were initially drawn to the Chamblee-Doraville area because of the availability of low-cost housing, especially the large number of moderately priced rental units. The opening of two subway stops in the 1980s made the area even more attractive to immigrant workers dependent on the low-wage jobs scattered throughout the metropolitan region. By 1990 the Chamblee-Doraville area had become one of the most ethnically diverse in the Southeast (excluding Florida). The ethnic transformation was particularly pronounced in Chamblee. In 1980 non-Hispanic whites composed 89 percent of Chamblee's population; African Americans, Asians and Latinos together composed only 11 percent. In 2000 whites composed only 24 percent of the Chamblee population, while Latinos had become the majority group with 54 percent of the population; Asians made up another 14.5 percent and African Americans 5 percent.[7]

In contrast to previous U.S. historical patterns in which immigrants settled in urban neighborhoods, recent immigrants in Atlanta have settled in suburban areas outside the inner city. They are living in apartment complexes located on multilane highways, alongside shopping plazas and convenience stores. Buford Highway, a busy six-lane highway that runs through Chamblee and Doraville, is the commercial center of the area. Numerous aging strip malls that line the highway have been converted to large ethnic and multiethnic shopping plazas with names like Chinatown Square, Asian Square Mall, Plaza Fiesta, and Plaza

Latino. In many ways immigrants have breathed new economic, social, and cultural life into an area that had suffered economic stagnation and population decline.[8]

The Latino population in Chamblee and the rest of metro Atlanta has diverse national and regional origins. The largest group by far is Mexican, but there are significant numbers of Central American, South American, and Caribbean newcomers. According to the 2000 census Mexicans made up 61 percent of metro Atlanta's Latino population; Central Americans, mostly from Guatemala and El Salvador, formed 8 percent; Puerto Ricans made up another 7 percent; and South Americans 6 percent.[9] A significant portion of the Latino immigrant population is undocumented. A 2004 report by the Urban Institute estimated that between 40 and 49 percent of all immigrants in the state of Georgia in 2000 were undocumented.[10] The percentage would be noticeably higher if only Latino immigrants were counted. Jeffrey Passel's 2005 report, "Unauthorized Migrants," estimates that nationally Latin Americans make up 81 percent of the unauthorized population.[11]

Latinos, regardless of legal status, have formed an integral part of the labor force in metropolitan Atlanta since 1990. Most have worked as laborers in the construction and service industries. More than 60 percent of Latino workers were employed in these industries in 2000, with 30 percent in construction and 35 percent in services, which includes hotel and restaurant work, landscaping, and janitorial service. Another 12 percent of Latino workers are employed in manufacturing, largely in carpet and poultry-processing factories.[12] The growth and prosperity of key economic sectors in Atlanta has depended on the labor of Mexican and Central American workers.

Spatial Regulation of Latino Immigrants

Despite their importance to the region's economy, many Latin Americans in Atlanta, particularly the large number of undocumented immigrants, lead precarious lives. Although immigrant workers provide a crucial source of labor to employers, U.S. immigration policies prohibit the legal entry of most Mexican and Central American workers and deny them a legitimate role in U.S. social and civic life. According to David Bacon, U.S. labor and immigration policies in effect create a "special category of residents in the U.S. who have significantly fewer rights than the population as a whole; they cannot legally work or receive social benefits, and can be apprehended, incarcerated, and deported at any time."[13]

A central way of limiting the rights of Latino immigrants has been to restrict their access to social space and thereby limit their ability to build and sustain social and community life. Regulation of immigrants' access to space has taken various forms in metropolitan Atlanta. Federal immigration officials have conducted periodic raids of workplaces, apartment complexes, and other gathering spots to round up and deport undocumented immigrants. Surveillance and control of immigrants has also occurred at the level of local government: the growing presence of Latino immigrants in metro Atlanta has unsettled many residents and local authorities and prompted numerous measures to restrict their movement and exclude them from particular places and neighborhoods. The various ordinances and policies limit immigrants' access to housing, higher education, employment, and transportation. Not all are directed explicitly against undocumented immigrants, but the reality is that the populations of legal and unauthorized residents among Latino immigrants are so intertwined (e.g., undocumented parents with U.S.-born children) that laws affecting one group necessarily affect the other.

A closer look at the regulation of day laborers and access to driver's licenses illuminates the conflicts over social space between Latino immigrants and local authorities. A drive through metropolitan Atlanta on any weekday morning starting at seven o'clock will reveal numerous street corners where groups of Latino immigrant men wait to be hired by local employers to perform a range of labor-intensive jobs: painting walls, building homes, clearing debris, moving furniture, weeding, and mowing lawns. Most of the men who wait for work are undocumented; immigrants with work permits have access to steadier and more secure forms of employment. Many local employers in the lawn maintenance, construction, and restaurant industries depend on day laborers for their businesses to survive. Although they provide a needed source of labor, these workers are often viewed with suspicion by local residents and merchants who complain that laborers scare off customers and threaten the peace and security in their neighborhoods.

As a result of such complaints, a number of city councils have passed ordinances forbidding laborers from gathering on street corners. The city of Chamblee passed an ordinance in 1996 prohibiting people from "assembl[ing] on private property for the purpose of soliciting work as a day laborer without the permission of the property owner." In 1998 the city of Roswell in Fulton County passed a similar law, followed in 1999 by Marietta in Cobb County.[14] In March 1999 police in Roswell arrested five workers waiting at a day-labor pickup spot in front of an apartment complex after the managers of the complex complained to authorities. That same year Immigration and Naturalization Service (INS) agents conducted a raid at a day-labor site in Marietta, arresting sixty-four migrant workers with the help of local police. Undercover agents had posed as contractors looking for workers.[15] Such mass arrests do not happen often, but they underscore the vulnerability of undocumented workers in public spaces.

In an attempt to address the tensions around day laborers, a Methodist church group established a day-labor center in Gwinnett County, initially located in a church basement, to provide a safe, legal place for workers to wait for employers. In 2001 the city of Roswell opened Georgia's first publicly financed center for day laborers, devoting $40,000 to the project. The center came about through the efforts of Latino community leaders, especially Jose Bernal, a local businessman who provided additional financial support for the center and led the formation of the Roswell Intercultural Alliance, a nonprofit organization created to address immigrant labor issues. The center provided a waiting area for workers, matched employers with laborers, and provided English classes and "seminars on state laws and other issues to help Hispanics assimilate."[16]

Despite the promising initial collaboration between Latino immigrants and city and police officials, the Roswell City Council bowed to public opposition and closed the center after just one year of operation. The Georgia Coalition for Immigration Reform (one of several anti-immigrant organizations established in the state since the late 1990s) protested the opening of the center in letters to Roswell city leaders, as well as to federal immigration officials in Atlanta. Coalition members complained about the use of public funding for a center that served "illegal" workers and called on immigration officials to uphold the law by arresting and deporting the workers who gathered there.[17] Even though the day-labor center no longer exists, workers continue to gather on street corners and local employers continue to hire them.

The use of automobiles and public roads has been another arena of struggle between Latino immigrants and local authorities. Latino immigrants frequently use buses and taxi services, but the South's low-density suburban development, dispersed job locations, and limited public transportation systems virtually require the use of personal vehicles. Many immigrant workers in metro Atlanta have to travel long distances to get to job sites; they depend heavily on automobiles to go shopping, visit health facilities, and take children to and from school. Yet Georgia, like most states in the country, has prohibited unauthorized immigrants from obtaining driver's licenses by requiring proof of legal residence or valid social security cards as identification. Thousands of immigrants in Georgia have been arrested, fined, and sometimes jailed for driving without a valid license.

Latino community leaders and immigrant advocacy groups in Atlanta have engaged in political efforts to legalize driving for unauthorized immigrants in Georgia. State Representative Pedro Marin of Gwinnett County, one of the first Latino legislators in the state, coauthored a bill in the house in 2003 (Ga. HB 578) that would have enabled unauthorized immigrants to obtain a driver's license with certain restrictions. Under the proposed act immigrant drivers would have to renew their license annually and could use it only for transportation to work, school, church, and medical clinics.

The measure provoked such public opposition that it was soundly defeated, and two years later state legislators passed Ga. HB 501, which mandated that only legal residents of the state could obtain driver's licenses.[18] Federal legislation passed in 2005 reinforced Georgia's stance on the issue. Legislators in the U.S. House of Representatives attached a provision (called the Real ID Act) to a military spending bill that prohibits states from offering driver's licenses to immigrants who cannot provide identification approved by the U.S. Department of Homeland Security, effectively barring unauthorized residents from obtaining driver's licenses.[19]

Claiming Social Space

For immigrants the roads, neighborhoods, and public places in Atlanta have been arenas of conflict where they have struggled in various ways against the spatial restrictions imposed by local and federal authorities. During the late 1980s and early 1990s immigrants in Chamblee-Doraville challenged these restrictions by claiming a Latino religious space. Through a process of negotiation and struggle with local government officials and the Catholic Archdiocese of Atlanta, immigrants formed a Latino Catholic mission where they could practice their faith in a familiar, welcoming environment and develop social and material resources to support their families and communities.

The Catholic Church, in contrast to federal immigration laws and local policies and ordinances that restrict and exclude undocumented immigrants, officially opens its doors to all people, regardless of nationality or legal status. The archdiocese was one of the first and continues to be one of the central institutions in the metropolitan area to address the problems confronting Latin American immigrants. Catholic Social Services provides job referral services, immigration counseling, and numerous other services, while the St. Vincent de Paul Society collects and sells clothing and household goods to immigrants at inexpensive prices.[20] Still the church—at both the archdiocese and parish levels—has had its own difficulties accepting an increasingly diverse immigrant Catholic population.

Most church officials have advocated the integration of immigrants into existing parishes. Although clearly more welcoming to immigrants than exclusion, the policy of integration as practiced in the Atlanta archdiocese still constituted a form of spatial restriction. Just as certain local and federal policies exclude immigrants and demand their invisibility from some public places, most church officials and priests in the Atlanta archdiocese expected immigrants to enter existing parishes, which are predominantly white, middle-class, and suburban, and conform to U.S. Catholic traditions and styles of worship.

Numerous barriers, however, stood in the way of this integration plan for Mexican and Central American immigrants in the late 1980s and 1990s. Many immigrants did not own cars and thus often relied on public transportation to go to Mass, yet few churches were located on convenient public transportation routes. Language, cultural, and class barriers also discouraged the participation of Latin American immigrants in existing churches. Many could not understand or speak English and did not feel welcome among the more prosperous, white members of suburban Catholic churches. Moreover, mainstream Catholic churches discouraged the different religious practices and styles of worship of Mexican and other Latin American Catholics: the intense devotions to regional and national patron saints; the processions, celebrations and other forms of religious expression that take place outside of the church in the streets and neighborhoods; and the more informal, noisy atmosphere of Sunday Masses with families with young children and infants.[21]

Immigrants felt unwelcome at local Catholic churches, yet greatly desired a place where and community with whom they could practice their faith. In the summer of 1988 several young Mexican men asked one of the few Spanish-speaking priests in the archdiocese, Father Jorge Christancho from Colombia, to visit their apartment complex in Chamblee to say Mass for the Spanish-speaking men, women, and children who lived there. More than fifty people gathered to meet with the Latin American priest in the patio of one family's apartment. Father Christancho, who was assigned to a church some distance from Chamblee, tried to persuade the priests in the two nearby parishes to provide Spanish religious services for the immigrants in the neighborhood. When this attempt failed he decided to continue to meet with immigrants in Chamblee in addition to his regular duties.[22]

As the numbers of participants quickly expanded, the group found a larger space to meet: the basement of a small, Latino-owned grocery store in a local shopping plaza. Immigrants used the space to address the social and material needs of participants as well as their religious needs—by collecting and storing food and clothing to distribute to those in need and by renting a small apartment to provide temporary shelter for newly arrived immigrants. After a few months in this location, attendance at the Mass had grown to more than two hundred people.[23]

In summer 1989, due to complaints from local residents and other tenants in the shopping plaza, the owners of the plaza sought to prohibit the gatherings.

At this point Father Christancho attempted once again to gain the support of Catholic Church officials. At his invitation, in August 1989 the newly appointed archbishop, Eugene Marino, who was the first African American Roman Catholic archbishop in the United States, celebrated Mass for the Latino community in Chamblee. Archbishop Marino was so impressed by the number of people and their commitment and faith that he promised to provide archdiocesan support for a "Hispanic mission." In December 1989 the archdiocese rented a small hall in Chamblee for this purpose, which became known among immigrants as El Centro Católico de Chamblee.[24]

After almost two years in the new location, El Centro faced a growing number of complaints to the archdiocese from local residents and city officials that the religious gatherings violated noise and crowd ordinances. By this time Archbishop Marino had resigned. The new archbishop, also African American, was less sympathetic to the concerns of immigrants in Chamblee. More tied to the church's model of ethnic integration, he closed the Latino Catholic center and instructed immigrants to attend the churches in the parishes closest to Chamblee.[25]

Latino migrants did not passively accept the archdiocese's decision. In response to the closing of El Centro, they took the Mass to the streets. The crowds of Latino Catholics meeting in public roads, parking lots, and the local Baptist church for the next several months eventually convinced the archdiocese to provide a new meeting place for the group.[26] In fall 1992 the Misión Católica de Nuestra Señora de Las Américas opened its doors in a converted warehouse convenient to a subway stop. The Misión soon became a major religious and community center for Mexican and Central American immigrants in Chamblee, Doraville, and surrounding towns and suburbs. By 1999 it was holding four Masses every weekend with standing-room-only crowds (more than five hundred people per Mass) and performing hundreds of marriages and baptisms for its members each year. With a small paid staff and close to a hundred volunteers, the *misión* also offered English, computer, and job training classes, sponsored a health clinic and free job bureau, and collected food and clothing for needy immigrants.[27]

Appropriating this space enabled immigrants to develop collective resources to sustain their communities and to challenge the confines of discrimination, economic hardship, and legal marginality in the United States. Often discriminated against and excluded in the broader society, immigrants found a welcoming place in the *misión*. They came together not only to pray and attend Mass, but also to socialize, to celebrate important events, to get needed resources (food, clothing, health care) and to exchange information about jobs and housing.

For young male workers from Mexico and Central America, the *misión* offered a place where they could gather together without raising the suspicions of law enforcement officials. Whereas U.S. authorities often perceive young Latino men as potential criminals and restrict their movement in public, people at the *misión* recognized them as decent, hardworking men struggling to support their families. For undocumented migrants in particular the *misión* has been a haven. In the words of Father Carlos García-Carreras, a Cuban American priest who served the *misión* from 1994 to 2000: "It's a place where they can say, 'I'm not afraid.' . . . [This] is the only place where they can feel more at home, more understood, more among their own people . . . because they feel so bad . . . in the rest of their surroundings here in Atlanta."[28]

Participation in the *misión* also has helped immigrants integrate into U.S. social and civic life. Since its founding the Latino mission has offered free English classes, one of the most sought-after services among its members. Immigrants have taken part in a number of other activities at the Misión Católica that encourage their integration into U.S. society, such as computer classes, driving lessons, and various job training courses.[29]

Equally important are the possibilities for political participation that immigrants have pursued in the *misión*. They have joined petition drives to voice their opinions on various immigration laws and policies. Many participated in a regionwide petition drive in support of a proposal before the Georgia legislature to allow driver's licenses for undocumented immigrants. In July 1999 more than eight hundred people from the *misión* signed a letter protesting the arrest of the sixty-four day laborers in Marietta in an INS raid. The signers expressed their support for an expanded and improved guest worker program in the United States as a solution to the problem of "labor shortages, especially in jobs most Americans recoil from, and the presence of thousands of hard-working, undocumented immigrants from south of the border." Excluded from standard avenues of political participation in the United States, immigrants use the *misión* as an alternative public space from which to engage in political debate over issues that affect their lives.[30]

While the *misión* has facilitated immigrants' incorporation into U.S. religious and social life, it also has fostered ties with their homelands. They have sustained connections to their homelands through the practice of familiar faith devotions and rituals. According to Father García-Carreras many immigrants attended the *misión* instead of other Catholic churches in the metro area in order to honor and pray to their specific national and regional saints there. Such practices are "a remembrance for them of their own devotions in their country. . . . people would tell you when they come over here, 'Everything changes in our lives. The only thing that doesn't change is God.' So, religion for them is a relation with their own country or with their own traditions and being able to teach their children about the traditions in their country and being able to celebrate them over here."[31]

Initially mainstream Catholic parishes in Atlanta were uncomfortable with the diverse religious devotions of Mexican and other Latin American immigrants and discouraged their efforts to display images of patron saints in church, with the explanation that the devotions are private, rather than parish-wide.[32] The *misión*, by contrast, encouraged the display of and devotions to Latin American saints. The Blessed Sacrament Chapel in the *misión* displayed statues and images of at least ten different patron saints from Latin America including Our Lady of Guadalupe and Our Lady of Juan de los Lagos from Mexico, Our Lady of Peace from El Salvador, Our Lady of Suyapa from Honduras, Our Lady of Copacabana from Bolivia, Our Lady of Charity from Cuba, Lord of Miracles from Peru and Our Lady of Altagracia from the Dominican Republic. People visited the chapel regularly to pray and leave offerings for their saints.

The largest Catholic devotion among immigrants in the Chamblee-Doraville area is to Our Lady of Guadalupe. Although known originally and primarily as the patroness of Mexico, the Virgin of Guadalupe has also come to be known as the patron saint of all of Latin America. This devotion dates from the sixteenth century, when the Virgin Mary miraculously appeared to an indigenous man, Juan Diego, at Tepeyac, a place near Mexico City that had been sacred to an Aztec goddess. The Virgin appeared as an Indian and spoke to Juan Diego in his native language, Nahuatl. According to historian Jeffrey Burns, "To the Indian and Mestizo population, Guadalupe instilled a sense of personal dignity in the face of the affronts of the Spanish colonizers. She was not only a religious figure, but a national figure who gave birth to the Mexican faith and people. . . . To generation after generation the apparition of Our Lady of Guadalupe affirmed the Mexican people and provided solace to a people whose existence was often quite harsh, particularly in the United States."[33]

Mexican immigrants have carried this religious devotion with them to Atlanta. Images of Guadalupe adorn walls, T-shirts, trucks, and store windows throughout the neighborhoods where Mexicans have settled. Our Lady of Guadalupe has been a prominent presence at the *misión*. A statue of the brown-skinned Virgin surrounded by golden rays greeted people as they entered the building and a colorful painting of her hung in the Blessed Sacrament Chapel. Since the founding of the mission lay leaders have organized an impressive annual celebration and procession in honor of Our Lady of Guadalupe on her feast day. During the celebration in 1999 hundreds of people gathered on the evening of December 11 to celebrate Mass and sing the traditional songs, "las mañanitas," led by a mariachi band. The following morning a procession with decorated trucks, one carrying the large painting of Guadalupe, traveled from the *misión* down Shallowford Road for several blocks, marking a Latino immigrant presence in the neighborhood. Local police held back traffic to enable the truck floats and marchers to pass safely through the streets of Chamblee-Doraville.

With the formation of the Misión Católica, Latino immigrants challenged the policies of exclusion and restriction they faced from federal and local authorities, as well as the policy of assimilation promoted by the Catholic archdiocese. The appropriation of social space has been a critical means of empowerment for Latino immigrants in Atlanta. The need for social space has been especially pressing for undocumented immigrants who are most vulnerable to the laws, policies, and practices restricting immigrants' social and political rights. In the face of current immigration policies at the federal and local levels, ethnic religious institutions like the Misión Católica will continue to be an important means of immigrant community building and empowerment in Atlanta and elsewhere in the country.

Notes

1. "IHM Ministers at Centro Católico," *Georgia Bulletin*, April 11, 1991; "Hispanic Mission Serves Newcomers," *Georgia Bulletin*, Dec. 5, 1991; interview with Father Carlos García-Carreras, Jan. 21, 2000; interview with Gonzalo Saldaña, June 20, 2000.

2. Mary E. Odem, "Unsettled in the Suburbs: Latino Immigration and Ethnic Diversity in Metro Atlanta," in Audrey Singer et al., *Twenty-first Century Gateways: Immigrant Incorporation in Suburban America* (Washington, D.C.: Brookings Institution, 2008), 105–36; Audrey Singer, "The Rise of New Immigrant Gateways" (Washington, D.C.: Brookings Institution, Feb. 2004); U.S. Census Bureau, *Census of Population, 1980, 1990, 2000.*

3. Henri Lefebrve, *The Production of Space*, trans. Donald Nicholson-Smith (Oxford and Cambridge, Mass: Oxford University Press, 1974, 1991); see also Edward Soja, *Postmodern Geographies: The Reassertion of Space in Critical Social Theory* (London and New York: Verso, 1989); David Harvey, *Spaces of Capital: Towards a Critical Geography* (New York: Routledge, 2001).

4. Delores Hayden, *The Power of Place: Urban Landscapes as Public History* (Cambridge, Mass.: MIT Press, 1995, 1999), 22–23.

5. For a study that situates Latino Catholics in Atlanta in the broader history of immigrants in the U.S. Catholic Church, see Mary E. Odem, "Our Lady of Guadalupe in the New South: Latin American Immigrants and the Politics of Integration in the Catholic Church," *Journal of American Ethnic History* 23 (Fall 2004): 29–60. Although I focus on Latino immigrants' involvement in the Catholic Church, immigrants have also participated in large numbers in evangelical Protestant churches in Atlanta.

6. Odem, "Unsettled in the Suburbs"; Judith Waldrop, "The Newest Southerners," *American Demographics* 15 (1993): 38–43; Audrey Singer and Jill H. Wilson, *From "There" to "Here": Refugee Resettlement in Metropolitan America* (Washington, D.C.: Brookings Institution, 2006).

7. U.S. Census Bureau, *Census of Population, 1980, 1990, 2000.*

8. Odem, "Unsettled in the Suburbs"; Singer, "Rise of New Immigrant Gateways"; Susan M. Walcott, "Overlapping Ethnicities and Negotiated Spaces: Atlanta's Buford Highway," *Journal of Cultural Geography* 20, no. 1 (Fall/Winter 2002): 51–75.

9. U.S. Census Bureau, *Census of Population, 2000.*

10. Jeffrey S. Passel, Randolph Capps, and Michael E. Fix, "Undocumented Immigrants: Facts and Figures" (Washington, D.C.: Urban Institute, 2004). See www.urban.org/url.cfm?ID=1000587.

11. Jeffrey S. Passel, "Unauthorized Migrants: Numbers and Characteristics" (Washington, D.C.: Pew Hispanic Center, 2005). See http://pewhispanic.org/files/reports/46.pdf.

12. Rakesh Kochhar, Roberto Suro, and Sonya Tafoya, "The New Latino South: The Context and Consequences of Rapid Population Growth" (Washington, D.C.: Pew Hispanic Center, 2005).

13. David Bacon, "For an Immigration Policy Based on Human Rights," in *Immigration: A Civil Rights Issue for the Americas*, eds. Susanne Jonas and Suzanne Dodd Thomas (Wilmington, Del.: Scholarly Resources, 1999), 157.

14. *City Code of Marietta, Georgia*, sec. 10-4-130, www.municode.com, accessed June 20, 2007; City of Duluth, Georgia, *Code of Ordinances*, sec. 10-13, www.municode.com, accessed June 20, 2007.

15. Mark Bixler, "Day Laborers in Roswell Get a Place to Call Their Own," *Atlanta Journal-Constitution*, Dec. 19, 1999, 1D; Rick Badie, "Gwinnett Mulls Rules for Laborers," *Atlanta Journal-Constitution*, June 2, 2000, 1D; Pilar Verdés, "Roswell pone manos a la obra," *Mundo Hispánico*, Aug. 5, 1999.

16. Martha Durango, "Centro está por abrir sus puertas," *Mundo Hispánico*, Dec. 21, 2000; Rick Badie, "Gwinnett Seeks Rules for Laborers," *Atlanta Journal Constitution*, June 2, 2000, D1; Mark Bixler, "Few Employers Know about Day Laborers Center," July 9, 2001, B1.

17. Bixler, "Few Employers Know about Day Laborers Center."

18. Mark Bixler, "Illegal Immigrants' License Try Revs Up," *Atlanta Journal-Constitution*, Aug. 27, 2001, 1B; Georgia House Bill 501, enacted May 2, 2005. This was an amendment to Title 40, "Motor Vehicles and Traffic" of the Official Code of Georgia Annotated; the bill can be found at http://www.legis.ga.gov/legis/2005_06/fulltext/hb501.htm.

19. Eunice Moscoso, "Driver's Licenses for Illegals to End," *Atlanta Journal-Constitution*, May 5, 2005, A1.

20. Helen Blier, "A 'Catholic' Catholic Church: The Roman Catholic Community of Atlanta," *Religions of Atlanta: Religious Diversity in the Centennial Olympic City*, ed. Gary Laderman (Atlanta: Scholars Press, 1996), 68.

21. Interview with Father Jorge Christancho, July 30, 1999; interview with Gonzalo Saldaña, June 20, 2000; Martha Woodson Rees and T. Danyael Miller, *Quienes Somos? Que Necesitamos?: Needs Assessment of Hispanics in the Archdiocese of Atlanta* (Atlanta: Hispanic Apostolate of the Archdiocese of Atlanta, 2002).

22. Father Jorge Christancho, "Perspectives on the Hispanic Ministry," March 16, 1992, box 014/2, folder 15, Catholic Archdiocese of Atlanta Archives; "Brief History of Our Lady of the Americas Catholic Mission" (Doraville, Ga., Feb. 1999), prepared by staff members of the *misión* (copy in author's collection).

23. See both references in the previous note.

24. "Catholic Center Seeks a Home," *Dekalb Extra*, March 28, 1991; "Brief History of Our Lady of the Americas Catholic Mission."

25. "Catholic Center Seeks Home," *DeKalb Extra*, March 28, 1991; Most Rev. James Lyke to Rev. Jorge Christancho, March 14, 1991, box 014/2, folder 12, Archdiocese of Atlanta Archives; Interview with Father Jorge Christancho, July 30, 1999.

26. "IHM Ministers at Centro Católico," *Georgia Bulletin*, April 11, 1991; "Hispanic Mission Serves Newcomers," *Georgia Bulletin*, Dec. 5, 1991; interview with Father Carlos García-Carreras, Jan. 21, 2000; interview with Gonzalo Saldaña, June 20, 2000.

27. Interview with Father Carlos García-Carreras, Jan. 21 and 27, 2000; "Ideario de la Misión" (Doraville, Ga.: n.d.), prepared by staff members of the mission (copy in author's collection).

28. Interview with Father Carlos García-Carreras, Feb. 11, 2000.

29. Interview with Sister Ricarda, March 13, 2001; Rees and Miller, *Quienes Somos?*

30. *Atlanta Journal Constitution*, July 12, 1999, A8.

31. Interview with Father Carlos García-Carreras, Jan. 27, 2000.

32. Ibid.

33. Jeffrey Burns, "The Mexican Catholic Community in California," in *Mexican Americans and the Catholic Church, 1900–1965*, eds. Jay P. Dolan and Gilberto M. Hinojosa (Notre Dame, Ill.: University of Notre Dame Press, 1994); Timothy Matovina, "Guadalupan Devotions in a Borderlands Community," *Journal of Hispanic/Latino Theology* 4 (Aug. 1996): 6–26.

CHAPTER EIGHT

New Americans in a New South City?

Immigrant and Refugee Politics in Nashville, Tennessee

JAMIE WINDERS

In 2000 nearly one in three immigrants in the United States lived outside traditional immigrant-receiving communities.[1] For the first time in three decades, California, long seen as the center of contemporary immigration to the United States, witnessed a decline in the new-immigrant share of its overall population.[2] On the other side of the country, more than a million Mexicans were living in the southern states of Georgia, Tennessee, North Carolina, and South Carolina by 2000.[3] In 2001 the U.S. Office of Refugee Resettlement (ORR) chose three cities that were not modern immigrant gateways—Nashville, Tennessee; Portland, Oregon; and Lowell, Massachusetts—to participate in the federally funded Building the New American Community (BNAC) initiative as urban laboratories in which so-called New American communities of refugees and immigrants could be built from the ground up.[4]

What can be made of these changing geographies of immigration in the United States? What does it mean—theoretically, empirically, and methodologically—to have rapidly growing foreign-born communities in cities that have little, if any, contemporary experience with immigration? As these vignettes note, Nashville, Tennessee, is a key southern city whose daily dealings with such questions has garnered attention at local, regional, and national levels.[5] Tapping the growing streams of Latino men and women migrating to cities and towns across the U.S. South since the early 1990s, the Music City witnessed a 454 percent increase in its Hispanic population from 1990 to 2000; and all signs point to the continuation of this trend.[6] Latino migration to Nashville from both domestic and international locales has transformed parts of the city into Spanish-language districts and has changed the language of work at many hospitality, construction, and fast-food worksites.[7] In the process this migration has raised new questions about race, ethnicity, and cultural belonging in

Nashville and has problematized the racial binary that has long characterized the city.[8]

This emerging narrative of immigration and rapid community change is increasingly familiar across southern communities, but Nashville's version of it is more complex. Because of a small but politically visible refugee population, Nashville's "international community," as it is often described in public discourse, includes not only large numbers of Latino residents but also refugees from around the world. Nashville, thus, is learning to be part of the *nuevo* new South through a complex set of racial, linguistic, and ethnic politics and practices that address more than a homogenous Hispanic community.[9] Although primarily Mexican, Nashville's Latino population includes an established Cuban cohort, an active Colombian colony, and a growing Central American community. Its refugee population, too, is diverse, with one of the nation's largest Kurdish communities and groups from Sudan, Somalia, Bosnia, and elsewhere.[10] Despite this diversity within and between the different categories of recent migrants, refugees and Latinos are often joined through categories, such as "New Americans" and the "international" or "immigrant" community, which circulate throughout public discourse and policy in Nashville. In this way the multiple lines of difference between and within Nashville's so-called refugee and Latino populations are compressed into a unidimensional category of "internationals" that becomes legible through its difference from a native-born (and often presumably white) U.S. norm.

This chapter engages the processes through which this compression has taken place in Nashville's urban politics and public discourse and the complexities of new racial and ethnic configurations in New South cities like Nashville. I argue that refugee populations in southern cities must be included in the growing literature on the South's changing demographics, as refugees, though small in number, impact the changing racial formations and politics increasingly associated with Latino migration. To make this argument I review the general features of Latino migration to the South and to Nashville itself, situating refugee resettlements within these narratives. I then examine how the combination of small but politically visible refugee communities and large but politically less visible Latino communities has influenced the ways that Nashville has understood and addressed issues of racial and ethnic diversity, particularly through its social institutions and organizations. Susan Hardwick and James Meacham have recently suggested that the geographies of refugee resettlement in the United States have received only limited attention.[11] This chapter addresses that gap in geographic literatures by examining the politics of refugee resettlement, particularly in relation to Latino migration. Through an analysis of the social spaces and institutional contexts within which Latinos and refugees encounter each other in Nashville, it shows how the contours of the city's "international" community are produced, maintained, and contested through the daily practices of key civic and government organizations in particular. In doing so it argues for more critical attention from scholars to both interactions between Latino and refugee organizations and communities and the complexities and contradictions within New American communities across New South cities.

Music City, USA, with a Latino Beat

Although Latino, particularly Mexican, agricultural workers have been in some southern communities since the 1930s, the twentieth century's closing decades saw a new geography of Latino population growth that included rural and urban southern destinations.[12] Latino migration to parts of Georgia and North Carolina began in the late 1980s as a domestic migration of young Mexicans, primarily men, following the contours of economic growth from cities in Texas and California to locales across the South.[13] This domestic migration was rapidly joined—if not surpassed—by an international migration that came primarily from Mexico and soon included women and children. In a short time Latino migration to small towns in Georgia and North Carolina expanded into Tennessee, Alabama, and Arkansas and became a regional phenomenon whose impacts are only now being assessed.

Although Latino migration has received by far the most attention in discussions of southern communities' changing racial and ethnic demographics, Latino men and women are not the only new arrivals in the region. As the South increasingly goes global economically, populations in many southern communities are doing the same.[14] A number of recent studies have documented these linkages between growing ethnic and racial diversity in the South and global processes such as foreign direct investment by Asian and European investors and humanitarian flows of refugees.[15] During the 1980s Georgia experienced the nation's highest rate of increase in its non-English-speaking population at 113 percent; and this trend largely reflected the state's expanding refugee population.[16] In rural North Carolina the incorporation of Southeast Asian refugees and Guatemalan Mayans into the local economy has led the small town of Morganton "to think of itself as a southern town, but with a difference," as historian Leon Fink notes.[17]

The study on which this chapter draws its data set out to examine how Nashville, too, has become a southern city "with a difference."[18] It investigated the ways that Latino migration in particular has impacted understandings and practices of race, ethnicity, and cultural belonging across Nashville's public sphere and low-wage labor market. In the absence of a strong secondary literature, the study employed a variety of methodological approaches and data sources, including semistructured interviews with community leaders and representatives, attendance at organizational meetings and community forums for immigrant issues, review of newspaper coverage of immigrant and racial politics from the mid-1990s to the present, and analyses of census and economic data and documents on Nashville's foreign-born population.[19] Questioning the place of Latinos within Nashville's systems of racialized difference, the study examined how Nashville became a popular destination for Latino migrants in the late 1990s and how this migration had impacted racial formations, politics, and practices across the city. These two questions structured the interviews that comprised the central part of the study and provided a framework through which to investigate how and when Latino migration became a noticeable feature across Nashville and its social institutions, how Latinos had been drawn into the city's broader racial politics and relations, and what changes interviewees associated with the growth of Nashville's Latino population. From August 2002 to June 2003 interviews were conducted with approximately fifty key actors in Nashville's racial and immigrant politics—a group including Latino, white, and African American business and community leaders, activists and advocates, service providers, and social workers.[20]

Although this study was designed to analyze Nashville's changing racial politics vis-à-vis Latino migration, an unexpected theme emerged as I pushed further into interview material, field notes, city publications, and other sources. Across the study some discussions of Nashville's Latino population bled into discussions of Nashville's refugee communities, as questions of changing racial and immigrant politics, and questions about new demographics in the Music City, came to reference both Latinos and refugees, sometimes in contradictory ways. Some social-service providers, for example, discussed their daily adjustments to Nashville's new diversity in relation not only to newly arrived Mexican families but also to newly resettled Somali families. Community forums about Nashville's race relations addressed not only latent tensions between Latino residents and established black and white communities but also heightened scrutiny felt by Iraqi residents. Worksites that had recently turned to Latino workers to resolve low-wage labor shortages had relied on Southeast Asian refugees in the 1980s and Bosnian refugees in the 1990s. Because Latinos and refugees were often visibly marked as different from a native-born norm, both groups were framed as constituting the international community that distinguished Nashville's refugee and immigrant populations from its native-born population, which respondents referred to as "American." Although it was clear that Latino migration was impacting the black–white racial binary in Nashville, it was also clear that Latinos were institutionally and spatially overlapping with the city's refugee populations and, in the process, challenging more than a racial dichotomy.

The remainder of this chapter examines these spatial and discursive overlaps between Latinos and refugees in Nashville and their effects on emerging narratives of race, ethnicity, and belonging.

Relocating Nashville

Throughout the 1990s Nashville, like many emerging immigrant gateways, saw dramatic population growth and economic expansion.[21] As Middle Tennessee's economic geography shifted from a light-manufacturing base around Nashville to a service economy centered on the city, population growth followed the opposite trend, generating rapid residential and urban sprawl.[22] From the mid-1990s onward the concomitant growth of a service economy in Nashville and the demand for residential and commercial construction in adjacent counties created jobs that were increasingly filled by Latino workers. By 2000, remarked Mike Davis, "even Nashville ha[d] a new *sonido*," one that, in parts of the city, was increasingly Latin in rhythm and rhyme.[23]

Nashville's new *sonido* developed in the context of refugee resettlements that began in the early 1960s, when Operation Peter Pan quietly brought a small number of Cuban children and families to Nashville.[24] The emergence of the modern U.S. refugee resettlement program in the early 1980s, however, made Nashville a more popular relocation site; and the growing size of its refugee communities, then composed of Southeast Asians, made refugees more visible across parts of the city. Through this larger resettlement that marked a more notable ethnic and cultural difference from a white norm, Nashville was drawn into what one state government director involved with refugee resettlement in the city called the "unwritten southern strategy" of moving refugees from "impacted" northeastern cities with lower refugee retention rates and stiffer job competition into "second-tier" southern cities like Nashville with stronger economies and right-to-work legislation.[25] Through a national "scatter system" of refugee resettlement, Nashville and other southern cities emerged as popular refugee relocation sites.[26]

By the 1990s Nashville's reputation as a successful refugee relocation site was established. From 1990 to 1994 it outpaced the national average in the share of foreign-born residents in its total population; and this gap widened between 1995 and 2000.[27] In the late 1990s Nashville was chosen by the ORR as one of four "preferred communities" in the United States to receive special federal monies for refugee relocation and was subsequently awarded targeted federal assistance for the resettlement of large numbers of Kurds from the first Gulf

War. By this time the pattern for refugees arriving in Nashville had shifted from large numbers from one place to smaller groups from various global hot spots, reflecting national trends.[28] Although the events of September 11, 2001, radically changed the climate of refugee resettlement and national quotas have not yet matched levels prior to that date, refugees continue to arrive in Nashville from Sudan, Somalia, and Iran, making the politics and cultural terrain of the city's international community increasingly intricate.[29]

As Nashville's visibility as a relocation site increased, particularly among national and federal agencies, the city itself began to recognize the complex ethnic, racial, religious, and national configurations that contoured its refugee population. This recognition is evident in the institutional arrangements the city created to address refugee populations during the late 1990s. Refugees in Nashville, as elsewhere around the United States, are initially sponsored by voluntary agencies, such as World Relief and Catholic Charities, which are responsible for immediate residential and occupational establishment.[30] In Nashville, however, the majority of refugee services were handled until 2005 through Nashville–Davidson County's Metro Refugee Services Program (MRSP), the only refugee program in the United States operated by a local government. Although voluntary agencies provide immediate aid to refugees arriving in the city, from the mid-1990s until 2005 changes to the structure of metro government, MRSP had a substantial role in long-term adjustment strategies for refugees. In particular MRSP has reworked a multiorganizational system in which individual voluntary agencies contracted with the state of Tennessee to resettle refugees into a unified system in which MRSP itself received close to 80 percent of the state's total funding for refugee resettlement in Tennessee, despite its sole focus on Nashville's Davidson County.

The impacts of this structural difference on refugees' daily experiences in Nashville have yet to be examined, but other studies point to the state's influence on refugee community politics and practices at the local scale.[31] In Georgia, for example, the formalization and institutionalization of refugee resettlement through the state Office of Refugee Resettlement has reportedly "encouraged all refugee groups to forget their differences and work towards the common goal of refugee resettlement."[32] In Nashville the location of refugee resettlement services within local government—rather than solely within civil society—changed the linkages among refugee communities, local government, and advocacy organizations, even after metro government withdrew from direct service provision for refugees. Perhaps most importantly, official connections between the local government and refugee resettlement in Nashville raised the visibility of refugee populations beyond what their economic or demographic impacts could otherwise generate. This organized structure for handling refugee issues in Nashville contrasts sharply with the city's piecemeal system in place to deal with immigrant, particularly Latino, populations. This contrast becomes even starker when each community's actual size is considered. Figures from the Tennessee Department of Human Services show that 4,615 refugees were relocated to the Nashville metropolitan statistical area (MSA) from January 1996 to June 2005, with the great majority (4,381) resettled in Davidson County. Although these numbers do not include asylum seekers or secondary migrants from other U.S. states—both of which potentially constitute a large number because of Nashville's strong labor market and established refugee communities—this official refugee population pales in comparison to Nashville's Latino population, which numbers somewhere between official figures of 50,000 and community estimates of 200,000.[33]

Despite the relatively small size of Nashville's refugee communities, refugees in the city have developed a presence in public discussions and discourse that partially compensates for their more limited numeric and economic impact. Through a combination of the legal status refugees hold, the social capital and political activism they bring from home communities, and the institutionalized presence refugee resettlement has commanded as part of local government, refugees generate a visibility in Nashville's urban politics and social-service networks that surpasses their demographic or economic footprint. As we see below, refugee communities have garnered a place in Nashville's public sphere, one that the growing presence of Latinos simultaneously enhances and complicates.

Nashville's "Internationals"

Although Latinos and refugees have different legal standings, reach Nashville along different migration paths, and create different economic ripples across the city, the two groups are often fused in discussions of Nashville's international community. In a series of listening forums on racial justice in 2003, for example, sessions on race and diversity were organized into discussions of public schools, the international and immigrant communities, the business community, and the inner city, schematically representing the institutional cartographies of race, ethnicity, and nationality in Nashville.[34] That same year, an immigrant community assessment commissioned by Nashville–Davidson County's metro government was published.[35] Although its focus groups included both refugee and immigrant (that is, non-Latino and Latino, respectively) participants, its policy recommendations, as well as its overall findings, grouped the two into one constituency whose needs could be addressed through uniform policy recommendations.[36] Through such practices, Latinos and refugees—groups whose differences from Nashville's existing community are embodied in appearance, language, culture, and other ascriptives—are imbricated within ideas about the international or immigrant community circulating in public discourse.

This overlap is particularly evident in the public sphere, where the two components of Nashville's international community frequently share the stage in nonprofit organizations. The Task Force on Refugees and Immigrants (TFRI), for instance, a nongovernmental offshoot of a mayor's advisory committee from the late 1980s, provides a community forum for refugee and immigrant community leaders and advocates. Through monthly meetings, e-mail alerts, and newsletters, TFRI acts as an information clearinghouse for Nashville's international community. Within it refugee and Latino community representatives map out positions on topics such as racial and ethnic profiling and social-service provision, although the representation of refugee communities is far greater among attendees. Particularly through its meetings, TFRI acts as an unofficial access point to Nashville's foreign-born communities, creating an international community that can be reached and dealt with officially.

Similar processes are at work in the Tennessee Immigrant and Refugee Rights Coalition (TIRRC). Created in 2001, TIRRC describes itself as "a state-wide, immigrant and refugee-led collaboration" with a "mission . . . to empower and unify grassroots immigrant leaders in Tennessee to develop a unified voice, defend their rights, and create an atmosphere in which they are viewed as positive contributors to the state."[37] Headquartered in Nashville, TIRRC is composed of more than twenty-five immigrant groups across Tennessee and is unique in its statewide focus, as well as its combination of immigrant and refugee populations. Joining immigrants and refugees across the state through political lobbying and activism, TIRRC addresses the needs of Latinos and refugees through a united political and social front. It has brought refugees and Latinos together in public discussions of diversity and discrimination in Nashville and has begun to speak for an immigrant community united at least in public discourse and campaigns.[38]

Such institutional overlaps between Latinos and refugees have generated opportunities to lobby for increased political visibility and recognition for Nashville's international community. At the same time however, muted tensions have sometimes arisen between community leaders over which segment of the city's foreign-born will be more visible and therefore better able to secure scarce public resources. According to one former state director involved with refugees, some workers in refugee agencies fear that in the face of the "sheer number of Latinos," refugees might "get lost in the shuffle." Other persons involved with refugees in Nashville, however, felt just the opposite, believing that Latinos, through their numbers, raise the visibility of all ethnic groups, since being aware of Hispanics can translate into being aware of other foreign-born groups. "Thanks to the Hispanic influence," remarked one agency director, all ethnic groups are "catching the attention" of key political figures in Nashville.

These tensions over access to public visibility and representation can be seen in the Nashville New Americans Coalition (NNAC). In 2001 Nashville, along with Portland, Oregon, and Lowell, Massachusetts, was selected to participate in the Building the New American Community initiative funded largely by the ORR. This three-year initiative was jointly sponsored by the National Conference of State legislatures, the Migration Policy Institute, the National Immigration Forum, the Southeast Asia Resource Action Center, and the Urban Institute and focused on midsized cities that experienced relatively little recent immigration. Framing integration as a two-way process between refugee/immigrant and receiving communities, the NNAC was an experiment in public–private partnership designed to "foster the successful integration of refugees and immigrants at a community level."[39] It combined federal, state, and local support with academic and community research to develop local integration plans and address the needs of foreign-born communities.[40]

Because the Nashville Area Chamber of Commerce played a leading role in the coalition, NNAC activities were more strongly oriented toward workforce and business development than those in Lowell or Portland.[41] In accordance with the goals of the Building the New American Community initiative itself, the NNAC focused on building leadership capacity within refugee and immigrant communities and maintained a strong focus on civic participation.[42] As its name suggests, the NNAC devoted much attention to the production of what it referred to as New Americans, a category that linked Nashville's foreign-born and existing communities by attempting to transform the former into the latter through civic training. Determining where Latinos fit within the New American category, however, has been a delicate and often tense process of placing a group that is both domestic and foreign born, both immigrant and citizen, within a system predicated on being one or the other.

Although the NNAC included refugee and immigrant organizations in its institutional structure and plan of action, in reality its initiatives, such as training refugees and immigrants to serve on boards of directors and publishing guides for Nashville employers on "the international workforce," were directed almost exclusively at refugees.[43] This orientation toward refugee-serving organizations caused tensions across the three cities associated with the Building the New American Community initiative; and in Nashville, some NNAC leaders admitted that the coalition's lack of attention to Latinos put Latino community leaders and organizations "on edge and at odds."[44] Although BNAC's final report attributed these tensions to the "false division" between refugees and "other newcomer groups" created by funding structures, they also arose, I argue, because Latinos sit uneasily within the New American category itself.[45] Through the NNAC's focus on civic participation, Nashville's international community has been understood as a political and social reservoir of future citizens, or New Americans, that many Latinos can only partially join because of issues of legal documentation and different understandings of their place as transnational residents of Nashville.[46]

In this way, although refugees and Latinos are frequently lumped together within discussions of Nashville's international community, the two groups face different sets of issues and have markedly different levels of access to the state and its resources. Although this institutional separation of Latino and refugee populations partially reflects the fact that less than 1 percent of refugees in Nashville are Hispanic, it is primarily reproduced and sustained by legal status.[47] Because MRSP and voluntary agencies associated with refugee resettlement deal exclusively with documented refugees, the orientation programs and job-placement assistance available to refugees have no formal counterpart for Latinos, who, in the words of one Latina advocate in Nashville, operate in "extralegal" spaces within federal immigration policy. Through this division, as well as more informal ones, Latinos coming to Nashville and refugees relocated to the city are channeled into different social-service networks and toward different organizations.

These institutional differences aside, Latinos and refugees do meet in two main spaces outside the public sphere: urban neighborhoods and the local labor market. Because both Latinos and refugees often need affordable housing with flexible leases, both groups are drawn to and steered toward the same swaths of southeast Nashville, where housing costs are more reasonable and the available housing stock includes many rental units.[48] Through this residential overlap, apartment complexes and neighborhoods previously used by agencies to settle refugees are increasingly home to newly arrived Latinos. Recent assessments of Nashville's MSA, for example, note that in southeast Nashville, where both Latinos and refugees are clustered, "the foreign-born populations represent all world regions and are not dominated by one particular group."[49]

Although there is an overlooked scalar factor at work in this claim (that is, at the scale of the city block or apartment complex, a microgeography of ethnic, racial, and linguistic segregation may be apparent), this geography of immigrant and refugee settlement has important implications not only for how and where ethnic and racial diversity becomes visible in Nashville but also for how broader social relations are negotiated in the city. Through this uneven residential geography of race and ethnicity, immigrants and refugees live in neighborhoods with striking levels of ethnic diversity, while other areas in

Nashville remain racially homogenous.[50] Although the city's urban landscape becomes relatively integrated during the day when its hidden spaces of labor in hotel basements and fast-food kitchens fill with a multicultural workforce, the situation changes at night when segregated residential geographies once again materialize and southeast Nashville becomes a gathering place for the city's foreign-born population.[51]

In addition to encounters between refugees and Latinos on neighborhood street corners and in area grocery stores—encounters that are somewhat limited by microgeographies of ethnicity, race, and language—Latinos and refugees frequently meet in line for applications at the same low-wage workplaces. Nashville's local labor market, thus, operates as another site where Latinos and refugees come into contact and, in some cases, competition. Particularly in the search for low-wage employment, the availability of Latino workers, according to one director of refugee resettlement, "can be detrimental" to refugees, especially because most voluntary agencies measure success in terms of refugee "employability."[52] At some local worksites it has reportedly become "difficult to get anyone other than Hispanics hired." In this way Latinos and refugees are pitted against each other as pools of desirable, docile workers for low-paying jobs, which in turn sharpens divisions between Latino and refugee organizations. Particularly in the midst of mid-1990s immigration raids across Middle Tennessee, Latino workers as a group were often framed in Nashville as "unsafe" because of the legal consequences employers faced by hiring undocumented workers.[53] Although Latinos continued to be hired across the city, resettlement agency workers, in their efforts to find jobs for refugees, played the card of "dangerous" undocumented Latinos to "sell" the idea of hiring refugees to local employers. Through the events and aftermath of September 11, 2001, however, the rhetoric concerning Latinos and refugees has largely reversed.[54] Post–September 11, refugees, particularly those from the Middle East, have become "unsafe" foreign-born employees and Latinos by default have become "safe" options in Nashville, in the terminology of study respondents. As one director involved with refugees noted, the "positive" of working with documented refugees in Nashville has evaporated, and the concern is no longer about having too many Hispanics. Through this "displaced hatred," anti-immigrant sentiment previously directed toward Latinos has somewhat abated; and a new imaginative geography of nativist sentiment has been produced.[55]

A recent report commissioned by Nashville's Human Relations Commission found that Nashville "residents, governmental, and nongovernmental institutions, and corporate entities" need greater understanding "of the amorphous nature of what diversity is, what diversity means, and the potential impacts it has for this community."[56] The amorphous nature of diversity in Nashville is the focus of this chapter, which, in the absence of a secondary literature on this theme, lays out a conceptual framework through which to engage this new aspect of New South cities. Through a discussion of the institutional and spatial contexts within which Latinos and refugees in Nashville are brought together, I argue that the interactions and tensions associated with such encounters within Nashville's international community complicate emerging dialogues about immigration, race, and cultural belonging across new immigrant destinations. Although Latino migration is undeniably contesting the ability of a racial dichotomy to account for all that is transpiring within southern cities, a dualistic system of racialized difference, at least in Nashville, also operates in relation to a system of difference organized along lines of nativity. Latinos, by occupying an ambiguous place within Nashville's understandings of race and by occupying an uneasy position in the city's definition of its international population, call into question conceptualizations and practices of race, ethnicity, and cultural belonging. Somewhere outside the categories black, white, and even New American but somewhere within both the foreign-born and the domestic-born populations, Latino residents are forcing a new envisioning of difference in the Music City.

In the midst of these changes, refugee populations that predate the onset of Latino migration are grappling with living in southern cities with little recent immigration experience and in a wider post–September 11 context with fluctuating ideas about citizenship, race, and ethnicity.[57] Although the politics of refugee resettlement in southern cities have not received substantial attention, the presence of refugee communities in those cities challenges not only the racial binary so powerful across the South but also the equation of being "foreign" with being Latino.[58] Refugees in southern cities, I suggest, encounter a racial and cultural terrain whose contours are not equipped to include them and whose transformations to accommodate Latinos may still leave them somewhere outside the boundaries of community.

Questions about changing racial and immigrant politics in southern cities merit further study, and refugee communities must have a place in such research. In one of the only studies of refugee communities in southern U.S. cities, Deborah Duchon suggests that Hmong refugees relocated to Atlanta adjusted more successfully than those relocated to California.[59] This kind of observation points to the need to examine the place-specific experiences of refugee resettlement across U.S. cities and towns, particularly new destinations in the South and Midwest.[60] In places like Nashville the most recent linkages between southern places and other parts of the world are raising new questions about race and ethnicity and demanding new theoretical frameworks for understanding them.

Until those frameworks can account for challenges not only to a racial binary but also to notions of citizenship and cultural belonging, the "difference" that new southern destinations may chart in the cartographies and conceptions of immigrant and refugee migrations will remain unclear.

Notes

This article first appeared in slightly different form in *Social and Cultural Geography* 7, no. 3 (2006): 421–35, and is reprinted here by permission of the journal and its publisher, Taylor & Francis Ltd., www.tandf.co.uk/journals.

I thank Mary Anglin, Jennifer Hyndman, John Paul Jones III, Brian Rich, Susan Roberts, and Rich Schein for their input on this research. Ishan Ashutosh provided valuable assistance in the final stages of this article as well. I am particularly grateful for the helpful comments provided by editor Michael Brown and three anonymous reviewers. Earlier versions of this article were presented at the 2004 Urban History Conference in Milwaukee, Wisconsin. The insight of discussant Margo Anderson, as well as comments from audience members, greatly improved my arguments. This material is based on work supported by the National Science Foundation under grant no. 0302502, the Association of American Geographers, and the Graduate School at the University of Kentucky.

1. Audrey Singer, *The Rise of New Immigrant Gateways*, Living Cities Census Series (Washington, D.C.: Brookings Institution, 2004).

2. Dowell Myers, John Pitkin, and Julie Park, *California's Immigrants Turn the Corner*, Urban Initiative Policy Brief (Los Angeles: University of Southern California, 2004), 2.

3. Carol Schmid, "Immigration and Asian and Hispanic Minorities in the New South: An Exploration of History, Attitudes, and Demographic Trends," *Sociological Spectrum* 23 (2003): 139–57.

4. Brian K. Ray and Ann Morse, *Building the New American Community: Newcomer Integration and Inclusion Experiences in Non-traditional Gateway Cities*, sponsored by the Office of Refugee Resettlement (Washington, D.C.: Migration Policy Institute, 2004).

5. Daniel B. Cornfield, Angela Arzubiaga, Rhonda BeLue, Susan L. Brooks, Tony N. Brown, Oscar Miller, Douglas D. Perkins, Peggy A. Thoits, and Lynn S. Walker,. *Final Report of the Immigrant Community Assessment*, prepared under contract for the Metropolitan Government of Nashville and Davidson County, Tennessee, 2003; Ray and Morse, *Building the New American Community.*

6. On Latino immigration to the South see Altha J. Cravey, "Latino Labor and Poultry Production in Rural North Carolina," *Southeastern Geographer* 37 (1997): 295–300; Altha J. Cravey, "Toque una ranchera, por favor," *Antipode* 35 (2003): 603–21; Karen D. Johnson-Webb, "Employer Recruitment and Hispanic Labor Migration: North Carolina Urban Areas at the End of the Millennium," *Professional Geographer* 54 (2002): 406–21; Marcela Mendoza, David H. Ciscel, and Barbara E. Smith, "El impacto de los inmigrantes latinos en la economía de Memphis, Tennessee," *Revista de Estudios Migratorios Latinoamericanos* 46 (2000): 659–75; Raymond A. Mohl, "Globalization and the *Nuevo*

New South," *Journal of American Ethnic History* 22, no. 4 (2003): 31–66; Arthur D. Murphy, Colleen Blanchard, and Jennifer A. Hill, eds., *Latino Workers in the Contemporary South* (Athens: University of Georgia Press, 2001); Jamie Winders, "Changing Politics of Race and Region: Latino Migration to the U.S. South," *Progress in Human Geography* 29 (2005): 683–99.

7. Mike Davis, *Magical Urbanism: Latinos Reinvent the US City* (London: Verso, 2000).

8. Bobby L. Lovett, *The African-American History of Nashville, Tennessee, 1780–1930: Elites and Dilemmas* (Fayetteville: University of Arkansas Press, 1999).

9. Mohl, "Globalization and the *Nuevo* New South."

10. Ray and Morse, *Building the New American Community*.

11. Susan W. Hardwick and James E. Meacham, "Heterolocalism, Networks of Ethnicity, and Refugee Communities in the Pacific Northwest: The Portland Story," *Professional Geographer* 57 (2005): 539–57.

12. Barbara Ellen Smith, *The New Latino South: An Introduction* (Memphis, Tenn.: Center for Research on Women at the University of Memphis, the Highlander Research and Education Center, and the Southern Regional Council, 2001); "The Tennessean Illegal Worker Crackdowns Near," *Tennessean*, 3 Oct. 1995, 4B.

13. Jorge Durand, Douglas S. Massey, and Fernando Charvet, "The Changing Geography of Mexican Immigration to the United States: 1910–1996," *Social Science Quarterly* 81, no. 1 (2000): 1–15; Leon Fink, *The Maya of Morganton: Work and Community in the Nuevo New South* (Chapel Hill: University of North Carolina Press, 2003); Rogelio Saenz, Katharine M. Donato, Lourdes Gouveia, and Cruz Torres, "Latinos in the South: A Glimpse of Ongoing Trends and Research," *Southern Rural Sociology* 19, no. 1 (2003): 1–19. Particularly in rural areas, employer recruitment practices also strongly contributed to this new geography of Latino migration and settlement. See Cravey, "Latino Labor and Poultry Production"; Karen D. Johnson-Webb, *Recruiting Hispanic Labor: Immigrants in Non-traditional Areas* (New York: LFB Scholarly Publishing, 2003); William Kandel and Emilio A. Parrado, "Hispanics in the American South and the Transformation of the Poultry Industry," in *Hispanic Spaces, Latino Places: Community and Cultural Diversity in Contemporary America*, ed. Daniel Arreola (Austin: University of Texas Press, 2004), 255–76.

14. James C. Cobb, "Beyond the 'Y'all Wall': The American South Goes Global," in *Globalization and the American South*, ed. James C. Cobb and William Stueck (Athens: University of Georgia Press, 2005), 1–18.

15. On foreign investment see Rebecca J. Dameron and Arthur D. Murphy. "An International City Too Busy to Hate? Social and Cultural Change in Atlanta: 1970–1995," *Urban Anthropology* 26, no. 1 (1997): 43–69; Sayrui Guthrie-Shimizu, "From Southeast Asia to the American Southeast: Japanese Business Meets the Sun Belt South," in Cobb and Stueck, *Globalization and the American South*, 135–63; David M. Reimers, "Asian Immigrants in the South, in ibid., 100–134.

On refugees see Deborah A. Duchon, "Home Is Where You Make It: Hmong Refugees in Georgia," *Urban Anthropology* 26, no. 1 (1997): 71–92; James R. Elliott and Marcel

Ionescu, "Postwar Immigration to the Deep South Triad: What Can a Peripheral Region Tell Us about Immigrant Settlement and Employment?" *Sociological Spectrum* 23 (2003): 159–80.

16. Dameron and Murphy, "International City Too Busy to Hate?" Elliott and Ionescu, "Postwar Immigration to the Deep South Triad."

17. Fink, *Maya of Morganton*, 10.

18. Jamie Winders, "(Re)working the U.S. South: Latino Migration and the Politics of Race and Work in Nashville, Tennessee," Ph.D. diss., Department of Geography, University of Kentucky, Lexington, 2004. Throughout the chapter, unsourced quotations are from this work.

19. The majority of interviews in this study were not tape recorded, both because fieldwork was conducted in an immediate post–September 11, 2001, context in the midst of growing anti-immigrant sentiment and because many participants, particularly those from governmental agencies, were not comfortable being recorded. For these reasons I relied primarily on note taking during and after interviews and in this chapter, more frequently paraphrase interview content than quote extensively from interview transcripts. A portion of the study not discussed here consisted of case studies of workplaces that had recently transitioned toward Latino labor and a multicultural workforce.

20. Wrap-up interviews and conversations concerning this chapter also took place in July 2005.

21. Singer, *Rise of New Immigrant Gateways*.

22. Jamie Winders, "Placing Latinos in the Music City: Latino Migration and Urban Politics in Nashville, Tennessee," in *Latinos in the New South: Transformations of Place*, ed. Heather A. Smith and Owen J. Furuseth (Burlington, Vt.: Ashgate Publishing, 2006), 167–90. Albert E. DePrince Jr. and Kathleen Vinlove, "Supply Shocks, Confidence, and the State of the Economy," *Midstate Economic Indicators* 11, no. 3 (2001): 1–4; Ellis A. Eff and Emel C. Eff, "Sprawl-inducing Migration in Tennessee: The Impact of Income and Price Differentials," *Tennessee Housing Outlook* 5, no. 1 (2002): 14–17.

23. Davis, *Magical Urbanism*, 4.

24. Operation Peter (or Pedro) Pan was the large-scale airlift of children from Cuba to the United States after Fidel Castro assumed power in Cuba in 1959. Coordinated by what would become Catholic Charities, a leading refugee resettlement agency in the United States, the operation ran from 1960 to 1962 and transported more than 14,000 Cuban children. Many children were eventually reunited with their families in the United States.

25. Carole E. Hill, "Contemporary Issues in Anthropological Studies of the American South," in *Cultural Diversity in the U.S. South: Anthropological Contributions to a Region in Transition*, ed. Carole E. Hill and Patricia D. Beaver (Athens: University of Georgia Press, 1998), 12–33.

26. Duchon, "Home Is Where You Make It," 85.

27. Katherine Lotspeich, Michael Fix, Jason Ost, and Dan Perez-Lopez, *A Profile of the Foreign-born in the Nashville Economic Market: The Urban Institute for the Building the New American Community Project* (Washington, D.C.: Urban Institute, 2003), 5.

28. David Martin, "The US Refugee Program in Transition," *Migration Information Source* (Washington, D.C.: Migration Policy Institute, 1 May 2005).

29. Cornfield et al., *Final Report of the Immigrant Community Assessment*. On pre–September 2001 quotas see Martin, "US Refugee Program in Transition."

30. Nawyn, "Faithfully Providing Refuge"; Erin Patrick, "The US Refugee Resettlement Program," *Migration Information Source* (Washington, D.C.: Migration Policy Institute, 1 June 2004).

31. Nawyn, "Faithfully Providing Refuge: The Role of Religious Organizations in Refugee Assistance and Advocacy," Working Paper 115, San Diego: Center for Comparative Immigration Studies, University of California, 2005.

32. Dameron and Murphy, "International City Too Busy to Hate?" 59.

33. These numbers can be situated within Davidson County's overall population of just over half a million residents, 26 percent of whom are African American. In Nashville's wider MSA there are 1.25 million residents, 15 percent of whom are African American.

34. B. N. Williamson, "Human Relations Commission: Campaign to Promote Racial Justice Listening Forums," *Series Report* (Nashville, Tenn.: Human Relations Commission, 2003).

35. Cornfield et al., *Final Report of the Immigrant Community Assessment*.

36. Within the study, 74 percent of participants were refugees (ibid.), another indication of the institutional visibility of Nashville's relatively small refugee population.

37. Tennessee Immigrant and Refugee Rights Coalition, http://www.tnimmigrant.org/, accessed 22 July 2005.

38. It should be noted that these organizations with a dual focus on immigrants and refugees are accompanied by several Latino organizations, including socially oriented nonprofit organizations and multiple Hispanic chambers of commerce.

39. Ray and Morse, *Building the New American Community*, ii.

40. Lotspeich, Fix, Ost, and Perez-Lopez, *Profile of the Foreign-born in the Nashville Economic Market*, 5.

41. Ray and Morse, *Building the New American Community*.

42. Ibid.

43. Ibid. This orientation reflects the fact that, like voluntary agencies (Nawyn, "Faithfully Providing Refuge"), the NNAC could only fund refugee-focused organizations (Ray and Morse, *Building the New American Community*).

44. Ray and Morse, *Building the New American Community*. African American community leaders, too, were largely left out of NNAC activities, despite their experience with many overall goals of the initiative (ibid.).

45. Ibid., 53.

46. Linda Basch, Nina Glick-Schiller, and Cristina Blanc-Szanton, *Nations Unbound: Transnational Projects, Postcolonial Predicaments, and Deterritorialized Nation-states* (Langhorne, Pa.: Gordon & Breach, 1995); Allison Mountz and Richard A. Wright, "Daily Life in the Transnational Migrant Community of San Agustín, Oaxaca, and Poughkeepsie, New York," *Diaspora* 5 (1996): 403–28; Roger Rouse, "Mexican Migration and the Social Space of Postmodernism," *Diaspora* 1 (1991): 8–23.

47. This percentage reflects national trends. Since 1975, fewer than 80,000 refugees from Latin America and the Caribbean have been resettled in the United States; of these 80,000, more than 50,000 were Cuban, http://www.state.gov/g/prm/rls/fs/2004/28211pf.htm, accessed 23 Jan. 2004.

48. Hardwick and Meacham, "Heterolocalism, Networks of Ethnicity."

49. Lotspeich, Fix, Ost, and Perez-Lopez, *Profile of the Foreign-born in the Nashville Economic Market*, 7.

50. Cornfield et al., *Final Report of the Immigrant Community Assessment*.

51. Rebecca Dameron and Arthur Murphy have documented a similar pattern in Atlanta, Georgia, where "new immigrants have built an enclave economy based not on distinct ethnic groups, but on the 'other' Atlanta used to differentiate those who do not fit into the categories of black and white" ("International City Too Busy to Hate?" 55). What they note, however, is an economic entity is, at least in Nashville, also a spatial entity that stretches across parts of the city.

52. Nawyn, "Faithfully Providing Refuge."

53. P. Donsky, "Immigration Arrests 72 Workers," *Tennessean*, 23 May 1997, 1B+; L. A. Moore, "Workers Arrested Yesterday Filled a Need, Employers Say," *Tennessean*, 26 Sept. 1996, 1A+; "Tennessean Illegal Worker Crackdowns Near," 4B.

54. Ray and Morse, *Building the New American Community*.

55. Nawyn, "Faithfully Providing Refuge." It should be noted that anti-immigrant sentiment toward Latinos and Latinas is again growing.

56. Williamson, "Human Relations Commission," 3.

57. Inderpal Grewal, "Transnational America: Race, Gender and Citizenship after 9/11," *Social Identities* 9 (2003): 535–61.

58. Duchon, "Home Is Where You Make It," 85; Fink, *Maya of Morganton*, 10.

59. Duchon, "Home Is Where You Make It."

60. Katherine Fennelly and Nicole Palasz, "English Language Proficiency of Immigrants and Refugees in the Twin Cities Metropolitan Area," *International Migration* 41, no. 5 (2003): 93–125.

CHAPTER NINE

Popular Attitudes and Public Policies

Southern Responses to Latino Immigration

ELAINE LACY AND MARY E. ODEM

In the spring of 2006 millions of Latino immigrants and their supporters across the United States engaged in peaceful marches protesting the U.S. House of Representative passage of HR 4437, a bill that included enforcement-only provisions and criminalized assistance to undocumented immigrants. Thousands of protestors marched in cities throughout the South, some carrying placards with messages such as those in Columbia, South Carolina: "We clean your hotels," "Civil rights for immigrants," and "Destroy the border: No one is illegal." In Jackson, Mississippi, demonstrators sang "We Shall Overcome" in Spanish, evoking comparisons to marches led by Martin Luther King Jr. decades earlier. In North Carolina organizers urged immigrants to engage in an economic boycott. One Latina leader in Charlotte, North Carolina, said, "If you need people to do the work, to buy, then give them a legal channel to get here."[1] Atlanta's April 10 march drew fifty thousand people, making it one of the largest demonstrations for social justice in the South since the civil rights era. Protestors in Atlanta and other cities across the Southeast criticized proposed state and federal legislation that would deny unauthorized immigrants access to employment and public benefits and would enlist state and local police in enforcing federal immigration laws, among other punitive measures.[2]

As was the case in other regions of the United States, these large, well-organized immigrant rallies heightened southerners' awareness of the growing Latino population in the Southeast, and further polarized the debate over immigration and immigration legislation reform. While some southerners stress the benefits this new immigrant cohort bring to the region, especially in terms of their high productivity and willingness to work for wages that allow employers to remain competitive, others portray Latino immigrants as "illegals" who take jobs from natives, depress wages, burden taxpayers, increase crime rates, and pose a threat to national unity and regional identity.

The failure of the U.S. Congress to enact immigration legislation reform in 2006 and 2007 led to pressures on state and local officials across the Southeast to pass laws and ordinances aimed at limiting undocumented immigrants' access to jobs, social services, housing, and education, among other measures. The surge of Latino immigrants to the region also has become fodder for a growing number of hate groups in the South, including a revitalized Ku Klux Klan. At the same time a number of churches and outreach organizations have taken on advocacy roles to protect immigrants' rights. By the time presidential primaries were taking place in early 2008, public attitudes toward immigrants and Latino immigrants in particular had become so emotional that immigration reform was the most important campaign issue for most voters in the Southeast.[3]

Even though nativist (anti-immigrant) sentiment reemerged in traditional immigrant-receiving areas in the United States—including California, Illinois, New York, and Texas—in the 1980s, it has only recently appeared in the Southeast. The scant attention given new immigrants in the region during the 1990s tended to be positive, more often than not depicting the newcomers as potentially transient workers who benefitted the area in various ways. For example, a 1998 series of newspaper articles on Latinos in South Carolina described the comings and goings of Mexican immigrants to the state, quoted employers who extolled their work habits, and described community efforts to integrate the new residents, including English- and Spanish-language classes offered in some areas. That same year, an Atlanta newspaper featured a story about Latino newcomers in Dalton, Georgia, that included the statement, "Because [Latino workers] are so important to the economy, business owners and elected officials are working hard to help the newcomers adjust to Dalton and Dalton to them."[4]

By the early twenty-first century, however, attitudes toward the newcomers had hardened. A number of factors contributed to growing anti-immigrant sentiment in the South, among them the September 11, 2001, attacks, deteriorating economic conditions in the region, the rapid growth rate of Latino immigrant numbers (and thus their increased visibility), and increased national attention to undocumented immigration.

The effects of the 2001 attacks in coloring public perceptions of the foreign born and in increased determination to secure U.S. borders have been well documented. National public opinion polls taken after September 11 revealed a growing hostility toward immigrants, particularly the unauthorized.[5] Added to these concerns is the national economic downturn. After two decades of economic growth, job security declined in the South by 2005, and by the third quarter of 2007 fewer jobs were created than in any period since 2003.[6] A number of studies have shown that negative attitudes toward immigrants increase during periods of economic recession and when individuals or groups feel economically threatened, and the Southeast was no exception.[7] As economic conditions worsened in late 2007 and early 2008, Internet blogs and letters to newspaper editors began to include charges that immigrants were contributing to the economic decline.

The heated national discussion over immigration reform in Congress in recent years has brought a heightened awareness of immigration and contributed to the polarization of attitudes towards Latino immigrants in the Southeast. The national media's attention to unauthorized immigration picked up steam in the early twenty-first century, and some pundits' anti-immigrant rhetoric reached such a pitch that in early 2008 the National Council of La Raza, the largest civil rights organization for Latinos in the country, asked CNN, MSNBC, and Fox News to stop providing a forum for hate speech.[8]

This chapter examines popular attitudes toward and perceptions of Latino immigrants in the Southeast, as well as local and state governments' responses. The chapter's focus is Georgia and the Carolinas, three of a handful of U.S. states that have experienced the most rapidly growing Latino population in recent years. The reaction to Latino immigration in the three states underscores southerners' concerns over a variety of issues related to immigration, and reveals a resistance to social and cultural change in a region that is accustomed to black-white society and where "southern" identity remains strong, especially in smaller communities and rural areas where many immigrants have settled.

Popular Responses to Latino Newcomers

Immediately after the April 2006 immigrant rallies in the state, a Greenville, South Carolina, woman called a local newspaper to complain about the "illegal" immigrants who had demonstrated on the streets of her city. The caller, who resided in the county with the largest number of Latino immigrants in the state, said that what bothered her about the public protest was not that the demonstrators were Latinos: it was how they got here. Her biggest worry, she said, was that terrorists could take advantage of "the looseness of our border with Mexico."[9] The caller expressed her fear that others around the world who won't want to wait for legal permission to enter the United States could do so via that border.[10]

Since September 11, 2001, concerns over national security have shaped southerners' attitudes toward all immigrants, but the issue that most often vexes the native-born population is Latino immigrants' legal residency status. In letters to newspapers, op-ed pieces, public meetings, radio talk shows, Internet blogs, on-line chat rooms, and elsewhere, residents of the Southeast have linked immigrants' legal standing to complicity in regional economic and social ills. The list of charges against them usually includes the following: they are here without authorization and therefore are criminals; they are a drain on the economy due to the additional burdens they place on education and health care providers, law enforcement, and social services; they don't pay taxes; they increase crime rates; they take jobs that should go to U.S. citizens; they depress wages; and they pose a threat to U.S. or regional culture and values. While those who harbor such sentiments generally say their real objection is to "illegal aliens," many of their charges are aimed at *all* Latino immigrants.

Some of the anti-immigrant rhetoric, especially in Internet blogs and chat rooms where one's anonymity is protected, is clearly extreme. Extremist rhetoric is also utilized by the growing number of "hate" groups that target immigrants. As is the case in some other parts of the United States, some racist and "hate" groups in the Southeast have been reenergized by the immigration issue, and, according to the American Defamation League, some "mainstream advocacy groups" have adopted the tactics of hate groups, "resorting to hateful and dehumanizing stereotypes and outright bigotry to demonize immigrants."[11]

Between 2000 and 2008 the number of hate groups increased by 48 percent (to 888 groups in mid-2008) across the United States. In the ten southern states (excluding Florida), 292 hate groups are operating, more than any other region of the country if we also exclude Texas and California, where the majority of Latino immigrants reside.[12] Virtually all these groups have an anti-immigrant focus, according to the Southern Poverty Law Center.[13] The fact that nativists (those opposing immigration) tend to target Latinos is apparent in the 35 percent increase in the number of hate crimes against Latinos between 2003 and 2006.[14]

Although most public discourse regarding Latino immigrants in the Southeast avoids extremism, the social and economic cost of the new immigration is often exaggerated. A number of southern politicians, most of whom have reduced the issue of immigration to the impact of "illegals," resort to inflammatory claims about Latinos. In a 2006 public hearing in Forsyth County, North Carolina, U.S. Representative Virginia Foxx (R-N.C.) said that illegal immigration can be compared to an "invasion" with a "major negative impact on education, health care, Social Security, taxes, employment, wages, the environment, crime and countless other areas of American life."[15] In early 2008 South Carolina State Representative Bobby Harrell said South Carolinians' concerns about the state's "rapidly growing illegal alien population" are justified because "illegal immigration is costing South Carolina taxpayers more than $186 million a year."[16] He has provided no proof of such costs. The 2008 presidential primaries further inflamed southern emotions on the issue. Virtually all Republican candidates in the primary races competed with one another for the strictest border security plan (sometimes in contradiction to their previous positions), and most said they would not include "amnesty" or guest worker provisions in federal immigration legislation reform.

Public discourse regarding Latino immigration echoes these politicians' concerns. During 2007 hearings over proposed state immigration legislation, non-Hispanic residents of Saluda and Charleston, South Carolina, argued that unauthorized Latinos in their areas take jobs from Americans, come to the United States to have "anchor babies," and that many live on government benefits.[17] A University of Georgia student leader wrote in an op-ed column after Georgia's strict state legislation passed in 2006, "[this act] was a much-needed response to the ever-increasing number of illegal immigrants in Georgia who benefit from the state's taxpayer-supported programs while avoiding paying into the system."[18] Such sentiments are echoed daily in a variety of public venues.

Despite the widespread nature of such allegations, scant evidence exists to support them. Beginning in 1996, welfare reform laws have prohibited unauthorized immigrants from receiving federal social benefits in the United States. Further, a recent study completed by researchers at the University of South Carolina found no evidence of burdensome health or educational costs to the state as result of Latino immigration, and suggested that wage depression (which many economists say typically accompanies massive immigration) appears to be the only negative economic effect of increased immigration.[19] And, immigrants *do* pay taxes: they pay sales tax and property tax; employers withhold FICA, federal income taxes, and sometimes state taxes from paychecks, and even undocumented immigrants pay income taxes using an ITIN number (Individual Taxpayer Identification Number).[20] They quickly learn that if state taxes are not withheld automatically they must pay them in order to get an ITIN, which is required in many areas to purchase autos or homes in lieu of other official documentation. Economists estimate that 55 to 65 percent of Latino workers are paid "on the books," despite nativists arguments that they are "all" paid "under the table."[21]

Latino buying power comprises another benefit of the Latino presence that nativists ignore. In a 2007 report, the Selig Center for Economic Growth at the University of Georgia estimated that Latino buying power nationwide would exceed $860 billion in 2007 and projected their spending at over $1.2 trillion by 2012. Four of the five most rapidly growing Latino markets were in the South: Arkansas, North Carolina, Tennessee, and Georgia. Finally, as Johnson and Kasarda contend (this volume), immigrants contribute to local and national economic growth through job creation (estimated at almost 90,000 new jobs in 2005).

In addition to concerns over the economic costs of the new Latino immigration, many southerners have expressed frustration over cultural differences between themselves and the new immigrants.[22] Residents of two South Carolina communities testified in early 2007 that local "illegals" refuse to learn English, have no respect for American culture, have poor hygiene and spread disease, and sacrifice animals in religious ceremonies.[23] A Georgia resident whose family had lived in the area since the nineteenth century said in 2006 that the new Latino immigrants "threaten everything that matters" and expressed the fear that "white" southerners would soon be outnumbered and irrelevant.[24] Speaking of the dramatic changes brought to the small town of Saluda, South Carolina, which has the largest ratio of Latinos (mostly Mexican and Guatemalan) to whites in the state, a former state representative said, "as the percentage [of Latinos] is getting higher [in Saluda], folks who have lived here their entire lives . . . are concerned about how their community is changing, and they don't have any control over it."[25] A North Carolina County Council passed an ordinance in 2007 that included the charges that undocumented immigration by Latinos to the county increased crime rates and that their "lack of social and personal health care standards" negatively affected the community.[26]

Charges that immigrants increase crime rates and carry diseases have surfaced in earlier periods of immigration to the United States. As the number of immigrants soared in the late nineteenth and early twentieth centuries, eugenicists stressed the importance of maintaining a "sound" racial stock in this country, and early-twentieth-century immigration legislation reflected such concerns. A 1903 law listed among those who would be barred from the United States "persons afflicted with a loathsome or with a dangerous contagious disease," and/or "who have been convicted of a felony or other crime or misdemeanor involving moral turpitude."[27] During other periods of massive immigration, some who enter have been, as one study expressed it, "stigmatized as the etiology of a wide variety of physical and societal ills. Anti-immigrant rhetoric and policy have often been framed by an explicitly medical language, one in which the line between perceived and actual threat is slippery and prone to hysteria and hyperbole."[28] Today, as in other periods of perceived national crisis, "biological generalizations" have resurfaced, aided by the Internet and political talk shows.[29]

For some southerners immigrants pose a threat to individual or group culture and identity. While some hostility to Latino immigrants clearly reflects racism, much of the opposition is based on fear: immigrants' Otherness poses a threat to those who do not wish to see local or regional culture and society altered by outsiders. Historians Edward Ayers and Peter Onuf argue that Americans "nurture" identification with the region in which they live "because it offers something that appears to be hard to find in a mass society: a form of identity that promises to transcend ethnic boundaries, to unite people across generations."[30] Many who live in smaller southern communities where the new Latino immigrants often settle have a strong sense of identity with their community and its culture, and Latino newcomers, whose language and cultural practices differ from those of the local community, can appear to threaten this identity. Aristide Zolberg argues that nativism represents "the conservative position on an 'identity' continuum. . . . Rather than thinking of 'Americans' as going 'nativist,' one should think of such episodes as confrontations between different actors who position themselves variously on the 'identity' dimension."[31]

Georgia's Peach State Poll of 2001 revealed that longer-term residents of the state expressed more negative attitudes toward immigrants, likely because these residents are more sensitive to social and cultural changes and "have a more developed sense of what the surrounding community 'ought' to look like."[32] In particular, long-term southern residents are accustomed to a black-white society, and "shifts in community characteristics challenge traditional notions of what defines the community."[33] Those in rural areas and smaller communities can also be sensitive to social change: as Angela Stuesse puts it (chapter 6, this volume), "the recent arrival of Latinos to rural areas complicates traditional hierarchies."

The flash point for those who fear cultural change is often the use of the English language. As numerous studies have demonstrated, the English language is perceived as a symbol, a "salient component of American identity," and new immigrants who do not speak English or do not speak it well are often perceived as challenging the nation's cultural identity, values, and beliefs.[34] New-language acquisition proves challenging for many immigrants, however: economic migrants, or those who relocate predominantly to improve their economic standing, are more likely to learn the new host-country language than are other types of migrants (such as political refugees or those who move to join relatives), but adults face more challenges in the process than do young people.[35] A study of Mexican immigrants in South Carolina revealed that the majority of adults wanted to learn English but that long work hours, the lack of transportation, and difficulty in locating classes prevented many from learning English quickly. Some persevered however, listening to English-language television and radio, and purchasing English-language learning materials on tapes or CDs.[36] Generational differences in English acquisition among immigrant groups have been widely studied, revealing the fact that third-generation Americans are fluent in English and often do not speak their grandparents' language.[37]

Clearly not all residents of Georgia and the Carolinas embrace negative attitudes toward Latino immigrants. For many, the economic benefits Latino immigrants bring to the Southeast outweigh all other factors. Employers in the agricultural and construction sectors of the economy have emphasized their dependence on this highly productive labor force for their own economic survival. A number of southern journalists and newspaper editors have pointed to both economic and cultural contributions of Latino immigrants and have criticized the hostility directed at immigrants by citizens and politicians. Church leaders in many parts of Georgia and the Carolinas view the Latino immigrant population as a source of new membership, and some community leaders (such as those in Dalton, Georgia, described in chapter 3 of this book) have recognized the economic revitalization that new immigrants have brought their towns. Still, public pressure from those hoping to rid the area of unauthorized immigration or to limit the number of immigrants coming to the region, among other factors, have led lawmakers throughout the South to address immigration as a legal issue. The pressure on local authorities has increased also because of federal inaction on immigration reform.

Latino Immigration and Public Policy

In response to political demands, state and local leaders have enacted laws and policies that range from exclusionary to accommodating of the new immigrants. During the initial period of immigration to the South, authorities tended to ignore immigrant populations, possibly assuming that they were a temporary phenomenon and would soon return home or move on to another region. Such attitudes have historical foundation in the United States, particularly toward Mexican immigrants. According to Camille Guérin-Gonzales, "Americans [have] constructed Mexicans as 'birds of passage,' [and] the proximity of the border made that even more believable."[38]

EXCLUSIONARY POLICIES

Most official rhetoric and policy in the Southeast in recent years have been exclusionary and seek to limit especially unauthorized immigrants' access to employment, transportation, housing, health care, higher education, and public benefits. The ultimate aim of many local ordinances and state laws is to discourage undocumented immigrants from coming to that locale or to drive out those already there. Still, some policies, such as "English-only" laws, affect both authorized and unauthorized immigrants.

New legislation related to immigrants and immigration is not unique to the Southeast. By late 2007 legislators in all fifty states had introduced a total of 1,562 bills pertaining to immigration, three times the number in 2005. Of that number, 244 were made law by lawmakers in forty-six states, most pertaining to immigrants and health, employment, identification, driver's and other licenses, public benefits, and human trafficking.[39]

STATE LEGISLATION

Georgia took among the most aggressive and comprehensive actions of any state in the United States to control unauthorized immigration with the passage in 2006 of the Georgia Security and Immigration Compliance Act, an omnibus bill that addressed virtually all policy areas. Considered at the time to be the most sweeping immigration bill enacted by a state, Senate Bill 529 (Ga. SB 529) addresses a range of issues related to unauthorized immigration. The act

- requires contractors and subcontractors doing business with the state to ensure that all of their workers have legal authorization to work, using the federal program E-Verify (formerly the Basic Pilot Program);[40]
- denies tax-supported benefits, including health care, to adults (eighteen years of age and older) who cannot prove their legal residency;
- requires police to check the legal status of anyone who is arrested for a felony or driving under the influence (DUI) and to report those who are undocumented to federal immigration authorities;
- authorizes the state to work with the federal government to train Georgia law enforcement officers to enforce immigration laws;
- and prohibits employers from claiming as a state tax deduction wages paid to undocumented workers.

The final form of Ga. SB 529 reflects a compromise between those seeking aggressive action to end unauthorized immigration to the state and business groups seeking to maintain an available pool of low-wage immigrant labor. After consulting with business lobbyists, legislators crafted the bill so that companies would not be held responsible if an employee used fake documents or if a subcontractor hired unauthorized workers without the knowledge of the company. More aggressive measures were considered but ultimately not included in the 2006 act, such as denying undocumented children access to public education and health care, and charging undocumented immigrants a 5 percent tax on money transfers.[41]

Other than the provisions that penalize employers for hiring undocumented immigrants, which will be phased in during 2008, Ga. SB 529 went into effect on

July 1, 2007. While it is too soon to know the full social and economic impact of the law, it is clear that the measure has created a climate of uncertainty and fear among Latino immigrants in the state. Realtors, car dealers and retailers in immigrant neighborhoods have reported a noticeable decline in Latino customers, which they attribute to the sense of economic and social vulnerability that immigrants feel in light of the new law. Police involvement in the enforcement of immigration law, as authorized by Ga. SB 529, has made Latino immigrants even more fearful and less willing to notify law enforcement when they are victims of or witnesses to crime.[42] The further impact of the law in Georgia warrants close attention, for the measure has already become a model for legislators in other states who are developing their own immigration policies.

Fearing an influx of undocumented immigrants from Georgia, South Carolina state legislators passed H4400 in June 2008.[43] The law, which state lawmakers claim is the nation's strictest, requires that both public and private employers verify the legal status of all employees using either E-Verify or ensuring that potential employees have a valid state driver's license or the documentation to get one. Private employers who do not comply face stiff fines, and if they hire an undocumented worker they lose their "implied right to hire." An authorized employee who is displaced by an undocumented worker can bring civil suit under the new law. South Carolina's law prohibits undocumented immigrants from attending public colleges, and follows federal laws in penalizing those who "aid and abet" undocumented immigrants and in prohibiting those in the country illegally from owning firearms. It is like Georgia's legislation in regard to allowing state and local law enforcement offices to enter into MOUs (memoranda of agreement) with the federal government to enforce immigration laws. The South Carolina Commission for Minority Affairs was designated as the agency that will maintain a twenty-four-hour hotline for anyone to report the presence of immigrants who they believe to be in the country illegally.

As was the case in Georgia, lawmakers in South Carolina made an effort to satisfy both constituents who believed unchecked immigration is ruining the state and employers who rely on the new labor pool. Still, in a relatively poor state experiencing an economic downturn in 2008, legislators provided insufficient funding to enforce all aspects of the legislation.

Legislators in North Carolina have passed several laws aimed specifically at curbing unauthorized immigration and restricting privileges of those already in the state. Signed into law in mid-2006, N.C. HR 2692 approved the establishment of an immigration court in North Carolina to speed up deportation of unauthorized immigrants, pressured the U.S. Congress to make impaired driving (by legal and unauthorized resident alike) a deportable offense, and supported the Department of Homeland Security's program that allows local law enforcement personnel to identify unauthorized immigrants who have been previously deported or who are sought for felony offenses.

Like Georgia and South Carolina, North Carolina now restricts driver's licenses to those who provide a valid Social Security number. The state also requires that all new hires in state government prove their legal residency, and put in place regulations against human trafficking. In 2007 North Carolina Governor Mike Easley signed Ga. SB 229 into law, enabling those operating jails or other places of confinement to check the immigration status of anyone arrested for felony or impaired driving charges.

COUNTY AND LOCAL ORDINANCES

Some counties and local governments in the Southeast, frustrated with state and federal delays in passing restrictive laws, have drafted their own local ordinances. Most of the local legislation includes restrictions on employment and housing for unauthorized immigrants, English-only provisions, and cooperation with federal agents to deport those in the area illegally.

Among the first pieces of such legislation were anticongregating ordinances directed at day laborers. Local residents and merchants across the Southeast complain that day laborers, the mostly Latino workers who congregate in urban areas waiting to be hired for hourly wages, scare off customers and threaten the peace and security of the neighborhood where they amass. In Georgia, the municipalities of Chamblee, Marietta, and Roswell passed anticongregating laws in the late 1990s.[44] These regulations reflect not only local residents' perceptions that immigrants engage in criminal activities but also their concerns that immigrant workers lower wages and take jobs from "real Americans." While communities in North Carolina are considering anti–day labor site ordinances, in most cases there and across the region local complaints against day laborers are handled by local police, who typically urge laborers to congregate elsewhere.

Many local ordinances attempt to restrict unauthorized immigrants' access to jobs by penalizing employers who hire them. A statement in a 2006 North Carolina newspaper reflects the popular perception that employers are the real culprits in the immigration fiasco: "Businesses are the biggest beneficiary of illegal immigration and are the reason unauthorized foreigners are here in the first place."[45] Although the Immigration Reform and Control Act of 1986 prohibits the hiring of undocumented workers and establishes sanctions for employers who do so, the federal government has not enforced the legislation in a serious way. Because the 1986 act does not allow state and local government to establish penalties that go beyond the federal law, a number of southern states, counties, and municipalities have pursued other measures to prohibit the employment of undocumented workers.

Several local ordinances have been modeled on provisions in Georgia's 2006 immigration law. The Georgia law targets unauthorized employment in two ways: state government refuses to conduct business with contractors who have not verified the legal status of their employees, and employers are prohibited from claiming as a state tax deduction wages paid to undocumented workers. Several counties in Georgia and the Carolinas have passed ordinances mandating use of E-Verify, refusing to do business with employers who knowingly hire unauthorized immigrants, or seizing licenses of businesses who do not comply with these regulations.[46] Beaufort County, South Carolina, was the first in that state to enact such legislation, based on the county's determination that "the employment of unauthorized aliens harms the health, safety and welfare of persons authorized to work in Beaufort County."[47]

Some southern localities also have sought to control illegal immigration through housing regulations. Local governments typically create housing codes that define legally permissible housing, and in the South, as elsewhere in the United States, these codes generally seek to maintain low-density, suburban neighborhoods characterized by detached single-family homes set on large lots, and to discourage multifamily housing and dense population of neighborhoods.[48] Some communities in the Southeast have another goal, however: to discourage the settlement of undocumented immigrants.

By mid-2008, 105 localities in the United States had considered legislation aimed at restricting housing options for undocumented immigrants. These proposals typically would require landlords to verify the legal residency status of current and prospective tenants and would impose fines on landlords who knowingly allowed undocumented tenants to remain in their housing units. The first community in the United States to propose such regulations was San Bernardino, California, in 2006, and although that proposal failed, later that year Hazleton, Pennsylvania, passed a similar yet more detailed ordinance, which would become the model for most subsequent proposed housing restrictions, including those in Georgia and the Carolinas. Hazleton's ordinance was struck down in mid-2007, and as result, "most of the housing [anti-illegal immigrant] ordinances have either been enjoined by courts or repealed by local legislatures."[49]

These proposals as well as numerous other regulations regarding housing in Georgia and the Carolinas have come in response to a sea of complaints from local residents.[50] While some, like those in Georgia's Cherokee County, prohibit renting or leasing to unauthorized immigrants, others require a certain number of square feet per person in a residence or limit the number of unrelated people who can live together in one housing unit. The Cherokee County ordinance was immediately challenged by some local residents and businesses as a violation of state and federal laws, and a state court issued a temporary restraining order and preliminary injunction against its enforcement.

Underscoring concerns over cultural differences and immigrant assimilation (or lack thereof), some local legislation in Georgia and the Carolinas requires use of the English language in official documents and at times, in public signage. Over time twenty-nine U.S. states have made English their "official language," largely as a result of the political organizing efforts of U.S. English Inc., a national organization formed in 1983 with the aim of "preserving the unifying role of the English language in the United States."[51] All of the southeastern states are among the twenty-nine. Typically, pieces of legislation regarding use of the English language are symbolic gestures with limited impact on government practices and policies. That may change with new efforts to restrict non-English-speaker's privileges.

Since 2006 the language issue has been revisited by southern lawmakers, usually at the county and local levels.[52] However, state legislators in Georgia introduced bills in 2008 that would "strengthen" the state of Georgia's English-only law, and the South Carolina state senate passed a bill in 2008 that would require that all official documents, including the written exam for obtaining a driver's license, appear in English only. Senator Glenn McConnell (R-Charleston) reported that the purpose of the bill was "to preserve the common thread of our culture."[53] A subsequent *Columbia (S.C.) State* newspaper editorial pointed out that if such a bill became law, legal residents whose English skills are lacking would be penalized. Undocumented immigrants are unable to obtain driver's licenses, so the *State* newspaper's editor raised the question, "What is this bill about?"[54] The bill (s857) did not pass the South Carolina house.

Finally, some southeastern localities have begun to participate in a federal program to help deport unauthorized immigrants. U.S. Immigration and Customs Enforcement (ICE) is encouraging state and local law enforcement personnel to help with federal immigration enforcement in a program under the Immigration and Nationality Act, section 287(g). Congress authorized 287(g) in 1996 but state and local authorities got on board only in 2002. As of early 2008 thirty-four state and local agencies in fifteen states are participating in 287(g).[55] Several counties in North Carolina were among the first in the nation to participate in 287(g). Sixteen sheriff's offices and two police agencies in four North Carolina counties are currently cooperating with ICE, as are agencies in Saluda and York Counties in South Carolina, and law enforcement personnel from Hall, Whitfield, and Cobb Counties in Georgia.[56] On the other hand a number of law enforcement personnel in Georgia and the Carolinas have balked at spending officers' valuable time and scarce resources checking immigration status when the "real criminals" should be their focus.[57]

ACCOMMODATION

Nationwide, some states have made efforts to incorporate Latino immigrants, for example by providing in-state tuition and health care to undocumented immigrant students, and driver's licenses to unauthorized adult immigrants.[58] While southeastern states generally have not proven as welcoming, some official responses to immigration in the Southeast have aimed at accommodating new immigrants. In general, DeKalb County, part of the sprawling Atlanta metropolitan area, has welcomed the newcomers, especially in comparison to most other southern localities with significant foreign-born populations. DeKalb County's actions are likely due to several factors: its longer history of immigration, the greater racial and ethnic diversity of the county's population, and the predominance of Democrats in the government.[59] DeKalb County leaders have approved innovative school programs for foreign-born students, hired Latino law enforcement officials (at this writing there are at least fourteen Latino officers in the County Police Department) and supported ethnic entrepreneurs.[60]

The city of Dalton in northwest Georgia has also made efforts to integrate the thousands of Latino immigrants who provide the bulk of the workforce for the region's carpet industry. Most notable is the impressive Georgia Project, described by authors Víctor Zúñiga and Rubén Hernández-León in chapter 3 of this volume. For the most part Dalton authorities have not participated in the aggressive anti-immigrant backlash that has occurred in other parts of the state in recent years. A key reason, according to Zúñiga and Hernández-León, is that the local industrialists who own Dalton's carpet mills have played a central role in city and county governance. They and their political supporters "have signaled their distaste for overt anti-immigrant movements, effectively discouraging them, and have given their blessing to initiatives such as the Georgia Project and the building of a new Catholic church."[61]

Even in localities that have been ambivalent or hostile to immigrants, certain public institutions, notably schools, could not ignore or exclude the rapidly growing population of foreign-born students. In the 1990s the number of school-aged children (pre-K–12) enrolled in limited English proficient (LEP) programs in the Southeast increased dramatically: between the 1994–95 school year and that of 2004–5, their numbers increased by 714 percent in South Carolina, 372 percent in North Carolina, and 292 percent in Georgia, while in the United States as a whole they grew by only 61 percent.[62]

Schools were among the first public institutions to develop programs and policies of accommodation and incorporation of immigrant newcomers. Public schools are mandated by federal law to provide equal educational opportunity to immigrant and language minority students.[63] In the 1980s the states of South Carolina and Georgia passed legislation to establish and fund a state educational program for K–12 students whose native language is not English. First established to serve the children of Cambodian and Vietnamese refugees, these programs greatly expanded in the 1990s to meet the needs of rapidly growing Latino and Asian immigrant student populations. Following trends in the rest of the country, southern legislators and education officials have rejected bilingual education and supported instead programs that place primary emphasis on learning English as quickly as possible. English for Speakers of Other Languages (ESOL) and English as a second language (ESL) programs offer English-language instruction combined with content classes in math, sciences, social studies, and language arts for English-language learners (ELL), as they are called. The population of ELL students is dispersed throughout the rural and metropolitan South, and their numbers range widely from just a few students in some rural school districts to over 10,000 in the Gwinnett County district in metro Atlanta in the 2004–5 school year.[64]

In addition to ESL and ESOL programs, several school districts in the South have established additional programs to ease the transition for immigrant children. For example, the DeKalb, Cobb, and Gwinnett school districts in Georgia have established International Welcome Centers that provide orientation, translation services, and language assessment and placement for newly arrived, foreign-born students. Other types of welcoming programs in the Carolinas offer extracurricular English and cultural-content classes to the children of Latino immigrants.[65]

In other policy areas, North Carolina passed legislation in 2007 guaranteeing public benefits to victims of human trafficking, and the state's community college system mandated in late 2007 that unauthorized immigrants be admitted to any of the state's fifty-eight community colleges (rather than allowing each campus to make that decision on its own). In response to a public outcry over that decision, Governor Mike Easley supported the action, saying it was the best for the students and for the future of the state.[66] Still, the state's community college system stopped admitting undocumented students in 2008.

Despite the desires of some local officials and residents, it is too late to undo immigration in the Southeast. The number of Latino immigrants, both documented and undocumented, continues to increase in the region, spurred by continued immigration and by births to Latinos already living in the area.

Despite an economic slowdown new immigrants continue to enter the region to take jobs in those industries where finding and keeping workers has proven challenging. The question is not *whether* new immigrants will become a part of southern society, but rather *how* they will be incorporated.

While the key issue for the majority of southerners who advocate immigration reform is immigrants' legal status, their objections go beyond documentation status to economic considerations such as job displacement, wage depression, and the burden on the local economy. The widespread misperception that unauthorized immigrants do not pay taxes and are not only eligible for but take advantage of welfare and other social programs compounds such concerns. Others claim that immigrants pose a threat by increasing rates of crime and disease. Another common fear is that local culture and regional identity will be undermined by massive immigration. Some southerners harbor feelings of helplessness over what they see as an "invasion" of immigrants whose culture is different from their own.

Regardless of the myriad of reasons why many in the Southeast seem bent on ridding the region of Latino immigrants, the immigrants themselves are well aware of how they are perceived. A 2007 study by the Pew Hispanic Center reveals that an increasing proportion of recent Latino immigrants say that they or someone they know has experienced discrimination, and sixty-four percent of Latinos surveyed said that the national debate over immigration has made life more difficult for Hispanics in the United States.[67]

In a recent study of southern identity among the region's increasingly diverse population, authors Larry Griffin, Ranae Evenson, and Ashley Thompson found that Latinos identify as southerners much less frequently than do other minorities (whether religious or ethnic) in the South. One reason, the authors conclude, is that Latinos "may feel themselves unwelcome by those purporting to be 'authentic' southerners—those whites and Protestants so freely affirming their identification with the region—and hence reject an identity that, in their minds, has rejected them."[68] Further, Griffin raises the question of "whether southern identity, at the end of the twentieth century, is entirely free of its past exclusionary color- and religious-coding."[69]

As was made clear in the 2006 demonstrations, Latinos in the Southeast see themselves as contributing to the region's well-being, and many are hopeful of eventual acceptance by residents of the region. Studies have demonstrated that immigrants who are marginalized and face discrimination become acculturated at a slower rate and in a different manner than do those who are more accepted.[70] So ironically, southerners' practice of demonizing immigrants because they do not fit in and "refuse to assimilate" impedes the process of assimilation or incorporation.

Notes

1. "Tens of Thousands Join Immigration Rally," Associated Press, 10 April 2006, at http://www.msnbc.msn.com/id/12250356/.

2. For a summary of immigrant rallies across the country in spring 2006, see Ted Wang and Robert C. Winn, *Groundswell Meets Groundwork: Recommendations for Building on Immigrant Mobilizations*, Four Freedoms Fund, July 2006, at http://www.mrss.com/news/Groundswell-Report_Final.pdf.

3. Ryan Lizza, "Return of the Nativist: Beyond the Republicans' Anti-Immigration Frenzy," *New Yorker*, 3 Feb. 2008, at http://www.newyorker.com/reporting/2007/12/17/071217fa_fact_lizza.

4. Pat Butler wrote a series of articles on Latino immigration in March, April, and May 1998 in *Columbia (S.C.) State*; Shelia M. Poole, "How Latinos Have Settled into Three Southern Communities," *Atlanta Journal-Constitution*, 3 May 1998.

5. John S. Lapinski, Pia Peltola, Greg Shaw, and Alan Yang, "The Polls-Trends, Immigrants and Immigration," *Public Opinion Quarterly* 61 (summer 1997): 356–83; poll results from 2004 conducted by National Public Radio, the Kaiser Family Foundation, and Harvard's Kennedy School of Government, at http://www.kff.org/kaiserpolls/upload/Immigration-in-America-Summary.pdf.

6. MDC Inc., *The State of the South* (Chapel Hill, N.C.: 2007), 15, at http://img-srv.dtcbuilder.com/engine/builder/images/2/0/6/1/8/7/file/2.pdf; U.S. Department of Labor, Bureau of Labor Statistics, at http://www.bls.gov/; Federal Reserve Bank of Atlanta, "Employment Slows from Its Robust Growth," *Econ South* 9 (2007), at http://www.frbatlanta.org/invoke.cfm?objectid=1D687B2E-5056-9F12-12B93EE37BCE6951&method=display_body.

7. Alejandro Portes, "Migration and Underdevelopment," *Politics and Society* 8 (1978): 1–48; George Sanchez, "Face the Nation: Race, Immigration and the Rise of Nativism in Late Twentieth Century America," *International Migration Review* 31 (winter 1997): 1009–30; John Higham, *Strangers in the Land: Patterns of American Nativism, 1860–1925* (New Brunswick, N.J.: Rutgers University Press, 2002).

8. Ariel Alexovich, "A Call to End Hate Speech," *NYT Blog*, 1 Feb. 2008, at http://thecaucus.blogs.nytimes.com/author/aalexovich/?scp=1&sq=ariel+alexovich+la+raza&st =blog.

9. Jeanne Brooks, "Illegal Immigrants Are Still Lawbreakers, Caller Says," *Greenville (S.C.) News*, 18 April 2006.

10. Although the Center for Immigration Studies (Washington, D.C.) and other conservative groups have repeatedly presented our "unsecured" border with Mexico as a security threat since 11 September 2001, law enforcement agencies seem more concerned with lack of security at our border with Canada. No credible evidence has been presented to prove that terrorists are entering the United States from Mexico.

11. "Anti-Immigrant Groups Borrow from Playbook of Hate Groups to Demonize Hispanics," American Defamation League Press Release, 23 Oct. 2007, at http://www.adl.org/PresRele/CvlRt_32/5154_32.htm.

12. The Southern Poverty Law Center's Hate Group Map is at http://www.splcenter.org/intel/map/hate.jsp.

13. Franco Ordoñez, "Surprising and Troubling Resurgence: Immigration Furor Boosts Klan Chapters in Carolinas," *Charlotte Observer*, 9 Feb. 2007.

14. Southern Poverty Law Center, "Intelligence Report: Hate Groups Up By 48% Since 2000," at http://www.splcenter.org/news/item.jsp?aid=300.

15. Dan Galindo, "On Illegal Immigration, Statistics are a Real Problem," *Winston-Salem Journal*, 16 April 2006.

16. "State Lawmakers Ready to Tackle Illegal Immigration in '08," *Hilton Head Island Packet*, 20 Jan. 2008.

17. Testimony before South Carolina House Committee regarding H3148, Feb. 2007.

18. Jeff Emanuel, "Georgia's New Immigration Law Should Serve as Natural Model," op-ed, *Athens Banner Herald*, 4 May 2006.

19. Elaine Lacy et al., "The Economic and Social Implications of the Growing Latino Population in South Carolina" (Columbia, S.C.: Consortium for Latino Immigration Studies, University of South Carolina, 2007) at http://www.sph.sc.edu/cli/documents/CMAReport0809.pdf.

20. Bianca Vazquez Toness, "U.S. Tax Program for Illegal Immigrants Under Fire," NPR, 5 March 2007, http://www.npr.org/templates/story/story.php?storyId=7718604&sc+emaf.

21. Doug Campbell, "The (Illegal) Immigration Effect," *Region Focus* (summer 2006): 19–23, at http://www.richmondfed.org/publications/economic_research/region_focus/summer_2006/pdf/feature1.pdf.

22. Lapinski et al.

23. Testimony before South Carolina House Committee.

24. Rachel L. Swarns, "In Georgia, Immigrants Unsettle Old Sense of Place," *New York Times*, 4 Aug. 2006.

25. Noelle Phillips, "New Town, New Hope. The Changing Face of Saluda," *The State*, 2 July 2006.

26. "Immigration Watch for November 14, 2006," Southern Poverty Law Center, at http://www.splcenter.org/intel/news/item.jsp?aid=90.

27. 32 Stat. 1214, sec. 2, 1903 *US Statutes at Large*.

28. Howard Markel and Alexandra Minna Stern, "The Foreignness of Germs: The Persistent Association of Immigrants and Disease in American Society," *Milbank Quarterly* 80 (2002): 757–88.

29. Dorothy Nelkin and Mark Michaels, "Biological Categories and Border Controls: The Revival of Eugenics in Anti-immigration Rhetoric," *International Journal of Sociology and Social Policy* 18 (1998): 35–63.

30. Edward L. Ayes and Peter S. Onuf, preface, *All Over the Map: Rethinking American Regions* (Baltimore: Johns Hopkins University Press, 1996), vii, quoted in Larry Griffin, Ranae Evenson, and Ashley Thompson, "Southerners All?" *Southern Cultures* 11 (spring 2005): 22.

31. Aristide R. Zolberg, *A Nation by Design: Immigration Policy in the Fashioning of America* (New York: Russell Sage Foundation, 2006), 8.

32. Micki Neal and Stephanie A. Bohon, "The Dixie Diaspora: Attitudes toward Immigrants in Georgia," *Sociological Spectrum* 23 (2003): 205.

33. Ibid., 205.

34. Carlos Garcia and Loretta E. Bass, "American Identity and Attitudes Toward English Language Policy Initiatives," *Journal of Sociology and Social Welfare* 34 (March 2007): 63–82; T. J. Espenshade and C. A. Calhoun, "An Analysis of Public Opinion Toward Undocumented Immigration," *Population Research Policy Review* 12 (1993): 189–224; V. M. Esses et al., "The Immigration Dilemma: The Role of Perceived Group Competition, Ethnic Prejudice, and National Identity," *Journal of Social Issues* 57 (2001): 389–412.

35. Gustavo Mesch, "Language Proficiency among New Immigrants: The Role of Human Capital and Social Conditions," *Sociological Perspectives* 60 (spring 2003): 43.

36. Elaine Lacy, *Mexican Immigrants in South Carolina: A Profile* (Columbia: Consortium for Latino Immigration Studies, University of South Carolina, Jan. 2007), at http://sph.sc.edu/cli/pdfs/final_final[1].pdf.

37. Richard Alba, "Bilingualism Persists, But English Still Dominates," Migration Policy Institute, Feb. 2005, at http://www.migrationinformation.org/Feature/display.cfm?ID=282.

38. Nina Bernstein, "100 Years in the Back Door, Out the Front," *New York Times*, 21 May 2006.

39. National Conference of State Legislatures, "2007 Enacted State Legislation Related to Immigrants and Immigration" (Nov. 2007), at http://www.ncsl.org/print/immig/2007immigrationfinal.pdf.

40. E-Verify is an employment eligibility verification program headed by the U.S. Department of Homeland Security and the Social Security Administration. Using E-Verify, employers can verify the legal residency of new employees through an online government database.

41. Lawrence Downes, "In Immigrant Georgia, New Echoes of an Old History," *New York Times*, 6 March 2006.

42. Linda Carolina Pérez, "Aplican leyes perforadas," *Mundo Hispánico*, 26 July 2007; Mary Lou Pickel, "Last Stop for Immigrants," *Atlanta Journal-Constitution*, 30 July 2007.

43. A state legislator said before the bill's passage: "Georgia is our next-door neighbor. If our state does not take action while our neighboring states continue to, South Carolina will become a safe haven for illegal aliens, and our taxpayers will heavily bear that cost" ("State Lawmakers Ready to Tackle Illegal Immigration in '08," *Hilton Head Island Packet*, 20 Jan. 2008).

44. *Atlanta Journal-Constitution*, 17 April 1997; *Atlanta Journal-Constitution*, 3 May 1998; *Mundo Hispánico*, Dec. 2000.

45. Karin Rives, "Illegal Immigration: Who Profits, Who Pays," *News and Observer*, 26 Feb. 2006, at http://www.newsobserver.com/1155/story/411982.html.

46. Lincoln and Forsyth Counties in North Carolina; Beaufort, Aiken, Dorchester, and Pickens Counties in South Carolina; and Cherokee and Gwinnett Counties in Georgia are among those that have passed legislation aimed at employers of undocumented immigrants.

47. An ordinance to Add a New Section 19 to Beaufort County Ordinance No. 99/36 Pertaining to Business and Professional Licenses So to Add the "Beaufort County, South Carolina, Lawful Employment Ordinance," to Provide an Effective Date, Severability and Other Matters Relating Thereto, at www.bcgov.net.

48. Ivan Light, *Deflecting Immigration: Networks, Markets, and Regulation in Los Angeles* (New York: Russell Sage Foundation, 2006).

49. Rigel Christine Oliveri, "Between a Rock and a Hard Place: Landlords, Latinos, Anti-Illegal Immigrant Ordinances, and Housing Discrimination," *Vanderbilt Law Review* 62 (2008): 60–61.

50. A Duluth, Georgia, zoning inspector said in 2001, "About 98 percent of the calls [regarding housing violations] are in reference to immigrants" (*Atlanta Journal-Constitution*, 22 July 2001). A Cobb County housing employee made a similar comment in 2005; see *Atlanta Journal-Constitution*, 20 June 2005. Gwinnett County and Cobb County, Georgia; Roswell in Fulton County, Georgia; Gaston County in North Carolina; and Gaston, South Carolina are among the localities that have passed housing regulations pertaining to immigrants as of early 2008.

51. U.S. English Inc., "Making English the Official Language," at http://www.us-english.org/inc/.

52. Laws requiring the exclusive use of English in official documents and sometimes on signage have passed in Cherokee County, Georgia; Beaufort County, South Carolina; and Davidson, Landis, Forsythe, and Rowan Counties in North Carolina.

53. "Senate Passes English-Only Bill," South Carolina Senate Republican Caucus, at http://scsenategop.com/senate-passes-english-only-bill.htm.

54. *The State*, 22 Jan. 2008. Some English-only efforts pertain to public signage. Several counties and municipalities in Georgia and the Carolinas require English-language signs and sometimes billboards other than those required by state or federal mandates. So far all efforts to challenge the legality of such legislation have failed.

55. Daniel C. Vock, "With Feds Stuck, States Take on Immigration," Stateline.org, 13 Dec. 2007, at http://www.stateline.org/live/details/story?contentId=264483.

56. The North Carolina counties include Mecklenburg, Alamance, Gaston, Lincoln, and Cabarrus. See Elizabeth DeOrnellas, "Localizing Efforts to Process Illegals," *Daily Tarheel.com*, 31 Oct. 2007, at http://media.www.dailytarheel.com/media/storage/paper885/news/2007/10/31/StateNational/Localizing.Efforts.To.Process.Illegals-3068108.shtml.

57. "Common Sense on Immigration," *Durham Herald-Sun*, 21 Sept. 2007.

58. Daniel C. Vock, "With Feds Stuck, States Take on Immigration."

59. DeKalb County is one of the most racially and ethnically diverse counties in the state, with a population in 2006 that was roughly 33 percent white, 54 percent black, 9

percent Latino, and 4 percent Asian, according to 2007 American Community Survey data.

60. *Mundo Hispánico*, 22–28 Feb. 2007.

61. Víctor Zúñiga and Rubén Hernández-León, ch. 3, this volume; Hernández-León and Zúñiga, "Appalachia Meets Aztlán," in Zúñiga and Hernández-León, eds., *New Destinations: Mexican Immigration in the United States* (New York: Russell Sage Foundation, 2006), 244–62; Edmund T. Hamann, "*Un paso adelante:* The Politics of Bilingual Education, Latino Student Accommodation, and School District Management in Southern Appalachia," in Stanton Wortham, Enrique G. Murillo, and Edmund T. Hamann, eds., *Education in the New Latino Diaspora: Policy and the Politics of Identity (Sociocultural Studies in Education Policy Formation and Appropriation)*, vol. 2 (Stamford, Conn.: Ablex Publishing, 2003), 67–99.

62. Migration Policy Institute, *Educational Data on LEP and Immigrant Children in the Southeast: Numbers, Funding, and Outcomes.* Preparatory materials for "Improving the Educational Outcomes of Immigrant Children in the Southeast: A Roundtable Discussion," University of North Carolina at Chapel Hill, 23–24 May 2007.

63. Title 6 of the 1964 Civil Rights Act prohibits discrimination on the basis of race, color or national origin in federally funded programs and in 1982 the Supreme Court ruled that the Fourteenth Amendment guarantees free public education to all immigrant children, regardless of their parents' legal status (*Plyler v. Doe*).

64. Georgia Department of Education, "ESOL Fall 04 FTE Counts," at http://public.doe.k12.ga.us/ci_iap_esol.aspx?PageReq=PD.

65. "The Changing Face of Metro Atlanta: A Decade of Change," *Atlanta Journal-Constitution*, 23 March 2001; DeKalb County School System, "International Student Center," at http://www.dekalb.k12.ga.us/schools/centers/international/index.html.

66. Benjamin Niolet and Jack Betts, "Easley: Let Immigrants in Colleges," Charlotte.com, 1 Dec. 2007.

67. Pew Hispanic Center, "2007 National Survey of Latinos: As Illegal Immigration Issue Heats Up, Hispanics Feel a Chill," at http://pewhispanic.org/files/reports/84.pdf.

68. Ibid., 14.

69. Ibid., 23.

70. Richard Alba, "Immigration and the American Realities of Assimilation and Multiculturalism," *Sociological Forum* 14 (March 1999): 3–25; Ruben G. Rumbaut, "Assimilation and Its Discontents: Between Rhetoric and Reality," *International Migration Review* 31 (winter 1997): 923–60; Richard Alba and Victor Nee, "Rethinking Assimilation Theory for a New Era of Immigration," ibid.: 826–74; Min Zhou, "Segmented Assimilation: Issues, Controversies, and Recent Research on the New Second Generation," ibid.: 975–1,008; Susan K. Brown and Frank Bean, "New Immigrants, New Models of Assimilation," in *The Second Generation* (Washington, D.C.: Migration Policy Institute, 2006).

CONTRIBUTORS

ROSÍO CÓRDOVA PLAZA is a research professor at the Instituto de Investigaciones Histórico-Sociales at the Universidad Veracruzana, Veracruz, Mexico. Her publications include *Los peligros del cuerpo: Género y sexualidad en el centro de Veracruz* (Mexico City: Plaza y Valdés/Benemérita Universidad Autónomo de Puebla, 2003); and she is coauthor, with Cristina Núñez and David Skerritt, of *Migración internacional, crisis agrícola y transformaciones culturales en la región central de Veracruz* (Mexico City: Universidad Veracruzana/Plaza y Valdés/Centro de Estudios Centroamericanos y Mexicanos del Embajada de Francia, 2008).

RUBÉN HERNÁNDEZ-LEÓN is assistant professor of Sociology at the University of California, Los Angeles. He is the author of *Metropolitan Migrants: the Migration of Urban Mexicans to the United States* (Berkeley: University of California Press, 2008) and coeditor with Víctor Zúñiga of *New Destinations: Mexican Immigration in the United States* (New York: Russell Sage Foundation, 2005).

JAMES H. JOHNSON JR. is Kenan Distinguished Professor of Entrepreneurship in the University of North Carolina Kenan-Flagler Business School and director of its Urban Investment Strategies Center. He has published many scholarly articles on urban labor markets, demographics, and competitiveness issues. Among his most recent publications are "Jobs on the Move: Implications for U.S. Higher Education" (with John D. Kasarda), *Planning for Higher Education* (spring 2008); and "Economic Globalization and the Future of Black America," *Journal of Black Studies* (spring 2007).

JOHN D. KASARDA is Kenan Distinguished Professor of Management at the University of North Carolina Kenan-Flagler Business School and director of its Frank Hawkins Kenan Institute of Private Enterprise. He has published many scholarly articles and books on demographics, economic development, and business issues. Among his most recent publications are "Airport Cities and the Aerotropolis: New Planning Models," *Airport Innovation* (spring 2007); and "Jobs and People on the Move" (with James H. Johnson Jr.), *Planning for Higher Education* (summer 2008).

ELAINE LACY is professor of History and assistant to the executive vice chancellor for academic affairs at the University of South Carolina, Aiken. She has published numerous articles on Latino immigration to the United States and on Mexican cultural politics. Some of her reports on Latino immigration to South Carolina are available on the website of the University of South Carolina Consortium for Latino Immigration Studies. Among other recent publications are "Katrina-Related Health Concerns of Latino Survivors and Evacuees" (with DeAnne Messias), *Journal of Healthcare for the Poor and Underserved* (May 2007); and "Comunidades mexicanas en Carolina del Sur: Vidas transnacionales y ciudadanía cultural," in *In God We Trust: Del campo mexicano al sueño americano*, ed. Rosío Córdova Plaza, María Cristina Núñez Madrazo, and David Skerritt Gardner (Mexico City: Plaza y Valdés Éditores/Universidad Veracruzana, 2007).

RAYMOND A. MOHL is distinguished professor of History at the University of Alabama at Birmingham. He is the author or editor of numerous books and articles on U.S. urban and immigration history, including *The Making of Urban American* (Wilmington, Del.: Scholarly Resources, 1997); *South of the South: Jewish Activists and the Civil Rights Movement in Miami, 1945–1960* (Gainesville: University Press of Florida, 2004); and "The Interstates and the Cities: The U.S. Department of Transportation and the Freeway Revolt, 1966–1973," *Journal of Policy History* (spring 2008).

MARY E. ODEM is associate professor of History and Women's Studies at Emory University in Atlanta, Georgia. She is the author of numerous publications on the subjects of women, gender, immigration, and ethnicity in U.S. history. Her recent publications include "Unsettled in the Suburbs: Latino Immigration and Ethnic Diversity in Metro Atlanta," in *Twenty-First Century Gateways: Immigrant Incorporation in Suburban America*, ed. Audrey Singer, Susan W. Hardwick, and Caroline B. Brettell (Washington, D.C.: Brookings Institution Press, 2008); and "Our Lady of Guadalupe in the New South: Latin American Immigrants and the Politics of Integration in the Catholic Church," *Journal of American Ethnic History* (fall 2004).

ANGELA C. STUESSE received her doctorate in anthropology from the University of Texas at Austin in 2008 and currently holds a postdoctoral fellowship at the Institute for Research on Labor and Employment at the University of California, Los Angeles. While there she is preparing a book manuscript based on her doctoral research, "Globalization 'Southern Style': Transnational Migration, the Poultry Industry, and Implications for Organizing Workers across Difference." She has written several scholarly and popular articles on the subjects of politically engaged research, neoliberal globalization, and transnational migration, race, and labor.

JAMIE WINDERS is assistant professor of Geography in the Maxwell School of Citizenship and Public Affairs at Syracuse University. Her work examines Latino migration, community transformation, and racial politics in the U.S. South. Among her recent publications are "Bringing Back the (B)order: Post-9/11 Politics of Immigration, Borders, and Belonging in the Contemporary U.S. South," *Antipode* (2007); and "'We're Here to Stay': Economic Restructuring, Latino Migration, and Place-Making in the U.S. South" (with Barbara Ellen Smith), *Transactions of the Institute of British Geographers* (2008).

VÍCTOR ZÚÑIGA is dean of the School of Education and Humanities at the Universidad de Monterrey, Mexico. His recent publications include *New Destinations: Mexican Immigration to the United States* (New York: Russell Sage Foundation, 2005), which he coedited with Rubén Hernández-León; "Peut-on parler d'une diaspora mexicaine aux États-Unis," *Géographie et Cultures* (2005); and "From Nuevo León to the USA and Back Again: Students in Mexico" (with Edmund T. Hamann), *Journal of Immigration and Refugees* (2008).

INDEX

Adaptation, immigrant, xvi, xxii, 19, 23–26, 113
Advocacy, immigrant: and business owners, 59–60; and churches, 58, 62–63, 144; and organizations, xxv, 41–42, 62–65, 117, 131, 133–34, 144, 146
African Americans, 1–2, 65, 149; buying power of, 56; in Catholic leadership, 120; in Chamblee-Doraville, 114; and civil rights, 94, 98; in Dalton, 44; Latino fear of, 22–23; in Southeast, 92, 93. *See also* Black-Latino relations
Agriculture: dependency of, on immigrant labor, 150; Latino labor in, xiv, xvii, xxi, 4, 13, 51, 54–55, 99; in North Carolina, 74, 84; in Veracruz, 20, 30, 32n13. *See also* Migrant workers
Aiken, S.C., 1, 12
Alabama, 51–65; cultural impact of immigrants on, 64–65; immigrant labor in, xiii, xiv, 51–56; as new immigrant settlement area, 21, 51–53, 128; response of, to new immigrants, 57–63
Alabama English Committee, 57, 59. *See also* English language
America First Committee, 57–58. *See also* Hate: groups
American Defamation League, 146
Anti-immigrant sentiment: in Alabama, 57–60; in Georgia, 45–46, 117; and Ku Klux Klan, 52, 58–59, 144; in Nashville, 136, 140n19; in South Carolina, 6–7, 11; in Southeast, xvi, xxv, 144–50, 158; in traditional Latino settlement areas, 144. *See also* Discrimination; Nativism
Argentina, immigrants from, 93, 99, 100
Arkansas: as immigrant destination, x, xvii; immigrant labor in, xiv, 128, 147; poultry industry in, 106n1
Asia, immigrants from, ix, xiv, 114, 130, 137
Assimilation, 2, 6, 11–12, 123, 155, 158
Atlanta, Ga., 112–23; church in, xiii; industry in, xiv, xvi; population of, 113; pro-immigrant rallies in, 143; settlement in, xvii, 37, 137

Barbour County Hispanic/Latino Coalition, 63. *See also* Advocacy, immigrant
Birmingham, Ala., xiv, xvii, 52–65
Birmingham Civil Rights Institute, 62. *See also* Advocacy, immigrant
Black-Latino relations, xxii, xxiv, 7, 23, 40, 53, 60–62, 65, 91–92, 97, 99–105. *See also* African Americans
Border, 42–43; enforcement, xvi, 4, 19, 21–22, 57–58, 131; security, 4, 9, 21–22, 30, 46, 59, 131, 144–45, 147, 159n10
Bracero Program, 21, 32n19
Building the New America Committee, 126, 134–35. *See also* Advocacy, immigrant
Businesses: and E-Verify, 151–52, 154, 161n40; Latino ownership of, 9, 41–42, 52, 56, 74, 80–81; and legislation regarding undocumented workers, 45, 151–54, 162n46; perceived as undocumented-immigration beneficiaries, 41, 59–60, 116, 153–54
Buying power, Latinos and, 56–60, 76–78, 84, 88n21, 90n34; and leakage, 84–86. *See also* Economic impact, Latino immigrants and

Calhoun, Ga. *See* Dalton, Ga.
California, Latino immigration and, xvi, 3, 21, 36–38, 54, 126, 128, 137
Carpet industry, xxii–xxv, xxiii; in Alabama, 55, 62; in Georgia, 35, 37–40, 47, 156; and work force shifts, 43, 46

Catholic Church: assistance of, to immigrants, xxiii, 62, 118; Catholic Family Services, 58, 63; Catholic Social Services, 118; and integration of Latino immigrants, 118–22; and Latino settlement processes, xxiii, 44, 156; and Spanish-language Mass, 62–63, 112. *See also* Churches
Census: definition of Hispanic in, xxv; undercount of Latino population in, 2–3, 53–54, 92
Central America, immigrants from, ix, xv, xvi, xvii, xviii, xx, 8, 53, 60, 94, 99–100, 112, 115, 120, 122. *See also* Guatemala, immigrants from
Chain migration, xvi–xvii, 1, 52, 56, 61
Chamblee-Doraville, Ga., xxiii, 112, 114, 123. *See also* Atlanta, Ga.
Churches: assistance of, to immigrants, xxv, 63, 118, 144, 150; and community building, xxiii, 8–9; immigrant affiliation with, 150; immigrant ties to, in sending communities, 10; Spanish-language services of, 8–9, 51, 62, 63. *See also* Catholic Church
Citizenship: cultural, 2, 7, 11–13; definition of, 15n23
Cobb County, Ga., 116; Marietta, 116, 121, 153
Construction, Latino labor in, xiv, xvi, 37, 150; in Alabama, 54, 56, 59–60; in Atlanta, 112, 115, 116; in Nashville, 126, 130; in North Carolina, 73, 74, 83–84; in South Carolina, 4
Crime: against migrants, 23, 30, 152; assumptions of immigrant engagement in, xxv, 22, 144, 146, 148, 153–54, 158
Cubans, and Cuban Americans, 121, 130

Dalton, Ga., xxii–xxiii, xxv, 34–48, 156; Whitfield County, 35–47 passim, 55
Davidson County, Tenn., 132. *See also* Nashville, Tenn.
DeKalb County, Ga., 114, 156, 162n59. *See also* Atlanta, Ga.
Demographic profile of immigrants: in Alabama, 55–56; in Georgia, xvii, 34, 43, 113, 114, 147; in Mississippi, 92; in Nashville, 126–30, 132; in North Carolina, 70–71, 74; in South Carolina, 3–4
Deportation: from Alabama, 59; fear of, 19, 23; and federal-state cooperation, 153–55; from North Carolina, 152; threats of, 1
Discrimination, 6–8, 96, 113, 120, 133, 158, 163n63
Disease, association of immigrants with, 7, 148, 158
Domestic violence, 28–29. *See also* Gender relations
DREAM Act, 1, 13n1. *See also* Legislation, immigration and
Driver's licenses, 6–7, 24, 117–18, 151, 155–56; restrictions on, 57, 59, 153

Economic impact, Latino immigrants and, xxi–xxii, 90n34; in Alabama, 52, 56, 58–60; and Latino buying power, 76–78, 84, 147; negative perceptions of, 145–47, 154; in North Carolina, 78–86; as positive, 5, 53, 62, 81–84, 144, 148, 150; and taxes, 76, 80–81, 85, 89n28
Education: costs associated with, 63, 85, 146; and ESL or ESOL training, 6, 40–41, 58, 63, 157; and immigrant incorporation, 157; in-state tuition for, 156; legislation affecting, 152, 157; and LEP Program, 156; levels of, among immigrants, 4; perceptions regarding immigrants' effect on, 154; as valued by immigrants, 6, 10, 52
El Salvador, immigrants from, ix, xv, xvii, 112, 115, 122. *See also* Central America, immigrants from
Employment and labor: competition for, xiv, 4, 36, 37, 46–47, 60–62, 97; and

contractors, 60, 101–2; and day laborers, 58, 116, 153; in forestry, xxi–xxii, 56, 61–62, 74; in garment industry, 54, 55, 61; gender division in, 74; and industries hiring Latinos, 4, 37–38, 54–55, 73; in meatpacking industry, 54; in North Carolina, 71; organizing, 60–61, 93–94, 97; recruitment for, xvii, 37–38, 54–55, 73, 96–97, 101; U.S. demands for Mexican, xiv, 4, 21. *See also* Carpet industry; Construction, Latino labor in; Manufacturing, Latino labor in; Poultry processing
English language: ability to speak, 8, 149; classes, 6; desire to learn, 11, 58, 120, 148–49; difficulty in learning, 149; and employment, 97; and identity, 149; and immigrant isolation, 24, 100; mixed with Spanish, 11; perception that immigrants "refuse to learn," 148; pride in learning, 6, 27
English Only: legislation, 57, 150, 153, 155, 162n52, 162n54; movement, 7. *See also* English language
Ethnic: diversity, 40, 128–29, 134–37; enclaves, 5; tensions, 40, 93, 99, 136
E-Verify, 151–52, 154, 161n40. *See also* Legislation, immigration and

Families: communication within, 6, 9–10; males' desire to control, from afar, xxi, 26–28; males' desire to leave, in Mexico, 28–29; movement of, 3–4; reunification of, 4, 19, 38, 113; separated by migration, xx–xxiii, 26–29, 30
Female immigrants, 3–4, 8, 12, 38, 39, 74. *See also* Gender relations
Fiestas, traditional Mexican, 8, 64, 122–23
Forestry, xxi–xxii, 56, 61–62, 74
Franklin County Coalition for the Hispanic Community, 63. *See also* Advocacy, immigrant

Gainesville, Ga., 46
Garment industry, 54, 55, 61
Gender relations, xx, 19, 26–31, 74
Georgia, x, 34–50, 112–23; educational programs for immigrants in, 156–57; local legislation in, 45, 116, 117, 153–55; nativist sentiment in, 147–49. *See also* Atlanta, Ga.; Dalton, Ga.
Georgia Coalition for Immigration Reform, 117. *See also* Anti-immigrant sentiment; Nativism
Georgia Peach State Poll, 149
Georgia Project, 35, 41–42, 46, 156. *See also* Education
Georgia Security and Immigration Compliance Act (SB529), 45, 151–52, 154. *See also* Georgia; Legislation, immigration and
Globalization: and migration, xiv–xv, 3, 18, 65, 73; neoliberal, and poultry industry, 94–97, 104; and transformation of South, xiv–xv
Greenville, S.C., xvii, 4, 145
Guatemala, immigrants from, ix, xv, xvii, xxiii, 93, 99–100, 112, 115, 128, 148. *See also* Central America, immigrants from

Hate: crimes, 146; groups, 52, 59, 144, 146. *See also* Discrimination; Nativism
Health care: access to, 25, 63, 120; costs of, xxii, 6, 45, 52, 76–82, 146–47; legislation affecting, 151; for undocumented immigrants, 59, 150, 156
Hispanic: definition of term, xxv; use of term, in South, 99–100
Hispanic immigrants. *See* Immigration, Latino; *and specific nationalities*
Hispanic Interest Coalition of Alabama, 63. *See also* Advocacy, immigrant; Birmingham, Ala.
Honduras, immigrants from, xvii, 122
Hoover, Ala., 58, 59, 63, 65

Housing: and census, 3; conditions, xviii, 4, 55; and discrimination, 6; legislation pertaining to, 153–55, 162n50; and overcrowding, 4, 55, 101. *See also* Legislation, immigration and
H2B visas, 56, 58, 61, 121, 147
Human rights, xxiv–xxv, 7, 15n23, 22, 26, 30, 93, 97–105, 123, 133. *See also* Advocacy, immigrant
Human trafficking, 151, 153, 157
Huntsville, Ala., 54, 59, 63, 64, 65

ICE. *See* Immigration and Customs Enforcement
Identity: Latino, 7–8, 12, 64, 98, 148–49, 158; southern, x, 42, 144–45, 148–49, 158
Illiteracy, 4, 6, 100. *See also* Education
Immigration, Latino: and chain migration, xvii, 52, 56; circulatory migration patterns of, xx, 99; factors driving, xiv–xv, 20–21, 54; historic perception of, ix, 18, 55, 64, 114, 144, 148; increase in, in South, xvi, xvii, xxiii, 2–3, 20, 36, 53–54. *See also* Mexican immigration
Immigration and Customs Enforcement (ICE), 47, 57, 71, 116, 121, 155
Immigration and Naturalization Services (INS), 47, 57, 71, 116, 121, 155
Immigration Reform and Control Act (IRCA), xvi, 19, 35–37, 52, 57, 153–54
Indigenous: communities, xv, 20, 99; languages, 99
INS. *See* Immigration and Naturalization Services
Integration, immigrant, xxv, 5, 11–13, 128, 156–57; cultural, 56–58, 92, 134; economic, xv, 19, 56–57, 74; religious, 118–22
IRCA. *See* Immigration Reform and Control Act

Job displacement, 60, 101, 146–47, 153, 158

Ku Klux Klan, 52, 58–59, 144. *See also* Anti-immigrant sentiment; Nativism; Race

La migra, 24, 26. *See also* Immigration and Naturalization Services; Law enforcement
Latino Association of Business, 56. *See also* Businesses
Latino immigrants. *See* Immigration, Latino; *and specific nationalities*
Law enforcement, 6, 143, 146, 151–53, 155–56; in Georgia, 116, 121. *See also* Immigration and Naturalization Services; Police
Legislation, immigration and: in Alabama, 58; on border security, 46; on day labor, 153; federal, 1, 22, 58–59, 118, 143–44, 153; in Georgia, 116–18, 151–52, 154; local, 144, 153–56; in North Carolina, 152–54; presumed flaws in, 147; proposed federal, 1, 143; in South Carolina, 152–54; state, 59–60, 144, 151–53, 158, 161n43; in Tennessee, 130

Manufacturing, Latino labor in, 4, 34, 46, 61–62, 73–75, 95, 115
Marietta, Ga., 116, 121, 153
Masculinity, 27–31, 33n24. *See also* Gender relations
Meatpacking, 54. *See also* Poultry processing
Media: in Atlanta, 114, 144; coverage of immigration, xxiv–xxv, 1, 23, 41, 46, 58, 145; in North Carolina, 73; Spanish-language, 8–9, 45, 64–65
Mexican immigration: and cultural change in South, 43–45; to Dalton, 36–39; and deaths of Mexican migrants, 21–22; factors in Mexico leading to, xiv–xv, 3, 19–21, 30, 31n6; new destinations of, in U.S., xvi, 18, 21, 36–38, 115; origins of, 3, 5, 18, 32n10, 99; other

Latinos' perceptions of, 100; to South Carolina, 1–17; and victimization, 30–31
Mexico, immigrants from: cultural impact of, 42–43, 44–45; enclaves of, 8, 51; independence celebrations of, 43; population of, in Atlanta, 115; religious practices of, 9, 44, 119–20, 122–23; vulnerability of, 19–22
Migrant workers, 14n10, 20, 55, 56, 63
MIRA. *See* Mississippi Immigrants' Rights Alliance
Mississippi, 92–105
Mississippi Immigrants' Rights Alliance (MIRA), 93, 98, 104–5, 107n12, 109n37. *See also* Black-Latino relations; Employment and labor
Mobile, Ala., 54, 57, 63
Montgomery, Ala., 54, 59, 62
MPOWER, 93–94, 98, 104–5, 107n12. *See also* Black-Latino relations
Music, ix, 9, 11, 24, 45, 64

NAACP (National Association for the Advancement of Colored People), 62
NAFTA (North American Free Trade Agreement), xv, 30, 35
Nashville, Tenn., xvii, 37, 126–38
Nashville-Davidson County Refugee Services Program, 131, 135. *See also* Advocacy, immigrant; Refugees
Nashville New America Coalition, 134, 135. *See also* Advocacy, immigrant
National Association for the Advancement of Colored People (NAACP), 62
National Council of La Raza, 145. *See also* Advocacy, immigrant
Nativism, 7, 22, 58, 146, 148–49; in Alabama, 51–52, 57–59, 65; factors driving, 144–45; in Georgia, 40, 45–47, 149; in South Carolina, 7, 145–49; in Tennessee, 136
Neoliberal reforms, xiv, xxiv; definition of, 95; effects of, 3; in Mississippi, 93–105. *See also* Economic impact, Latino immigrants and; Globalization
North Alabama Hispanic Association, 63. *See also* Advocacy, immigrant
North American Free Trade Agreement (NAFTA), xv, 30, 35
North Carolina, 70–85; and economic benefits of immigration, 76, 77, 147–48; Hispanic growth in, 70–71; immigrant impact on budget of, 81–83; and immigration legislation, 152–55, 157; industries hiring Hispanics in, 73–74; labor force in, 73–74, 87n12, 128; nativism in, 146

Occupational Safety and Health Administration (OSHA), 96, 105. *See also* Employment and labor
Office of Refugee Resettlement, 126, 130, 131, 134. *See also* Advocacy, immigrant; Refugees
Operation New Birmingham, 62. *See also* Advocacy, immigrant
OSHA (Occupational Safety and Health Administration), 96, 105. *See also* Employment and labor

Peru, immigrants from, xx, xxiii, 99, 122
Police: and day laborers, 116, 153; as enforcers of immigration law, 47, 143, 151–53, 155; immigrant assistance from, 25; immigrant perceptions of, 7, 23, 26; and Spanish-language instruction, 6, 63
Poultry processing, 4, 60–61, 96; in Georgia, 46, 112; and industrial-strategy shift, 54, 91–97, 194, 111n56; and labor organizing, xxiv, 97–105; in Mississippi, 92–105; and recruitment of Latino workers, 51, 54–55; in Southeast, xiv, 106n1; workforce changes in, 52, 55, 91–92
Public Policy, Latinos and, 150–58

Puerto Rico, immigrants from, xvii, 87n8, 115

Race: in Nashville, 127–30, 137–38; and racial stereotyping, 100, 103; and racism, 2, 22, 103; structure of, in Southeast, ix–x, xxiii–xiv, 2, 7, 52, 53, 91–93, 149
Raids, 116, 121. *See also* Law enforcement
Rallies for immigrant rights, in the South, 46, 59, 143, 145
Real ID Act, 118. *See also* Legislation, immigration and
Refugees, xv, 126–28, 141–42; advocacy organizations for, 128, 135; resettlement of, xxiv, 125–26, 127, 130–32
Remittances, 1, 9–10, 12, 28, 52, 56, 77, 84, 99, 101. *See also* Families
Roswell, Ga., 116–17, 153
Rural South: economy of, 84; Hispanic population in, 71
Russellville, Ala., 51–52, 54, 59, 63, 64

Scott County, Miss., 92–93, 102
Self-employment, Latinos and, 9, 42–43, 52, 56, 74, 80
Social capital, 2, 5, 12, 132
Social networks, xxiii, 114–15; and jobs, 5, 56, 101; and migration process, 3, 5, 19, 38, 52; and settlement in U.S., 5, 21, 23; and women, 8
Social services, 6, 147, 158. *See also* Catholic Church
Sojourner, 3, 11, 13, 16n34, 150
South Carolina, 1–16; and immigrant education, 157; and immigration legislation, 152–55; response of, to immigration, 7, 145–49
Space, social: changes in, as result of immigration, 47–48; immigrants use of, 118–22, regulation of, 113, 115–18; and spatial boundaries, 42–43; theory of, 113
Spanish language: church services in, 8–9, 51, 62, 63; instruction in, for public servants, 6, 63; marketing in, 56; media in, 8–9, 41, 45, 64–65; mixed with English, 11; in Nashville, 126; nativist objections to, 44, 52, 57; in southern communities, 51; in workplace, 8, 97–99
Sports, Latinos and, 9, 44, 64

Task Force of Refugees and Immigrants (TFRI), 133. *See also* Advocacy, immigrant
Taxes, 76, 80–81, 85, 89n28, 146–47, 158
Tennessee, 126–47; Nashville, xvii, 37, 126–38
Tennessee Immigration and Refugee Rights Coalition (TIRRC), 133. *See also* Advocacy, immigrant
TFRI (Task Force of Refugees and Immigrants), 133. *See also* Advocacy, immigrant
TIRRC (Tennessee Immigration and Refugee Rights Coalition), 133. *See also* Advocacy, immigrant
Transnationalism: activities, xx–xxi, 2; communities, 1, 3, 9–10, 12, 52–53, 135; religion, 121–23; transnational space, 9–11, 21, 26–31; worker flows, 65, 92, 95, 101
Transportation, 6, 7, 8, 15n19, 24–25, 117. *See also* Driver's licenses
Tuzamapan, Veracruz, 19

Undocumented immigration: in Alabama, 57; in Atlanta, 115, 116, 121; and detentions, 22; and false documents, 24–25; and fear, 23–26; and immigrant vulnerability, 19–22, 115; increase of, in numbers, 19; legislation pertaining to, 151; in North Carolina, 71; in South Carolina, 10–11; objections to status, 41, 145–46. *See also* Immigration, Latino; Mexican immigration

U.S.-Mexico relations, xiv–xv, 19–21, 30

Veracruz, Mexico, 8, 19–21, 23–31, 32nn12–13, 32n16
Virgin of Guadalupe, ix, 9, 13, 44, 64, 112, 122

Wages: depression of, 76, 84, 146–47, 153, 158; and industry savings, 83–84; levels of, 4, 22, 47, 55, 60–62, 101–2
White privilege, 40, 43. *See also* Race
Whitfield County, Ga., 35–37, 40, 41, 43, 47, 55. *See also* Dalton, Ga.